Capital Flight from Cameroon, Ghana, and Zambia

Léonce Ndikumana

Capital Flight from Cameroon, Ghana, and Zambia

Natural Resources and Perverse Global Connections

palgrave
macmillan

Léonce Ndikumana
Department of Economics
and Political Economy Research
Institute (PERI)
University of Massachusetts Amherst
Amherst, MA, USA

ISBN 978-3-032-22769-0 ISBN 978-3-032-22770-6 (eBook)
https://doi.org/10.1007/978-3-032-22770-6

This Palgrave Macmillan imprint is published by the registered company Springer Nature Switzerland AG
The registered company address is: Gewerbestrasse 11, 6330 Cham, Switzerland

Acknowledgements

We owe a deep debt of gratitude to institutions and individuals who contributed directly and indirectly to the research contained in this book and to bring the book to completion. We especially appreciate valuable comments and suggestions from experts and policy makers in Cameroon, Ghana, and Zambia who generously availed themselves, shared their knowledge, and provided us with valuable policy insights, data, and qualitative information for the case studies. We acknowledge with gratitude technical assistance from Dr. Didier Wayoro for the design of the maps contained in the book. While we cannot list the names of each of these institutions and individuals here, we trust everyone will recognize the fruits of their support in the content of this book.

We are deeply grateful to the Carnegie Corporation of New York for a fellowship grant (Award No. G-F-21-58369) that supported the research project, as well as research funding from the Political Economy Research Institute at the University of Massachusetts.

Contents

Notes on Contributors

Kwame Adjei-Mantey is a Lecturer at the Institute of Statistical, Social & Economic Research (ISSER), University of Ghana, Legon, Accra, Ghana and a Research Fellow at the Future Africa Institute, University of Pretoria. His research interests cover applied microeconomics and micro econometrics focusing on issues of development economics; the environment, climate change, and energy transitions; and behavioral economics. He has published articles in journals such as *Energy Policy*, *Environment and Development Economics*, *Energy for Sustainable Development*, and *Review of Economics of the Household*, as well as book chapters. Kwame obtained his BA in economics from Kwame Nkrumah University of Science and Technology, an MPhil in economics from the University of Ghana, and a PhD in economics from Kobe University in Japan.

William Godfred Cantah is a Lecturer in the Department of Data Science and Economic Policy and Co-ordinator at the Centre for Data Archiving, Management and Analysis (CDAMAA) at the University of Cape Coast, Ghana. He holds a PhD in economics from the University of Cape Coast. He is a member of the National Development Planning Commission (NDPC). He has served as a consultant for domestic and international organizations including the Ghana Statistical Service, the Economic Commission for Africa and the African Development Bank. His research interests cover monetary policy, international trade, foreign direct investment, external debt, and natural resources. He has published articles in various journals including *African Development*

Review, *Eastern Economic Journal*, *Global Business Review*, *International Economic Journal*, *Journal of Economic & Financial Studies*, and *Resources Policy*.

Bilen Gurara is a PhD student in economics at the University of Massachusetts Amherst, USA. She holds a BA in economics and an MSc in natural resource and environmental economics from Addis Ababa University in Ethiopia. She is an alumna of the Sié Fellowship at the University of Denver, where she earned an MA in global finance, trade, and economic integration. She worked as a researcher at the Ethiopian Development Research Institute. Her academic research interests are in the intersection of political economy with public health and climate change; economic development; and capital flight.

Juste Lokossou is a PhD student in economics at the University of Massachusetts Amherst, USA. He earned a Bachelor's degree from the University of Abomey-Calavi in Benin and holds two Master's degrees from South Dakota State University—one in Economics and the other in Data Science. His research interests include macroeconomics and finance.

Hans Tino Mpenya Ayamena is a Senior Lecturer in the Faculty of Economics and Applied Management, University of Douala, Cameroon. He holds a PhD in economics from the University of Youndé II. He is also a researcher in the Laboratoire d'Analyses et de Recherche en Economie Mathématique (LAREM) at the University of Youndé II. His research interests cover microeconomics analysis of development (welfare, inequality and poverty analysis, microfinance) and macroeconomics analysis of development (resources mobilization, natural resources, capital flight). He has published articles in several journals including the *Review of Development Economics*, *African Integration and Development Review*, and *African Development Review*.

Dale Mudenda is a Senior Lecturer in the Department of Economics at the University of Zambia where he has served as Chair. He holds a PhD from the University of Cape Town, South Africa and is a graduate of the University of Malawi and University of Zambia. His research interests primarily relate to international economics, industrial development, the economics of extractive industries, macroeconomics, and economic development in general. He has published articles in various journals including *African Journal of Economic Review*, *Foreign Trade Review*, *Zambia Social Science Journal*, and others.

Léonce Ndikumana is a Distinguished Professor of Economics and Director of the African Development Policy Program at the Political Economy Research Institute (PERI) at the University of Massachusetts Amherst, USA. He is an Honorary Professor of Economics at the University of Cape Town and the University of Stellenbosch in South Africa. His research focuses on African development and Macroeconomics and covers issues related to external debt and capital flight, extractive industries, financial markets and growth, macroeconomic policies for growth and employment, and the economics of conflict and civil wars in Africa. He is co-editor of *On the Trail of Capital Flight from Africa. The Takers and the Enablers* (Oxford University Press), which is also published in French as *La Fuite des Capitaux d'Afrique: Les Pilleurs et le Facilitateurs* (Amalion), and *Capital Flight from Africa: Causes, Effects and Policy Issues* (OUP). He is co-author of *Africa's Odious Debts: How Foreign Loans and Capital Flight Bled a Continent* (Zed Books), which is also published in French as *La Dette Odieuse d'Afrique: Comment l'endettement et la fuite des capitaux ont saigné un continent* (Amalion). He also published dozens of academic articles and book chapters. Léonce Ndikumana holds a BA in economics from the University of Burundi, an MA and a PhD in economics from Washington University in St. Louis.

Acronyms

ASGM	Artisanal Small-Scale Gold Mining
BEAC	Banque des États de l'Afrique Centrale [Bank of Central African States]
BoP	Balance of Payments
BSAC	British South African Company
CEPS	Customs, Excise, and Preventive Services
CHED	Cocoa Health and Extension Division
CIF	Cost Insurance and Freight
CMB	Cocoa Marketing Board
CMC	Cocoa Marketing Company
COCOBOD	Ghana Cocoa Board
CPC	Cocoa Processing Company
CRIG	Cocoa Research Institute of Ghana
CSPH	Caisse de Stabilisation des Prix des Hydrocarbures [Hydrocarbon Price Stabilization Fund]
EITI	Extractive Industries Transparency Initiative
ERP	Economic Recovery Program
FCFA or CFA franc	Communauté financière d'Afrique franc [franc of the Financial Community of Africa]
FINDECO	Finance and Development Corporation
FOB	Free on Board
GoldBod	Ghana Gold Bold
GRA	Ghana Revenue Authority
HNWIs	High-Net-Worth Individuals
IEA	International Energy Agency
IFC	International Finance Corporation

INDECO	Industrial Development Corporation
ITIC	International Transport and Insurance Costs of merchandise trade
MEMACO	Metal Marketing Corporation of Zambia
MINDECO	Mining Development Corporation
MMDA	Mines and Minerals Development Act
NADMO	National Disaster Management Organization
OECD	Organization for Economic Cooperation and Development
PAYE	Pay as You Earn income tax
PBC	Produce Buying Company Limited
PMMC	Precious Minerals Marketing Company
PNDC	Provisional National Defense Council
PPRC	Producer Price Review Committee
QCC	Quality Control Company
RST	Rhodesian Selection Trust Group
SCDP	Société Camerounaise des Dépôts Pétroliers [Cameroon Petroleum Depots Company]
SEREPCA	Société de Recherche et d'Exploitation des Pétroles du Cameroun [Cameroon Petroleum Research and Exploitation Company]
SNH	Société Nationale des Hydrocarbures [National Hydrocarbons Company]
SNI	Société Nationale d'Investissements [National Investment Company]
SONARA	Société Nationale de Raffinage [National Refinery Company]
SPD	Seed Production Division
SSNIT	Social Security and National Insurance Trust
UNCTAD	United Nations Conference on Trade and Development
UNECA	United Nations Economic Commission for Africa
ZCCM	Zambia Consolidated Copper Mines Limited
ZCCM-IH	ZCCM-Investor Holdings
ZDA	Zambia Development Agency
ZEITI	Zambia Extractive Industries Transparency Initiative
ZIMCO	Zambia Industrial and Mining Corporation

List of Figures

List of Tables

CHAPTER 1

Introduction: The Pernicious Nexus Between Capital Flight and Natural Resources in Africa

Léonce Ndikumana

Blessed With "Critical" Minerals

In *The Looting Machine*, Burgis (2015, p. 6) makes the following poignant observation: "Outsiders often think of Africa as a great drain of philanthropy, a continent that guzzles aid to no avail and contributes little to the global economy in return. But look closer at the resource industry, and the relationship between Africa and the rest of the world looks rather different." His observation portrays the pernicious nexus between capital flight and natural resources, which is the subject of this volume.

To cope with recurrent crises due to climate change, natural disasters, and pandemics, to combat poverty and inequality, to tackle the time-bomb problem of youth inequality, African governments need large and increasing amounts of financing. Where can they find the money? Naturally, they should turn to their natural resources, chiefly minerals and oil. They should exploit these resources, export them, collect royalty, rents, and taxes on the profits of the multinational companies operating in the extractive sectors. Most importantly, African countries should endeavor to move up the value chain in natural resource exploitation and stop exporting them in raw form. But, alas, this seemingly "natural" solution

L. Ndikumana, *Capital Flight from Cameroon, Ghana, and Zambia*, https://doi.org/10.1007/978-3-032-22770-6_1

has remained elusive, because African governments have failed to take control over those resources.

Indeed, Africa has been blessed with massive amounts of reserves of minerals and oil, which have historically been a source of envy and attraction of foreign actors since the pre-colonial era. With the current global drive to foster the transition to clean energy and fuel green growth, Africa has become yet a source of coveted attention for its critical minerals. The International Energy Agency (IEA) projected that from 2021 to 2030 the global demand for critical minerals will increase 3.5 times to more than 30 million tons under the 2050 net-zero emissions scenario (IEA, 2023). Africa accounts for 81% of the world production of platinum. It produces 74% of cobalt in the world, 72% of tantalum, and large fractions of other critical minerals such as manganese and chromium, as well as precious metals such as diamonds (62% of industrial diamonds and 35% diamond gems).[1] The Democratic Republic of Congo is the top producer of cobalt (71% of world total) and tantalum (31%), while South Africa is the number one producer of chromium (55%) and manganese (35%). The demand for these critical minerals is expected to rise substantially, which should generate export booms. But mineral export booms have come and gone, and African countries have had little to show for them. This has been the story of Africa's natural resources, as its first integration with the global trade economy long before the colonial era marked the end of its control over its resources.

Before the Western conquerors set foot on African soil, mineral resources belonged to the local kings and were exploited by the indigenous populations for their own use and to exchange the products through barter trade. Thus, the former kings of the territories that form today's Zambia owned the rights to the copper on their territory, and so did the kings of ancient Ghana own the rights to gold, as the kings of the Congo owned the rights to copper. But when the European traders arrived in African kingdoms, they systematically displaced African indigenous people from mining; in fact, it became illegal for Africans to mine in their own homeland (Martin, 1972; Musambachime, 2016). Thus, copper belonged to King Leopold II in the "Congo Free State," even before formal colonization of the Congo by Belgium. Colonization cemented and formalized the dispossession of African resources, with the rights

[1] *Source* Data from the World Bank, accessed online here: https://www.world-mining-data.info/?World_Mining_Data___Data_Section.

captured by the colonial state. The exploitation of minerals shifted into the hands of foreign corporations and served to mobilize government revenue for the colonial state and fuel industrialization in the West. The British South African Company (BSAC) was given by the British Crown the mining rights on the territories situated north of the Limpopo and the local chiefs lost their rights to grant mining concessions on those territories (Mudenda & Bardouille, 1988). Political independence did not reverse the dispossession of Africa's natural resources. Instead, control over the resources shifted from the colonial state to multinational corporations, perpetuated by fiscal regimes inherited from the colonial era and maintained by the post-independence African regimes in the name of attracting foreign capital and creating a "business-friendly" environment for mining.

The lack of control over its natural resources is a major reason why Africa remains the world's poverty capital despite its massive resource endowment. Indeed, Africa is the only continent where the number of poor people continues to rise despite national and global efforts to combat it. While Africa hosts only 15% of the world population, it accounts for 38% of the world's poor people. This share of Africa's population increased only by 2% points since 1990, but the continent's share in the world poor tripled during this period.[2] Clearly, Africa has failed to leverage its critical minerals for the benefits of its people.

Capital Flight and the "Curse"

Instead of benefiting from their endowment in minerals and oil, African countries have suffered heavy financial hemorrhage through capital flight. In fact, heavy dependence on minerals and oil exports is a key mechanism of the many faces of the "resource curse" in Africa. It is estimated that as of 2022, the continent has lost over $2.7 trillion (at 2022 constant US$) through capital flight (Ndikumana & Boyce, 2025). This amount refers to a sample of 30 African countries over the period 1970–2022. The amount represents nearly the sample's total GDP (99%) in 2022. The pace of capital flight has been increasing over time. Since 2010 the continent is losing an egregious $97 billion annually through unrecorded capital

[2] World Bank, World Development Indicators.

outflows. This exceeds the estimated resources needed for the continent to reach the sustainable development goals.

The data reveal a pernicious relationship between capital flight and natural resources. While all African countries are to some extent exposed to capital flight, those that are rich in natural resources appear to be particularly more exposed, especially the oil-rich nations. In the sample of 30 countries covered in the report by Ndikumana and Boyce (2025), six of the top ten countries with the highest amount of capital flight are oil dependent nations (Fig. 1.1).[3] Eleven of the top 15 countries are either mineral- or oil-rich. A key channel of the pernicious link between capital flight and natural resources is export misinvoicing, which is facilitated by weak enforcement of national regulations governing commodity trade, and the opacity of the international trading system notably due to the preeminent role of the so-called "trading hubs" such as those in Switzerland and the United Kingdom. An important facilitator of export misinvoicing is the economic power and complex structure of multinational mining and oil companies that take advantage of intra-company trading and their close links with tax havens. These mechanisms are a manifestation of the legacy of unequal exchange between Africa and advanced economies, and the continuation of a resource exploitation regime that robs the continent of its means of financing of its development agenda.

Capital flight robs a country of its wealth. But capital flight fueled by the plunder of a country's exhaustible natural resources is multiple times worse. It takes away both the natural resources and the proceeds from their exploitation. The resources are taken, and the monetary value goes with them! So, capital flight from resource-rich countries robs these countries not only the value of the resources but also the chances of using the proceeds of these resources to expand their production base through investments in new activities that would sustain the economy when the resources are exhausted. Thus, resource-fueled capital flight is one of the reasons why African resource-rich countries have failed to transform their economies, and why they will be "left in the cold" when their resources are exhausted.

The pernicious link between capital flight and minerals and oil in Africa is a key reason why African resource-rich countries have not been able

[3] The six countries are (in order of amount of capital flight): Nigeria, Algeria, Angola, Cameroon, Republic of Congo, and Ghana.

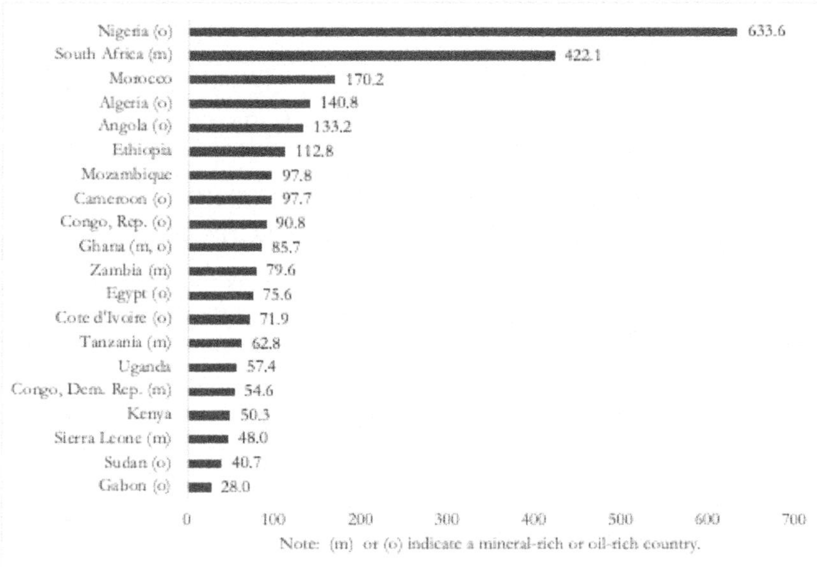

Fig. 1.1 Total capital flight from African countries over 1970–2022 (billion, constant 2022 US$) (*Source* Author's construction with data from Ndikumana and Boyce (2025). *Note* Out of a sample of 30 countries, the figure shows only 20 with the highest amount of capital flight)

to achieve their potential in terms of long-term growth and living standards of their populations. But the problem cannot be the minerals and the oil. And the problem is not African. Botswana is a leading producer of a coveted mineral—diamonds; yet it has posted sustained economic growth and is now an upper middle-income country (Matshediso, 2005; Robinson, 2013). Some African countries have been compared to peers in other regions that have comparable endowment and structural features but have performed much better notably in getting more out of their minerals and oil. In Chapter 7 of this book, we compare Cameroon to Malaysia, two countries with comparable features. At independence, per capita income in Malaysia was 1.4 times that in Cameroon. Today, a Malaysian citizen's income is nearly 8 times that of a Cameroonian. While Malaysia has been able to take advantage of its resources, Cameroon has not. The difference lies in the regime used to manage the resources to generate benefits in terms of employment creation, government revenue, foreign exchange earnings, value addition, investment of the revenue in non-resource sectors, and spillover effects on the rest of the economy. That is why Malaysia is a growth success while Cameroon is not.

Fiscal Regimes Perpetuating the Legacy of Unequal Exchange

A country's success in leveraging its natural resources to fuel its economic development depends on the type of compact signed between the government and private companies in the exploitation of its resources. The compact is known as the "fiscal regime," which determines three key elements. The first is the extent of direct engagement of the government in natural resource exploitation as a shareholder in mining and oil companies. Second are the payments to be made by companies to the government, and third is the set of incentives provided to companies to attract foreign investment. African countries have generally adopted fiscal regimes that prevent them from achieving optimal outcomes on the three dimensions. The dominant fiscal regime in Africa is the concession model, which provides little direct involvement of the government as a shareholder. Thus, the country relies on payments from companies in the form of royalties, corporate income tax, windfall taxes, and some non-tax levies. Given that the dominant players in the natural resource sector are multinational corporations with complex structures involving branches and affiliates located in tax havens, revenue generation from taxes and royalties is eroded through abusive transfer pricing, thin capitalization related to intra-firm borrowing, and export misinvoicing, which enable profit shifting and tax base erosion. Moreover, fiscal regimes in African countries are comparatively lenient with relatively low tax rates and long tax holidays, all in the name of attracting foreign capital into the extractive industry. This is despite the fact that fiscality is not a predominant deterrent of foreign direct investment in mining.[4] In the end, revenue generation remains sub-optimal, and the distribution of the benefits is tilted in favor of foreign companies.

[4] See IISD and OECD (2018) for "reasons not to offer income tax holidays to mining investors." The report states that "Tax holidays are lower priority for mining companies" (p. 22).

Externally biased fiscal regimes in African extractive industries are a legacy of the colonial era, which has been perpetuated by external pressures for liberalization and privatization in the post-independence era. Failed attempts at nationalization of mining as in the case of Zambia under President Kenneth Kaunda (Chapter 5 in this volume) have discouraged reforms of fiscal regimes toward a more balanced distribution of the gains from extractive industries. Under colonial rule, fiscal regimes that were biased in favor of private investors were internally consistent because the overall benefits accrued to the colonial state's economy. The colonial state issued mining rights to corporations from its country. Thus, tax and non-tax revenue as well as repatriation of corporate profits benefited the same colonial economy. In that context, even though tax evasion by mining corporations reduced the colonial state's revenue, the leakages were integrated into the same colonial economy. So, tax evasion and other leakages such as through export misinvoicing were "internalized" in the colonial economy. This internal consistency broke down with independence. The fiscal regimes in free African nations remained biased in favor of foreign investors, undermining revenue mobilization by a combination of tax evasion, profit shifting, and export misinvoicing. The gains from these economic malpractices accrue outside of African economies. So, the leakages are no longer internalized. This constitutes a major structural mechanism of the African resource curse.

Opaque International Commodity Trading System

The bulk of the gains from natural resources occur through exports which generate government revenue and foreign exchange earnings. Thus, we would expect that rising international demand and prices for commodities would generate export booms resulting in increased government revenue and foreign exchange accumulation in African resource-rich countries. This expectation has not materialized. International commodity booms have not generated meaningful and sustained gains for African resource-rich countries. One of the key reasons is the opacity—or dark spots—in the international commodity trading system. Analysis of commodity trade data reveals two systemic issues. The first is commodity export underinvoicing, whereby the value of African exports as recorded by the exporting country is substantially lower than the value of its trading partners' imports of the same commodity, even after accounting for the cost of insurance and freight. In such a situation, exporting companies artificially under-report their exports with the intention of retaining the undeclared foreign exchange earnings abroad, which constitutes capital flight. This appears to be a systemic problem for gold exports as it is illustrated in this volume in the cases on Ghana (Chapter 3) and Zambia (Chapter 6).

The second issue is the reverse scenario, whereby a substantial fraction of African commodity exports cannot be traced in the import statistics of the trading partners. It is as though some of African commodities have been sold to the planet Mars. A prime suspect is the so-called "trading hubs," where commodities are held and not declared as imports, and eventually on-sold to destination countries when the market prices are favorable. This phenomenon is illustrated in the case of copper exports recorded in Zambia's books as heading to Switzerland (Chapter 6 in this volume). Under such an opaque trading system, it is impossible to know the true market value of African commodities, and therefore we cannot tell whether the exporting countries are receiving a fair fraction of the value of their commodities. Obviously, if Africa can't even "count" how much minerals it is selling to the rest of the world, it is impossible to know how much it is losing through the opaque international trading system.

Why Cameroon, Ghana, and Zambia?

The issue of capital flight from Africa has been documented substantially in terms of the magnitude of the financial hemorrhage and the distribution across countries (Ajayi & Ndikumana, 2015; Ndikumana & Boyce, 2022, 2025; UNCTAD, 2020). We know that the problem is big, not new, and getting worse over time. What we still know much less about are the factors that drive capital flight, the mechanisms of the leakages of capital, the actors and the enablers, and the ultimate impact on African economies. Yet, the knowledge of these matters is critically important for designing policies aimed at combating capital flight. This book seeks to contribute to filling this gap, following in the footsteps of the studies published in Ndikumana and Boyce (2022). The book presents the findings from case studies on Cameroon, Ghana, and Zambia, three countries that have experienced high capital flight and are highly endowed in natural resources. But the three countries also exhibit substantial differences in the structure of their economies, the management of their extractive industries and overall performance of their economies, which makes them representative of the diversities and similarities across African countries.

Dubbed "Africa in miniature", https://discover-cameroon.com/en/about-cameroon/ accessed April 23, 2026, **Cameroon** is among the countries with the highest growth potential on the continent with a vast endowment in natural resources. It is highly dependent on primary commodities, with cocoa and petroleum accounting for 68% of its total exports. It has also suffered heavy hemorrhage through capital flight, with total unrecorded capital outflows standing at $97.7 billion in 2022, placing it in the 8th position among African countries (Ndikumana & Boyce, 2025). The country has failed to leverage its natural wealth to fuel economic development, an illustration of the typical African unfulfilled potential. The case study on Cameroon focuses on the oil sector which represents 52% of total exports. The case of Cameroon is both typical and unique in Africa along several important dimensions. It is a case where the organizational structure of the oil sector had the potential to leverage the country's oil endowment in two ways. But the potential has remained elusive.

First, the industrial organization of the oil sector gives the government a strong hand on the sector through the Société Nationale des Hydrocarbures (SNH), the company created with a dual mandate to both regulate oil activities and manage the government's investments in the sector including its shares in private companies. This is unique in Africa where governments typically sign concession agreements with extractive companies, whereby they only collect taxes and non-tax levies from these companies. In contrast, the Cameroonian fiscal regime allows the government to be an investor in oil exploitation, and therefore to harvest more benefits than under the typical concession model. As it will be clear in Chapter 7 in this volume, however, this model has not met the expectations, and Cameroon remains the typical case of a resource-rich country that has failed to leverage its resources to reach its economic and social development goals.

Second, departing once again from typical practice in Africa where countries exploit and sell unprocessed commodities, the Cameroonian government had the right idea to process oil domestically and supply the domestic market with processed oil products. But it made two strategic mistakes. It established the Société Nationale de Raffinage (SONARA) in 1973 to manage an oil refinery built to process light crude oil, which Cameroon does not produce. The heavy crude oil that Cameroon produces is exported. This design created serious problems including the reliance on imported crude oil, equipment, and material, which cannot be covered by the proceeds of oil processed by the national refinery as it is meant to be sold domestically. This creates a structural currency mismatch problem for SNH and SONARA. As a result, Cameroon has not escaped the legacy of African resource-rich countries that produce what they do not consume and consume what they do not produce. In that respect, Cameroon is indeed an interesting case study.

Ghana ranks tenth on the scale of capital flight which stood at $85.7 billion by 2022. It is also a typical resource-dependent economy where cocoa, gold, and oil account for about 80% of total exports. The case study on Ghana focuses on cocoa and gold, the country's traditional export commodities before the recent discovery of oil. The two sectors offer a unique opportunity to investigate the significant implications of the industrial organization and the fiscal regime governing an extractive sector. While cocoa wields top national attention as "the political crop" and is managed with a heavy presence of the government through its managing entity COCOBOD, the gold sector has traditionally been fully privatized and dominated by foreign corporations. The government has a strong hand in the regulation of the cocoa value chain from the farm-gate to the export counter, enabling it to secure a stable price for farmers and repatriate the foreign exchange proceeds of exports of cocoa beans. In contrast, gold mining companies have typically operated under mining agreements that grant them generous fiscal incentives and the ability to keep substantial fractions of their export proceeds offshore. The organization of the cocoa sector is certainly not perfect, especially given that the value of cocoa is concentrated at the top of the value chain, which is controlled by foreign processing companies. For gold, exports data are so murky that it is even impossible to trace large fractions of Ghana's gold exports in the statistics of its trading partners, especially South Africa. Under the concession model that governs the gold sector, the country is stuck on the short end of the bargain, thus eroding the gains accruing to the national economy. The establishment of the Ghana Gold Board (GoldBod) in the beginning of 2025, whose mandate is to manage the gold sector carries promises of improvements in the distribution of the benefits of gold exploitation. GoldBod is "the sole authority with exclusive rights to buy, sell, weigh, grade, assay, value and export gold and other precious minerals in Ghana."[5] This innovation has already been

[5] GoldBod: https://goldbod.gov.gh/.

credited for a sizeable increase in gold exports in the first quarter of 2025, with the value of exports nearly tripling in April relative to the same month in 2024.[6] To the extent that this momentum can be sustained, this will have beneficial consequences on the country's foreign exchange reserves and the exchange rate of the cedi. The comparative perspective on cocoa and gold sectors provides useful insights for policy and regulatory reforms that can help increase African countries' benefits from resource exploitation.

Zambia is a copper economy, and its Kwacha is "a commodity currency" whose value moves at the rhythm of copper prices and exports. Copper represents 70% of total exports, and it constitutes a vital source of government revenue. But even though copper is the dominant product, Zambia also has other minerals including gold and gemstones, which could potentially help to diversify the export base, create jobs, and stimulate economic growth. But this potential remains underleveraged as these other minerals have thus far remained peripheral to the country's development agenda. The case study on Zambia provides vivid illustrations of the problems associated with an opaque international commodity trading system exhibiting both export misinvoicing and "missing copper" that can't be traced in the records of the so-called "trading hubs" notably Switzerland. Similarly, Zambia's gold statistics cannot be reconciled with those of the main destination which is South Africa. These systemic discrepancies in trade statistics illustrate the chronic problem of export misinvoicing that plagues Zambia and most African resource-rich countries and serves as a major channel of the resource curse.

Together the three countries provide a rich laboratory for the investigation of the nexus between capital flight and natural resources in our quest to understand the drivers, mechanisms, actors, and facilitators of capital flight from African countries. The findings presented in this book are based on the analysis of a combination of secondary data and first-hand information collected through fieldwork in the three countries. While published literature and official government reports may offer substantial information on natural resources and capital flight, a big wealth of information is still unwritten, and it can only be learned by visiting the mining sites and talking to the managers and the engineers, visiting the cocoa

[6] In April 2024, Ghana exported $897.6 million of gold, nearly three times the $304.7 million exported in April 2024. Source: GoldBod's website: https://goldbod.gov.gh/goldbod-ghanas-forex-reserves-surge-amid-record-exports-under-mahama/.

farms, discussing the issues with experts at national universities and think tanks, and by talking to officials in government ministries and specialized bodies that are responsible for the formulation and implementation of sectoral regulations and macroeconomic policy. Information from site visits and interactions with various stakeholders helped us to put flesh on the findings from statistical analysis and to make sense of the apparent disconnect between resource endowment and economic outcomes, as well as the perverse connections between resource-rich countries and the global economy.

Indeed, fieldwork enabled us to hear directly from mining operators, cocoa farmers, as well as policy makers in various government institutions. For instance, a visit to cocoa farms in Nyankrom near the town of Swedru in Ghana's Central Region was an opportunity to hear from hard-working farmers about the demands of cocoa growing, and to witness the modest living conditions of those proud and tenacious farmers. That helped us to put into perspective the statistical illustrations of the impact of cocoa on living conditions presented in Chapter 4 of this book. Similarly, visits to the sites of artisanal and small-scale mining in Lufwanyama (emeralds) and Mwambwa (gold) in Zambia helped us to put into perspective the complexity of this subsector, the potential for growth, as well as the challenges associated with the regulation of the subsector. With inadequate regulation, opportunities for mobilizing government revenue and foreign exchange are lost as investors in the subsector claim to "never find" the gold or the gemstones, as the exploration stage seems to be endless. Witnessing first-hand the early stages of the construction of a gold marketing center in Mwambwa (Zambia) brought to light the potential impact of the formalization of gold mining and the development of domestic value chains, which augurs very well for the future of the sector.

Visits to large-scale mining sites in Zambia was a major learning experience as we listened to company managers about the complexity of mining from a business perspective, and to the smart mining engineers about the challenges these companies face from a technical perspective. This helped us to further understand some of the reasons for the dominance of foreign investors, notably the heavy capital requirements in a financially underdeveloped continent, and the intensive knowledge requirements in a continent that has not adequately invested the proceeds of its minerals to train its own engineers.

A major component of the fieldwork was the interactions with policy makers and the facilitation they provided in connecting us with the operators. Discussions with policy makers and regulators were both enlightening and humbling. They were enlightening because they helped fill gaps in our understanding of the sectors from our reading of the literature. But humbling as well because they exposed the complexities and challenges of regulation of the extractive industry and the balancing acts that policy makers must orchestrate in managing the sectors. It is only hoped that the learning from the exchanges with policy makers was to some extent reciprocal.

Structure of the Book

The book is organized in six substantive chapters besides this introduction and the conclusion. Chapter 2 presents the estimates of capital flight from Cameroon, Ghana, and Zambia from 1970 to 2022 and discusses the key drivers of the phenomenon. This sets the stage for the case studies aimed at uncovering the mechanisms and enablers of capital flight from Africa with a focus on the role of natural resources, with a view to shed light on possible strategies to curb further capital outflows in the context of efforts to scale up and diversify development financing to support recovery from global crises, the transition to green growth, and to boost sustainable development in Africa.

Chapter 3 presents the historical and institutional context of the development of the gold sector in Ghana and examines the contribution of the sector to the economy and its exposure to capital flight. The analysis sheds light on the important role that the regulatory framework and the fiscal regime that govern the gold sector have played in perpetuating a system of unequal distribution of the benefits from gold exploitation in terms of tax revenue and foreign exchange earnings in favor of foreign gold companies. The chapter presents the results of a statistical investigation of gold exports showing substantial discrepancies between Ghana's gold exports and the value of imports recorded by its trading partners. These differences point to export underinvoicing as a conduit of capital flight, while also exhibiting a systematic lack of transparency and inconsistencies, especially in the case of gold recorded as destined for South Africa which does not show up in the latter's import statistics. Overall, the analysis suggests that the benefits from the gold sector remain much below potential, calling for structural reforms in the governance of the sector. In this perspective, the recent creation of the Ghana Gold Board (GoldBod)[7] is a much welcome innovation.

Chapter 4 presents a case study of the cocoa sector in Ghana. It examines the industrial organization and fiscal regime that governs the sector, with a detailed discussion of the role of the Ghana Cocoa Board (COCOBOD) and how it regulates the operations in the sector. The chapter investigates the implications of this industrial organization for the performance of the cocoa sector, and how it helps to minimize the exposure to capital flight that may occur through export misinvoicing and to prevent the leakage of foreign exchange earnings from exports. The evidence presented in the chapter suggests that the benefits from the cocoa sector in terms of contribution to economic growth, tax revenue and poverty reduction remain suboptimal. This suggests that there is substantial room for improvement through targeted reforms and policy interventions at the sectoral level.

Chapter 5 presents a case study of Zambia's mining sector. It reveals that the expectations that Zambia's vast endowment in mineral resources would drive economic transformation and propel the country to higher levels of living standards remain elusive. The analysis shows that the contribution of mineral exploitation to employment, government revenue, foreign exchange earnings, economic growth, and poverty reduction remains suboptimal. Yet, the sector continues to attract substantial attention from foreign investors and remains dominated by foreign corporations. So, the chapter poses the question: if the people of Zambia are not reaping adequate benefits from mineral resource exploitation, then who is capturing the rents? To shed light on this question, the chapter provides a review of the history, industrial organization, and management of the mining sector, and explores the factors that have constrained the performance of the sector with an emphasis on the role of the ownership structure, the fiscal regime, exposure to external shocks, and lack of transformational orientation of the sector. The analysis helps to draw some policy suggestions for the improvement of the performance of the mining sector going forward.

Chapter 6 investigates mineral export misinvoicing as a channel of capital flight from Zambia, with a focus on copper, gold, and gemstones. The chapter highlights the potential importance of the gold and

[7] Government of Ghana, Ghana Gold Board Bill, 2025—Memorandum (26th February 2025).

gemstones subsectors, which traditionally have remained at the margin of the national mining development agenda. Statistical analysis reveals major discrepancies between Zambia's recorded exports and imports as recorded by its trading partners. In the case of copper, a large fraction of exports recorded in Zambia as headed to Switzerland does not appear in Swiss imports. The "missing copper" cannot be traced through triangular analysis of trade between Switzerland and its major partners either. Gaps in the opposite direction are observed in Zambia-China trade, suggesting export underinvoicing, a mechanism of capital flight. These do not offset the gaps observed in mirror trade statistics between Zambia and Switzerland, which remain a mystery. Similarly, whereas the primary destination of gold exports recorded by Zambia is South Africa, virtually no gold imports from Zambia are recorded in South Africa's trade statistics. The evidence presented in the chapter calls for urgent measures to curb misinvoicing of mineral exports and to address the structural opacity in the trade value chain for Zambia to maximize the benefits from the mineral exploitation.

Chapter 7 presents a case study of Cameroon with a focus on the oil sector. The study provides a detailed analysis of the historical emergence of the oil sector and the institutional and regulatory arrangements governing the sector to shed light on the causes of the country's failure to leverage its potential considering its impressive resource endowment. The chapter discusses the apparent "paradox of plenty" in the sense that while Cameroon is one of the most endowed African countries in a wide range of overground and underground natural resources, it has struggled to leverage these resources to secure decent living standards for its population. Thus, instead of boasting impressive development outcomes, Cameroon is among African resource-rich countries that are known for suffering high financial hemorrhage through capital flight, suggesting that capital flight is one of the mechanisms of the "resource curse." The evidence presented in the chapter may shed light on strategies to usher a new path toward a Cameroonian economy beyond oil.

Chapter 8 concludes the book by offering some policy options for combating capital flight and disabling the pernicious link between capital flight and natural resource exploitation in Africa.

References

Ajayi, I. S., & Ndikumana, L. (2015). *Capital Flight from Africa: Causes, Effects and Policy Issues*. Oxford University Press.

Burgis, T. (2015). *The Looting Machine*. HarperCollins Publishers.

IEA. (2023). *Critical Minerals Market Review 2023*. International Energy Agency.

IISD and OECD. (2018). *Tax Incentives in Mining: Minimizing Risks to Revenue*. International Institute for Sustainable Development.

Martin, A. (1972). *Minding Their Own Business: Zambia's Struggle Against Western Control*. Hutchinson.

Matshediso, I. B. (2005). A Review of Mineral Development and Investment Policies of Botswana. *Resources Policy, 30*(3), 203–207.

Mudenda, G., & Bardouille, R. (1988). *Technological Development and Educational Policy: The Case of the Mining Industry in Zambia* (IIEP Research Report No. 71). International Institute for Educational Planning.

Musambachime, M. C. (2016). *Wealth from the Rocks: Mining and Smelting of Metals in Pre-Colonial Zambia*. Xlibris Corporation.

Ndikumana, L., & Boyce, J. K. (2022). *On the Trail of Capital Flight from Africa: The Takers and the Enablers*. Oxford University Press.

Ndikumana, L., & Boyce, J. K. (2025, January). *New Estimates of Capital Flight From African Countries, 1970–2022*. Political Economy Research Institute.

Robinson, J. (2013). Botswana as a role model for country success. In A. Fosu (Ed.), *Achieving Development Success: Strategies and Lessons from the Developing World* (pp. 187–203). Oxford University Press.

UNCTAD. (2020). *Tackling Illicit Financial Flows for Sustainable Development in Africa*. Geneva, Switzerland: United Nations.

CHAPTER 2

Magnitudes and Drivers of Capital Flight from Cameroon, Ghana, and Zambia

Léonce Ndikumana

Introduction

African countries face daunting challenges in meeting the large and growing needs for financing their development agenda. The situation has been exacerbated by the Covid-19 pandemic and the war in Ukraine has caused a contraction in economic activity, reduced government revenue and capital flows, and undermined macroeconomic stability. African countries are experiencing financial stress associated with increasing external debt burden due to rising world interest rates and an increasing share of expensive private debt. Some countries have been forced to default, including Zambia, one of the countries covered by this study, while others such as Ghana have fallen into the debt distress category, which makes it harder for them to access additional external finance.

At the same time, African countries have experienced an acceleration of financial hemorrhage through capital flight since the turn of the twenty-first century. It is estimated that as of 2022, Africa had lost more than $2.7 trillion through unrecorded capital outflows (Ndikumana & Boyce, 2025). The financial hemorrhage has accelerated since the turn of the century, a period that ironically witnessed average higher growth rates across the continent. From 2010, the continent has lost about $97

L. Ndikumana, *Capital Flight from Cameroon, Ghana, and Zambia*,
https://doi.org/10.1007/978-3-032-22770-6_2

billion annually through capital flight.[1] These outflows vastly exceed the resources that flow into the continent in the form of official development aid, foreign direct investment, or external borrowing. The evidence suggests that strategies to boost development financing in Africa must put the problem of capital flight and other illicit financial flows at the center stage. Specifically, instead of focusing only on how to attract more external financing, African governments and their development partners must adopt strategies to curb illicit capital outflows and repatriate the wealth accumulated abroad that originates from capital flight.

While all countries are affected by capital flight, natural resource-dependent African countries experience comparatively more capital flight than their resource-scarce counterparts. According to the latest estimates, eight of the top fifteen African countries with the highest volume of capital flight are resource-dependent (Ndikumana & Boyce, 2021; see details in the next section).[2] This suggests that the causes of capital flight are country and context specific. This has motivated research that goes beyond the analysis at the aggregate and cross-sectional levels toward case studies to better understand the mechanisms, channels, enablers, and drivers of capital flight from the continent. This study follows in the tracks of the recent work by Ndikumana and Boyce (2022a) and their colleagues that investigated the cases of Angola, Côte d'Ivoire, and South Africa to uncover specific drivers of capital flight and the role of domestic and external enablers of the plunder of natural resources that fuels capital outflows.

This chapter focuses on the cases of Cameroon, Ghana, and Zambia, which are significantly endowed with natural resources and have experienced substantial capital flight over the past decades. Total capital flight over the 1970–2022 period amounts to $97.7 billion for Cameroon, $85.7 billion for Ghana, and $79.6 billion for Zambia. Key channels of capital flight in the three countries are external borrowing and trade misinvoicing, except for Ghana where the latter is minimal. While external borrowing directly and indirectly fuels capital flight, trade misinvoicing constitutes an important mechanism of unrecorded cross-border capital

[1] See estimates of annual losses through illicit financial flows, a broader concept than capital flight, in UNECA (2015).

[2] The top fifteen countries in order of highest amount of capital flight are: Nigeria, South Africa, Morocco, Algeria, Angola, Ethiopia, Mozambique, Cameroon, Rep. of Congo, Ghana, Zambia, Egypt, Côte d'Ivoire, Tanzania, and Uganda.

movement. In all three countries, capital flight has accelerated since the beginning of the twenty-first century, even as they confronted the effects of severe shocks associated with the COVID-19 pandemic and the war in Ukraine, which have negatively affected international financial flows and trade. The results at the country level shed light on possible strategies to curb further capital outflows in the context of efforts to scale up development financing to support the recovery from global crises and the transition to green growth and boost sustainable development in Africa.

The next section reviews the literature on the drivers of capital flight with a focus on how the analysis at the case study level can help advance knowledge on the subject. This is followed by a presentation of the data sources and the methodology used to estimate capital flight in Section 3. Section 4 presents and discusses the findings. Section 5 concludes with a summary of the findings and some policy recommendations.

Drivers of Capital Flight

The economic literature on capital flight has devoted substantial attention to understanding the nature of the phenomenon, measuring its magnitude, and exploring empirically its drivers over time and across countries. The empirical evidence has convincingly shown that capital flight is a severe problem for all developing countries, whose intensity continues to increase over time. Understanding the drivers of capital flight is essential for the design and implementation of policies to prevent it and encourage the repatriation of wealth stashed abroad through capital flight.

Thus far, however, most of the analysis has been undertaken primarily at the cross-sectional and aggregate level. Recently, however, efforts have been undertaken to delve into the complexity of the drivers and mechanisms of capital flight at the country level, considering domestic as well as external dimensions of the phenomenon. The volume edited by Ndikumana and Boyce (2022a) presents compelling evidence on the cases of Angola (Shaxson, 2022), Côte d'Ivoire (Merckaert, 2022), and South Africa (Aboobaker et al., 2022). Country-level analysis helps to shed light on the pertinence of the evidence accumulated from aggregate and cross-country studies. This section highlights key dimensions where the literature can benefit substantially from case studies, as a way of motivating the case study on Cameroon, Ghana, and Zambia.

Natural Resources and Capital Flight

The evidence from the empirical literature shows a close connection between capital flight and endowment in minerals and oil in developing countries. In the case of Africa, oil- and mineral-rich countries feature prominently on the top of the list of countries with the highest volume of capital flight (Ndikumana & Boyce, 2025). Table 2.1 presents the estimated total capital flight over 1970–2022 for the top fifteen countries along with indicators of the contribution of natural resources and manufactured products to total exports over 2018–2022. In thirteen of the top fifteen countries, primary commodities account for more than 60% of total exports. The two exceptions are Egypt (53.9%) and Morocco (27.4%). The share of primary commodities in total exports exceeds 90% for eight of the fifteen top countries. Minerals are the dominant commodities for South Africa (38.9% of total exports) and Zambia (78.5%). Agricultural commodities account for a sizeable share of total exports in Côte d'Ivoire (39.7%), Ethiopia (30%), and Ghana (15.7%). The flip side of heavy endowment in natural resources is lack of diversification as exhibited by the small share of manufactured products in total exports. Manufactured products represent less than 20% of total exports in these countries, with the exceptions of Egypt, Morocco, and South Africa.

The three countries covered in this book—Cameroon, Ghana, and Zambia—exhibit typical features of natural resource dependence and are therefore compelling cases for examining the extent of exposure to capital flight associated with natural resource endowment and governance of the natural resource sector.

In the case of Cameroon, crude oil exports represented an average of 50% of total exports over 2018–2022, while cocoa and tea accounted for 27%. The share of crude oil in total exports as well as its contribution to GDP have been declining over time. In 1986, crude oil accounted for 19.9% of GDP and 48.2% of total exports.

The Ghanaian economy is also dominated by primary commodities, which make up 94.7% of total exports. Ghana's exports have been traditionally dominated by gold and cocoa, and natural resource dependence has increased with the discovery of oil. In 2021, oil, gold, and cocoa accounted for 80.6% of total exports.

The Zambian economy is dominated by the mineral sector, primarily copper and cobalt, which accounted for 73.5% of total exports in 2020 (Bank of Zambia database). This share has fluctuated over time following

Table 2.1 Importance of natural resources (as a percentage of total exports) in African countries with the highest amount of capital flight (over 1970–2018)

	Capital flight (1970–2022) ($ billion)	*Fuels (% of exports)*	*Ores, metals, precious stones, and non-monetary gold (% of exports)*	*Coffee, tea, cocoa, spices, and manufactures thereof (% of exports)*	*All primary commodities (% of exports)*	*Manufactured goods (% of exports)*
Nigeria*	633.6	91.1	2.1	1.1	96.4	3.4
South Africa	422.1	10.5	38.9	0.2	61.9	37.9
Morocco	170.8	0.4	5.7	0.3	27.4	71.7
Algeria*	140.8	93.2	0.5	0.0	95.0	4.7
Angola*	133.2	92.8	5.1	0.0	98.3	1.7
Ethiopia	112.8	0.02	9.2	30.2	79.8	17.8
Mozambique	97.8	39.9	36.0	0.2	93.4	5.3
Cameroon*	97.7	50.3	5.8	14.4	93.6	6.3
Congo, Rep.*	90.8	68.8	18.7	0.4	92.6	7.0
Ghana*	85.7	28.0	41.4	15.7	94.7	5.0
Zambia	79.6	2.0	78.5	0.2	89.1	10.8
Egypt*	75.6	28.2	8.8	0.8	53.9	45.4
Côte d'Ivoire*	71.9	13.3	10.7	39.7	92.3	7.5
Tanzania	62.8	2.7	49.5	4.4	85.3	14.6
Uganda	57.4	3.8	30.4	20.5	83.4	16.3

Source UNCTAD database
Note * indicates an oil exporting country

variations in production and international prices of minerals. For instance, in 2010, it was at 81%, but it dropped to 65% in 2013.

The question is, what explains the relatively high exposure to capital flight for countries that depend on natural resources? The relationship between capital flight and natural resources involves both direct and indirect linkages, which can be conceptualized in various ways (Ndikumana & Sarr, 2019). First, abundance of natural resources, and especially high dependence on revenue from resource rents, tends to weaken the mechanisms of control and government accountability, because the resource rents reduce the government's need to collect taxes, which consequently weakens the state-people performance contract. Such an environment generates temptations for politicians to embezzle the resource rents, part of which are siphoned abroad for safe keeping. Kolstad & Søreide, 2009 put it as follows: "corruption is the development problem in resource-rich countries, rather than just one of a number of problems" (p. 14).

Second, when natural resource exploitation is dominated by multinational corporations (MNCs), the imbalance of economic power and technical capacity between the African state (the regulator) and the MNCs creates opportunities for violation and abuse of rules and regulations in the areas of taxation, trade, and foreign exchange transactions. In such an environment, capital flight may occur through trade misinvoicing by exporters as well as from embezzlement of government revenue by public officials.

Third, the outflow of capital through export misinvoicing is further facilitated by the ability of globally connected MNCs to trade commodities among related entities. In the case of African countries where extractive sectors are dominated by MNCs, we can expect a close connection between capital flight and natural resource dependence.

The aim of the case studies on Cameroon, Ghana, and Zambia is to further explore these linkages between natural resources and capital flight through detailed historical, institutional, and statistical analysis focusing on key natural resources in each country. The findings are presented in the subsequent chapters of this book.

Institutions, Natural Resource Governance, and Capital Flight

Even though most resource-endowed African countries have experienced relatively higher capital flight than their counterparts, there are a few exceptions that have not suffered a similar fate. A good example is

Botswana, which is the world's top producer of diamonds and yet experienced virtually no capital flight (estimated at a mere $1.2 billion over 1970–2022). This suggests that while endowment in natural resources may be a cause of vulnerability to capital flight, there are other factors that can help mitigate the risk. One prominent mitigating factor is the quality of institutions in general, and the quality of management of the extractive industries in particular. In other words, efficient natural resource governance prevents natural resource-fueled capital flight.

Cross-sectional econometric analysis on African countries supports this proposition: the interaction between resource rents and measures of institutional quality has been shown to be positively related with capital flight (Ndikumana & Sarr, 2019; Ndikumana et al., 2015). Case studies provide direct evidence on the role of institutions and governance of extractive industries for the linkages between capital flight and natural resources. The cases of Angola, Côte d'Ivoire, and South Africa are analyzed in detail in Ndikumana and Boyce (2022a, b, c). In Angola, oil has fueled capital flight and personal enrichment of politically connected individuals and corporations through export misinvoicing, embezzlement of export proceeds that "go missing," and funneling funds in offshore financial centers with the help of international commercial banks (Shaxson, 2022). The Angolan national oil company has been used by the political elites as a cash cow. Capital flight from Angola is a manifestation of the "resource curse" preventing the country from fully leveraging its oil endowment.

In Côte d'Ivoire, where the cocoa sector is fully privatized and dominated by foreign corporations, endemic opacity in cocoa export statistics is a signal of export misinvoicing as a channel of capital flight (Merckaert, 2022). Similarly, export misinvoicing plagues South Africa's mineral sector (Ndikumana et al., 2022), resulting in large volumes of capital flight. The case of South Africa presents an illustration of the complex network of domestic and international actors that participate in the plunder of public assets (including state-owned enterprises) to accumulate private wealth stashed abroad with the help of domestic and foreign banks.

One aspect of governance of natural resources that matters for the linkages between capital flight and natural resources is the ownership structure, and specifically the role of the public sector in extractive industries. The first question is whether extractive companies are national or foreign, and the second is whether they are privately owned, government-owned, or mixed. Ghana offers a useful case study in this respect, especially in comparing the organizational structure and regulation of the cocoa sector and that of the gold sector, and the implications for the performance of the two sectors and the overall impact on the economy. Chapter 3 in this book (by Ndikumana and Cantah) examines the gold sector while Chapter 4 (by Ndikumana and Adjei-Mantey) analyzes the case of cocoa. The two studies reveal significant disparities between the two sectors due to differences in the regulatory framework and organizational structure of the two sectors. While the cocoa sector is strictly regulated by the government with a dual role of COCOBOD as an operator and a regulator, the gold sector is fully liberalized, and it is governed by a business-friendly fiscal regime. The establishment of the Ghana Gold Board (GoldBod) in April 2025 constituted a major innovation in the governance of the gold sector (see Chapter 3 for details). The analysis of trade statistics shows a stark difference: while cocoa trade statistics do not exhibit large systematic discrepancies between Ghana's exports and its partners' recorded imports, gold statistics exhibit large discrepancies—especially in the case of gold exported to South Africa. Specifically, Ghana reports substantial gold exports to South Africa, but little Ghanaian gold shows up in South Africa's import statistics. To the extent that these discrepancies in gold trade with South Africa (overinvoicing of gold exports) are not compensated by symmetric discrepancies with other partners (underinvoicing), they would reduce the estimated amount of capital flight.

Moreover, while all the proceeds of cocoa exports are repatriated to Ghana by COCOBOD, a substantial fraction of earnings from gold exports is retained abroad by foreign companies following specific clauses in the Development Agreements signed between the government and individual gold companies (Chapter 3). The two modes of management and regulation have generated substantially different outcomes in terms of exposure to capital flight from the exploitation of cocoa compared to gold.

Evidence on the linkages between capital flight and natural resources through trade misinvoicing has also been established in other studies on African countries. A few examples are given here for illustrative purposes. Kwaramba et al. (2016) present evidence of export misinvoicing in Zambia in the cases of diamonds, gold, and nickel. Export misinvoicing in the oil and timber sectors in Cameroon has been examined in studies by Gankou et al. (2016) and Mpenya et al. (2016). Substantial export misinvoicing has been found in the diamonds sector in Central African

Republic, mainly attributed to weak governance (Yapatake Kossele & Njong, 2020). The evidence suggests that misinvoicing of exports of natural resources is a key mechanism of the strong link between natural resources and capital flight.

External Debt and Capital Flight

The empirical literature has documented close linkages between capital flight and external debt, especially since the debt crises of the 1980s (Ndikumana & Boyce, 2003, 2011a, b; Ndikumana et al., 2015). The relationships can be direct and indirect, and can run in both directions. External debt can directly fuel capital flight as borrowed funds are embezzled and converted into private wealth that is funneled abroad into bank accounts and physical assets such as real estate and other valuable objects. Econometric evidence has shown that in the case of African countries, more than half of each dollar borrowed flows back abroad as capital flight in the same year (Ndikumana & Boyce, 2003; Ndikumana et al., 2015). Additional leakages of borrowed funds continue in subsequent years.

External borrowing also causes capital flight indirectly through adverse effects on the economy that in turn induce capital flight. The accumulation of external debt increases investment risk and reduces the returns to investment, inducing wealth holders to transfer their assets abroad. These "debt overhang" effects are magnified by weak economic governance and political instability, which may presage high taxation or high risk of expropriation in the future. Wealth holders may seek to avoid such risks by funneling their wealth abroad, thereby fueling capital.

The debt-capital flight links merit serious attention given the recent rapid acceleration of external debts across the continent, with some countries facing severe debt distress and even default (Coulibaly et al., 2019; Ndikumana et al., 2020). Debt accumulation in Africa since the turn of the century has coincided with an explosion of capital flight. The trend worsened prior to the Covid crisis and was further exacerbated by its economic fallout.

The three countries covered in this study have experienced rapid increase in external debt from the turn of the century.[3] Another feature

[3] World Bank, International Debt Statistics.

of this period is that the rise in debt stock has coincided with substantial increase in US dollar-denominated debt, leading to rising costs of debt service due to steady appreciation of the US dollar against national currencies. Indeed, Zambia experienced an increase in the average interest rate on new external debt commitments and in nonguaranteed private debt, which raised the overall cost of debt. As a result of the rapidly rising burden of debt obligations in the context of a struggling economy, Zambia became the first African country to face debt default in the wake of the Covid crisis in 2020. This underscores the importance of carefully investigating the implications of debt accumulation for capital flight in African countries.

Globalization, Safe Havens, and Offshore Financial Centers

Globalization has increased the speed and scope of cross-border movement of goods and capital. With the acceleration of technological innovation, globalization is associated with increased difficulties in tracking and deterring illicit financial flows. These flows are facilitated by the expansion and sophistication of the so-called "safe havens" and offshore financial centers that help in the transfer and concealment of private wealth. The accumulation of private wealth from past capital flight from Africa has reached towering heights, making the continent a "net creditor" to the rest of the world in the sense that the accumulated stocks of wealth from capital flight exceed the continent's debts vis-à-vis the rest of the world. This illustrates the substantial opportunity costs incurred by the continent from capital flight, beyond the outflows that deplete domestic savings and undermine productive investment on an annual basis.

The global nature of capital flight and the forces that facilitate it imply that strategies to combat the problem must also be global. Specifically, preventing further capital flight and inducing the repatriation of private wealth held offshore will require a global compact anchored around enforcement of transparency and accountability in international trade and financial systems, supported by effective and universal automatic exchange of information on trade and banking on a country-by-country basis.

Estimation of Capital Flight: Methodology and Data

Capital flight is estimated following the latest methodology as presented in Ndikumana and Boyce (2025), which fine-tuned the algorithm used in previous studies (Ndikumana & Boyce, 2010, 2022b). For each country, capital flight is measured as unrecorded capital outflows, which is obtained as the difference between recorded sources of inflows and recorded uses of these inflows. Recorded inflows consist of net external borrowing (reported in the World Bank's International Debt Statistics database), foreign direct investment, portfolio investment, and "other investment" as recorded in the Balance of Payments. Net external borrowing (debt flows) is obtained as the change in debt stock adjusted for exchange rate fluctuations (based on the currencies in which the external debt is denominated), debt write-offs or forgiveness, and interest arrears accumulation. These inflows of foreign exchange are used to cover the current account deficit, with the balance added to the stock of foreign exchange reserves. For a country i in year t, the difference between recorded inflows and recorded uses provides a baseline measure of capital flight as a "balance-of-payments residual" as follows:

$$\begin{aligned} KF_{it} =& CDEBTADJ_{it} + FDI_{it} + PI_{it} + OIADJ_{it} \\ & - (CAD_{it} + CRES_{it}) \end{aligned} \tag{2.1}$$

where CDEBTADJ is the adjusted change in debt stock, FDI is foreign direct investment, PI is portfolio investment, OIADJ is "other investments" adjusted for debt forgiveness (see Ndikumana & Boyce, 2025 for details), CAD is the current account deficit, and CRES is net additions to foreign exchange reserves. The recorded value of "other investment" is adjusted to take into account the fact that debt forgiveness is recorded on this line of the BOP under "other debt instruments." This is normally also recorded under "Reserves and Related Items" as "exceptional financing" with offsetting signs. In that case using net "other investment" as recorded and "reserves and related items" (instead of "reserve assets") would not require any adjustment. Otherwise, not adjusting "other investment" for debt forgiveness (recorded with a negative sign) would reduce estimated capital flight in the concerned year. For countries that have received substantial debt forgiveness, this adjustment results in an increase in net capital flight relative to estimates that did not incorporate this adjustment.

To obtain a comprehensive measure of capital flight, we add net misinvoicing of exports and imports. This is obtained by comparing an African country's trade statistics to those of its trading partners. Following established methodology, we compute annual trade misinvoicing by scaling up the discrepancies relative to the group of industrialized countries (ICs) (labeled "advanced economies" in the BoP), using the inverse of the share of this group in the African country's exports or imports. A detailed description of the procedure is provided in Ndikumana and Boyce (2021, 2025).

The estimate of adjusted capital flight (ADJKF) is obtained by adding net trade misinvoicing (*MISINV*) to the balance of payments residual as follows:

$$\begin{aligned} KF_{it} = & CDEBTADJ_{it} + FDI_{it} + PI_{it} + OIADJ_{it} \\ & - (CAD_{it} + CRES_{it}) + MISINV_{it} \end{aligned} \quad (2.2)$$

Estimation Results

This section presents the results of capital flight estimations for each of the three countries covered by this book.

Capital Flight from Cameroon

Over the 1970–2022 period, Cameroon lost \$97.7 billion (in constant 2022 dollars) through capital flight (Table 2.2). The largest unrecorded capital outflows occurred in the 1980s (\$28 billion for the decade) and during 2010–2022 (\$33.5 billion), up from \$17.3 billion over 2000–2009. In 2020 and 2021 alone, the country lost \$6.5 billion through capital flight, or an average of \$3.2 billion per year, which is higher than the average annual loss recorded in the 1980s (\$2.8 billion per annum).

Key drivers of capital flight from Cameroon are external borrowing and trade misinvoicing. Over the period 2010–2022, net external debt inflows totaled \$15.3 billion, or an average of \$1.2 billion annually. Net trade misinvoicing added \$17.8 billion to the balance of payments residual.

On the side of sources of foreign exchange, in addition to external borrowing, Cameroon received significant foreign direct investment

Table 2.2 Capital flight from Cameroon by decade (total, constant 2022 US$, billion)

	1970–1979	*1980–1989*	*1990–1999*	*2000–2009*	*2010–2022*	*1970–2022*
CDEBTADJ	7.5	8.2	11.3	−6.3	15.3	36.0
FDI	0.7	2.2	0.2	3.8	10.3	17.2
PI	0.0	0.0	−0.3	0.0	−0.3	−0.7
OIADJ	1.3	9.5	7.7	10.1	12.1	40.7
CA	−7.1	−10.9	−5.9	−5.3	−18.9	−48.0
CRES	0.0	0.0	0.1	−4.5	−2.7	−7.1
BoP Residual	2.4	9.0	13.2	−2.3	15.7	38.0
Trade misinvoicing	2.1	18.9	1.3	19.6	17.8	59.7
Adjusted capital flight	4.4	28.0	14.5	17.3	33.5	97.7
Memorandum						
Sources of funds*	9.5	20.0	19.0	7.5	37.3	93.2
Uses of funds**	7.1	10.9	5.8	9.8	21.6	55.2
BOP Residual	2.4	9.0	13.2	−2.3	15.7	38.0
Private flows (FDI + PI)	0.7	2.2	−0.1	3.7	10.0	16.5
Average annual capital flight ($ bn)	0.4	2.8	1.4	1.7	2.6	1.8
Average annual capital flight/GDP (percent)	5.0	13.0	6.8	6.7	6.2	7.0

Note The symbols of the variables are defined in the text under Eq. 2.1
*Sources of funds = CDEBTADJ + FDI + PI + OIADJ; **Uses of funds = CA + CRES

totaling $17.2 billion over the four decades, and other investments totaling $40.7 billion over the study period. On the uses side, the inflows were offset in the BoP by the current account deficit, with some limited additions to the foreign exchange reserves.

In relative terms, total capital flight from Cameroon was equivalent to 220% of the country's 2022 GDP. On an annual basis, capital flight represented 7% of GDP on average over the past four decades, with the highest ratio recorded in the 1980s at 13%.

Capital Flight from Ghana

Over the past four decades from 1970 to 2022, Ghana lost $85.7 billion (in constant 2022 dollars) from unrecorded capital outflows (Table 2.3). The phenomenon exhibits an upward trend since 2010. During the last decade, the volume of capital flight increased substantially relative to the previous decade, from $27.7 billion to $44.6 billion. On average, over the study period, the country lost $1.6 billion per year, representing 3.2% of the country's GDP. Cumulative capital flight as of 2022 represented 115% of GDP that year.

External borrowing (change in the stock of external debt) and foreign direct investment inflows into Ghana more than balanced the current account deficits and accumulation of reserves on the uses side, generating net unrecorded capital outflows. External borrowing grew rapidly after the turn of the century and accelerated thereafter, with new inflows totaling $38.8 billion over the period 2010–2022. During the same period the country received large net FDI inflows totaling $44 billion, most of which most likely went into the oil and gold sectors.

Unlike the cases of Cameroon and Zambia (next section) reviewed in this chapter, net trade misinvoicing has not significantly contributed to total capital flight from Ghana. Important insights on this topic emerge from the analysis of two key sectors, gold (Chapter 3) and cocoa (Chapter 4). In the case of cocoa, disaggregated statistical analysis reveals relatively low export misinvoicing. To a significant extent, the limited export misinvoicing is attributable to the unique organizational and regulatory structure of the cocoa sector in which the state company COCOBOD is the only entity authorized to export cocoa

Table 2.3 Capital flight from Ghana by decade (total, constant 2022 US$, billion)

	1970–1979	*1980–1989*	*1990–1999*	*2000–2009*	*2010–2022*	*1970–2022*
CDEBTADJ	2.7	5.1	7.0	16.7	38.8	70.3
FDI	1.1	0.2	2.0	10.7	44.0	58.0
PI	0.0	0.0	0.0	1.0	14.6	15.6
OIADJ	1.5	4.0	5.8	16.1	−12.7	14.7
CA	−1.1	−2.9	−7.1	−15.5	−46.5	−73.1
CRES	−1.2	−0.6	−0.2	−3.6	−1.0	−6.7
BoP Residual	3.0	5.8	7.5	25.3	37.1	78.7
Trade misinvoicing	−0.8	−0.9	−1.3	2.4	7.5	6.9
Adjusted capital flight	2.2	4.9	6.3	27.7	44.6	85.7
Memorandum						
Sources of funds*	5.3	9.4	14.8	44.4	84.6	158.5
Uses of funds**	2.3	3.5	7.2	19.1	47.6	79.8
BOP Residual	3.0	5.8	7.5	25.3	37.1	78.7
Private flows	1.1	0.2	2.0	11.7	58.6	73.6
Annual average capital flight ($ bn)	0.2	0.5	0.6	2.8	3.4	1.6
Average annual capital flight/GDP (percent)	0.5	0.4	0.9	8.9	4.8	3.2

Note The symbols of the variables are defined under Eq. 2.1
*Sources of funds = CDEBTADJ + FDI + PI + OIADJ; **Uses of funds = CA + CRES

beans.[4] Thus, the usual incentives for export misinvoicing (for tax evasion and to conceal foreign exchange earnings offshore) do not apply. The cocoa sector therefore contributes relatively little to capital flight through export misinvoicing.

In contrast, the case of gold is quite complex, with the odd situation where gold exports appear to be overinvoiced in some trade routes where Ghana's recorded gold exports exceed its partners' recorded imports substantially beyond the cost of insurance and freight (Chapter 3). The extreme case is that of Ghanaian gold exports to South Africa, where gold does not appear at all in South Africa's import statistics. This suggests that overall gold export misinvoicing and overall discrepancies between Ghana's exports and its partners' imports may in fact contribute to reducing the estimated capital flight from Ghana.[5]

Capital Flight from Zambia

Total capital flight over the period 1970–2022 amounts to $79.6 billion, with average annual unrecorded outflows of $1.2 billion million over the past five decades (Table 2.4). Trade misinvoicing has played a significant role in capital flight, adding $16.9 billion to the BoP residual over the four decades under study.

The most recent decade witnessed an explosion of capital flight, with a total of $39.4 billion, strongly correlated with external borrowing ($28.9 billion) and trade misinvoicing ($10 billion). In addition to external borrowing, FDI was a major source of foreign exchange during the 2010–2022 period ($15.9 billion), with the two components together offsetting

[4] This contrasts significantly with the case of Côte d'Ivoire where cocoa exporting is dominated by private firms. Analysis of the sector reveals substantial discrepancies between recorded cocoa exports on the Ivoirian side and recorded cocoa imports from the partners' side (see Merckaert, 2022).

[5] Two points are worth noting here. First, given that our estimate of net trade misinvoicing is obtained by scaling up the discrepancies with respect to the group of industrialized countries, it does not reflect discrepancies with South Africa. Second, the fact that South Africa reports no gold imports from Ghana in fact tells us nothing about whether Ghana's gold exports data understate or overstate the value of gold exported to South Africa. Even if Ghana's gold exports were underinvoiced, the reported value would still exceed the value reported by South Africa given these peculiarities of South Africa's trade statistics.

Table 2.4 Capital flight from Zambia by decade (total, constant 2022 $, billion)

	1970–1979	*1980–1989*	*1990–1999*	*2000–2009*	*2010–2022*	*1970–2022*
CDEBTADJ	12.1	7.9	2.5	4.9	28.9	56.2
FDI	1.3	1.2	2.5	7.0	15.9	27.9
PI	0.0	0.0	0.0	0.2	6.0	6.2
OIADJ	1.2	11.3	1.6	−10.9	−30.8	−27.6
CA	−8.9	−9.3	−4.4	−4.3	8.0	−19.0
CRES	3.0	5.1	3.4	6.1	1.4	19.0
BoP Residual	8.8	16.1	5.5	3.0	29.4	62.8
Trade misinvoicing	−2.0	10.0	1.2	−2.3	10.0	16.9
Adjusted capital flight	6.8	26.1	6.7	0.7	39.4	79.6
Memorandum						
Sources of funds*	14.7	20.3	6.6	1.2	20.0	62.8
Uses of funds**	5.9	4.2	1.1	−1.8	−9.4	0.0
BOP Residual	8.8	16.1	5.5	3.0	29.4	62.8
Private flows (FDI + PI)	1.3	1.2	2.6	7.2	21.9	34.2
Annual average capital flight	0.9	1.6	0.6	0.3	2.3	1.2
Average annual capital flight/GDP (percent)	6.4	34.9	10.2	0.6	10.6	10.1

Note The symbols of the variables are defined under the equation providing the algorithm for computation of capital flight
*Sources of funds = CDEBTADJ + FDI + PI + OIADJ; **Uses of funds = CA + CRES

recorded outflows on the "other investment" line of the BoP (−$30.8 billion).

The case of Zambia illustrates the risks associated with high external borrowing in association with capital flight. While the country must meet rising debt obligations resulting from acceleration in the volume and cost of external borrowing, its debt service capacity is eroded by capital flight. Financial hemorrhage through capital flight precipitates debt distress and is one of the factors that can force a country into default, as witnessed by Zambia in 2020.

Conclusion

The objective of this chapter was to generate up-to-date estimates of capital flight from Cameroon, Ghana, and Zambia, and to examine the key drivers of the level and trend of capital flight. The results show that the three countries have experienced large unrecorded capital outflows, amounting to $97.7 billion for Cameroon, $85.7 billion for Ghana, and $79.6 billion for Zambia over the period 1970–2022 (in constant 2022 US dollars). Furthermore, all three countries have witnessed an acceleration of capital flight since the turn of the twenty-first century, in a context of severe, recurrent, and simultaneous crises that have worsened the shortage of development financing.

An important difference among the three countries that emerges from the results presented in this chapter is that while net trade misinvoicing contributes significantly to estimated capital flight in the cases of Cameroon and Zambia, it plays a limited role as a conduit of capital flight from Ghana. This reflects specific regulatory and management frameworks governing two key sectors of the Ghanaian economy, namely gold and cocoa. While the heavily regulated cocoa sector exhibits low export misinvoicing, the liberalized gold sector exhibits substantial discrepancies between Ghana's exports and its partners' imports, anomalously pointing to apparent export overinvoicing (which statistically reduces estimated capital flight). The inconsistencies in Ghanaian gold exports data merit further investigation.

The chronic nature of capital flight and its continued acceleration suggest that it is driven by structural factors with domestic and global dimensions. It implies that capital flight is not a problem that will simply go away on its own, but that it needs to be addressed with a robust strategy that is coordinated at the regional and global levels. National policy design can draw on policies to combat capital flight and illicit financial flows that are emerging in the academic literature and international agency reports (see Ndikumana & Boyce, 2015, 2022c; UNCTAD, 2020). Because capital flight and illicit financial flows are transnational phenomena, a strategy to combat them requires robust multilateral engagement to address their drivers and channels, including tax evasion, money laundering, corruption, lack of transparency in trade and financial systems, and institutionalized banking secrecy. In this respect, Africa in particular, and the world in general, will benefit immensely from better policy coordination and automatic exchange of information on trade, banking, and taxation at the global level.

At the country level, African governments urgently need to re-examine the management and regulatory frameworks governing natural resource exploitation. Policy design and reform efforts must be focused on increasing transparency, compliance with national regulations and laws including tax compliance, and incentivizing domestic investment in the natural resource sector. The goal of the suggested strategies is to reduce financial hemorrhage and maximize the gains from natural resource exploitation by curtailing trade misinvoicing, maximizing tax and non-tax revenue, and ensuring effective repatriation of foreign exchange generated from commodity exports. To achieve these goals, African governments and their development partners need to scale up investments in the "data infrastructure" (UNCTAD, 2020) with a focus on sector-level research and data generation. The tool kit for fighting capital flight includes various instruments, notably integrated digitalization of trade, financial, and tax systems, which will improve transparency, timely release of data, audit, monitoring of compliance, and detection of violations of trade, finance, and capital account regulations. In this context, development partners need to support Africa by scaling up financial resources and technical assistance into the digitalization of African economies.

References

Aboobaker, A., Naidoo, K., & Ndikumana, L. (2022). South Africa: Capital Flight, State Capture and Inequality. In L. Ndikumana & J. K. Boyce (Eds.), *On the Trail of Capital Flight From Africa: The Takers and the Enablers* (pp. 149–192). Oxford University Press.

Coulibaly, B. S., Gandhi, D., & Senbet, L. W. (2019). *Is Sub-Saharan Africa Facing Another Systemic Sovereign Debt Crisis?* Brookings Institution.

Gankou, J.-M., Bendoma, M., & Sow, M. N. (2016). The Institutional Environment and the Link Between Capital Flows and Capital Flight in Cameroon. *African Development Review, 28*(S1), 65–87.

Kolstad, I., & Søreide, T. (2009). Corruption in Natural Resource Management: Implications for Policy Makers. *Resources Policy, 34*(4), 214–226.

Kwaramba, M., Mahonye, N., & Mandishara, L. (2016). Capital Flight and Trade Misinvoicing in Zimbabwe. *African Development Review, 28*(S1), 50–64.

Merckaert, J. (2022). Côte d'Ivoire: Bitter Chocolate. In L. Ndikumana & J. K. Boyce (Eds.), *On the Trail of Capital Flight From Africa: The Takers and the Enablers* (pp. 99–148). Oxford University Press.

Mpenya, A. H. T., Metseyem, C., & Epo, B. N. (2016). Natural Resources and Capital Flight in Cameroon. *African Development Review, 28*(S1), 88–99.

Ndikumana, L., & Boyce, J. K. (2003). Public Debts and Private Assets: Explaining Capital Flight From Sub-Saharan African Countries. *World Development, 31*(1), 107–130.

Ndikumana, L., & Boyce, J. K. (2010). Measurement of Capital Flight: Methodology and Results for Sub-Saharan African Countries. *African Development Review, 22*(4), 471–481.

Ndikumana, L., & Boyce, J. K. (2011a). *Africa's Odious Debts: How Foreign Loans Capital Flight and Capital Flight Bled a Continent*. Bloomsbury Publishing.

Ndikumana, L., & Boyce, J. K. (2011b). Capital Flight from sub-Saharan African Countries: Linkages with External Borrowing and Policy Options. *International Review of Applied Economics, 25*(2), 149–170.

Ndikumana, L., & Boyce, J. K. (2015). Strategies for Addressing Capital Flight. In S. I. Ajayi & L. Ndikumana (Eds.), *Capital Flight from Africa: Causes, Effects and Policy Issues* (pp. 393–417). Oxford University Press.

Ndikumana, L., & Boyce, J. K. (2021). *Capital flight from Africa, 1970-2018: New estimates with updated trade misinvoicing methodology*. PERI Research Report (May).

Ndikumana, L., & Boyce, J. K. (Eds.). (2022a). *On the Trail of Capital Flight from Africa. The Takers and the Enablers*. Oxford University Press.

Ndikumana, L., & Boyce, J. K. (2022b). Capital Flight From Angola, Côte d'Ivoire, and South Africa: An Overview. In L. Ndikumana & J. K. Boyce (Eds.), *On the Trail of Capital Flight From Africa: The Takers and the Enablers* (pp. 10–36). Oxford University Press.

Ndikumana, L., & Boyce, J. K. (2022c). Conclusions: Capital Flight in the World Economy. In L. Ndikumana & J. K. Boyce (Eds.), *On the Trail of Capital Flight From Africa: The Takers and the Enablers* (pp. 234–246). Oxford University Press.

Ndikumana, L, & Boyce, J. K. (2025, January). *New estimates Capital flight from Africa over 1970–2022*. Political Economy Research Institute (PERI) Research Report.

Ndikumana, L., Boyce, J. K., & Ndiaye, A. S. (2015). Capital Flight from Africa: Measurement and Drivers. In S. I. Ajayi & L. Ndikumana (Eds.), *Capital Flight from Africa: Causes, Effects and Policy Issues* (pp. 15–54). Oxford University Press.

Ndikumana, L., & Sarr, M. (2019, October). Capital Flight and Foreign Direct Investment in Africa: An Investigation of the Role of Natural Resource Endowment. *Resources Policy, 63*, Article 101327.

Ndikumana, L., Mannah-Blankson, T., & Njuguna, A. E. (2020, November). *Looming Debt Crisis in Sub-Saharan Africa: Drivers, Implications and Policy Options* (Working Paper No. 529). Political Economy Research Institute.

Shaxson, N. (2022). Angola: Oil and Capital Flight. In L. Ndikumana & J. K. Boyce (Eds.), *On the Trail of Capital Flight From Africa: The Takers and the Enablers* (pp. 39–98). Oxford University Press.

UNCTAD. (2020). *Tackling Illicit Financial Flows for Sustainable Development in Africa. Economic Development in Africa Report 2020*. UNCTAD.

UNECA. (2015). *Illicit Financial Flows: Report of the High-Level Panel on Illicit Financial Flows from Africa*. UNECA.

Yapatake Kossele, T. P., & Njong, M. A. (2020). Capital Flight and Diamond Exports in the Central African Republic: The Role of Political Governance Crisis. *African Development Review, 32*(3), 362–374.

CHAPTER 3

Who Owns Gold in Ghana? The Legacy of Unbalanced Exchange

Léonce Ndikumana and William Godfred Cantah

Introduction

Ghana has historically been synonymous with gold—the "Gold Coast." At one point, it was deemed one of the richest territories on the African continent and a prime destination for foreign investment:

> "The Gold Coast," according to Sir Frederick J. Pedler, was "the richest territory in West Africa. It is, in this respect, the West African counterpart of Uganda on the Eastern side. Here are two countries which we ought to make into models of what African territories should be. If investment cannot be remunerative here, then all our Empire is just a hopeless slum." (Boakye, 2020a, b, p. 27)

Ghana is currently among the world leading producers of gold.[1] But, who owns gold in Ghana? What has Ghana done with its gold? In ancient times, Ghanaian kings had the monopoly over all the gold mined within their respective territories. The kingdoms had the exclusive right to trade

[1] Ghana is ranked 8th largest producers of gold in the world according to World Mining Data, https://www.world-mining-data.info/?World_Mining_Data___Data_Section. The US Geological Survey (USGSS) puts it at number 12. https://www.usgs.gov/centers/national-minerals-information-center/gold-statistics-and-information.

L. Ndikumana, *Capital Flight from Cameroon, Ghana, and Zambia*,
https://doi.org/10.1007/978-3-032-22770-6_3

gold and use the proceeds to finance the expansion of their territories. In those days of artisanal gold exploitation, the answers to the above two questions were quite straightforward: gold was owned by the Kings; they used it to expand and develop their territories. The story changed under modern era with the emergence of industrial mining, which is dominated by foreign companies, as will become clear through the analysis in this chapter.

Gold exploitation in Ghana originates from the pre-colonial era, where it fueled the growth of chiefdoms and kingdoms (including the kingdoms of Ashanti and Denkyira as well as the Fanti Confederacy) that together form part of present-day Ghana. Gold was a highly demanded commodity by European traders at the coast of Ghana, and by Arab and Hausa traders who came through the North of the country. Thus, gold mining became the main economic activity in the pre-colonial states such as Bono-Manso, Denkyira, Adanse, Assin, Akyim, and Ashanti (Ofosu-Mensah, 2013). Gold was mined from streams and rivers in the rain forest and coastal sands using traditional methods (Gocking, 2005; Kimble, 1963). Despite the long history of gold mining in Ghana, however, there seems to be no data on the amount of gold produced before the fifteenth century. However, various historical accounts indicate that gold mining contributed immensely to the development of the Ashanti Kingdom and fueled trade between people of southern Ghana and their northern neighbors (Allen, 1958; Aryee, 2001; Hilson, 2002; Ofosu-Mensah, 2013).

Today, gold is Ghana's top export product, accounting for 35% of total exports in 2021 (Bank of Ghana database). It is, therefore, an important potential source of export earnings, tax revenue and employment. The gold mining sector includes small-scale informal artisanal mining and large-scale industrial mining, the latter being controlled by private foreign corporations mainly from the Canada, South Africa, and United States.

The history of gold mining in Ghana is a story of alienation, foreign domination, and unequal exchange. From the beginning and through the colonial era, regulations were enacted to attract foreign investors and protect their interests, which made it difficult for indigenous people to gainfully participate in mining activities. The failure of the post-independent nationalization experiment led to the liberalization of the mining sector, consolidating the dominance of the sector by foreign corporations. Today large-scale mining firms account for over 60% of gold exports, and only two firms are owned by Ghanaians (Adamus Resources Ltd and Prestea Sankofa Gold Ltd).

The regulations of the gold sector enacted over time have consolidated a system of unbalanced exchange whereby the distribution of the gains from gold exploitation is biased in favor of foreign-owned large-scale mining firms to the disadvantage of small-scale mining firms, which are Ghanaian-owned. The dominance of foreign firms is partly the outcome of various mining laws (e.g., PNDC Law 153)[2] that provided tax incentives to attract foreign firms into the Ghanaian economy. In addition, foreign firms are given the privilege to keep substantial portions of the exports proceeds offshore, consolidating the system of unbalanced exchange in favor of foreign mining firms. The fiscal regime, therefore, favors rent extraction by foreign investors, while undermining tax revenue generation and foreign exchange reserve accumulation. It is an illustration of "legal capital flight" whereby the country's resources are extracted in a system of unequal distribution of the gains in favor of foreign corporations. This is in addition to capital flight leaking through various channels, especially export misinvoicing, which is documented in this chapter and in Chapter 2 of this volume.

This chapter presents the historical and institutional context of the development of the gold sector in Ghana and examines the contribution of the sector to the economy and its exposure to capital flight. It emphasizes the importance of the regulatory framework and the fiscal regime that govern the distribution of the benefits from the industry in the form of tax revenue, foreign exchange earnings, and the overall impact on the economy. This chapter specifically investigates discrepancies between Ghana's recorded exports and its partners' imports as an indicator of trade misinvoicing, which is a mechanism of resource-fueled capital flight.

The findings from this study provide insights into the complexity of the gold mining sector, and its thus far unfulfilled potential contribution to the Ghanaian economy. This chapter highlights how domestic and global regulatory and institutional mechanisms prevent the country from fully benefiting from its natural resources and perpetuate the alienation of local entrepreneurship and unfair exchange. The results indicate that the gold sector is exposed to capital flight through trade misinvoicing as

[2] PNDC = Provisional National Defense Council.

illustrated by substantial discrepancies between Ghana's gold exports and its partners' imports as recorded in Comtrade statistics. The evidence calls for strengthening the recording and monitoring of gold trade statistics to enhance transparency and reliability of the data as a way of minimizing capital flight through trade misinvoicing.

Evolution of the Gold Industry in Ghana

Gold exploitation is concentrated in the southern regions of the country, with some ongoing explorations in the North (map in Fig. 3.1). Gold exploitation and trade evolved through phases, from an unregulated regime in the pre-colonial era to a regulated regime during the colonial

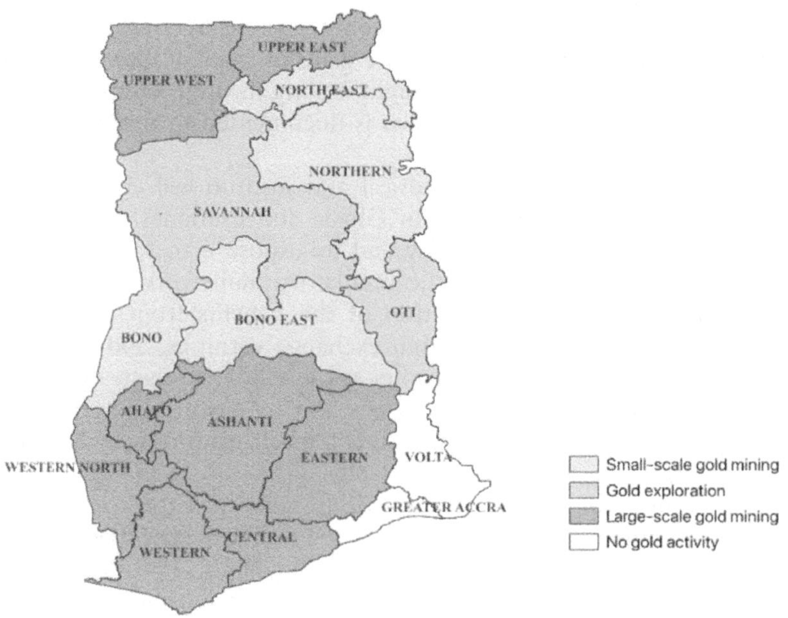

Fig. 3.1 Location of gold exploration and exploitation in Ghana as of 2024[3] (*Source* Authors' design with assistance from Dr. Didier Wayoro)

[3] The map reflects the start of large-scale mining in the Upper West region by Azumah Resources in 2024.

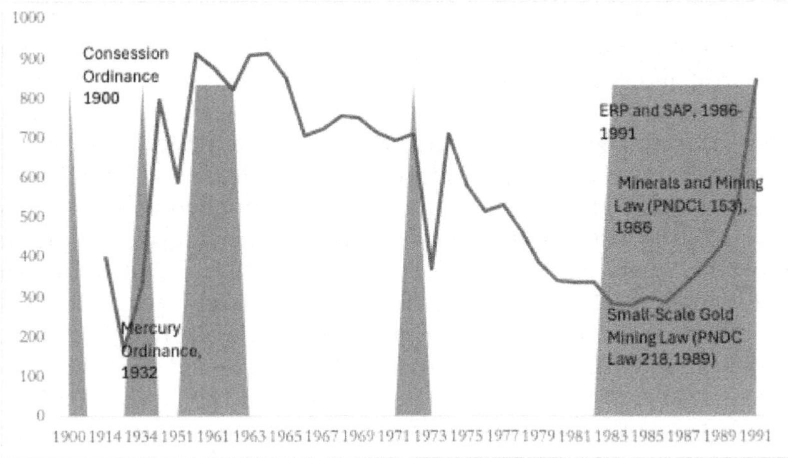

Fig. 3.2 Gold production in Ghana from pre-colonial era up to structural adjustment (1900–1991, '000 ounces) (*Source*: Authors' construction using data from Allen (1958), Hilson (2002), and Ghana Minerals Commission.)

regime and thereafter. This section traces this evolution, documenting the trends of production and exports over time, and highlighting the role of foreign actors in the sector.

Figure 3.2 presents a long-term evolution of gold production through various phases, marked by consecutive regulatory innovations, and major reforms notably in the context of the Economic Recovery Program and the Structural Adjustment Program of 1986–1991.

Unregulated Gold Trade During the Pre-colonial Era (1471–1843)

The last three decades of the fifteenth century witnessed an influx of European traders in the gold industry on the West Coast of Africa, which was motivated by high demand for gold as a source of wealth and power, a medium of exchange, an input in minting of coins, and to back paper notes in European economies (Carmichael, 1993). The Portuguese were the first to reach the coast of present-day Ghana in 1471 and started barter trade where they supplied local ethnic groups with manufactured products in exchange for gold (Hilson, 2002).

To monopolize the industry, the Portuguese controlled various gold trade routes, maintained positive working relationships with local chiefs in the area, and constructed a castle in Elmina which served as a military base to protect their interests from other Europeans. During the sixteenth century, Portuguese traders in Elmina secured about 13,000 oz of gold, with an estimated value of about £60,000 at that time (Hilson, 2002). They, however, were unable to maintain their monopoly on gold trade for long, as the gains from the trade attracted other European countries, notably the British and the Dutch. Indeed, by 1642, the Dutch had taken over Elmina from the Portuguese. However, the dominance of the Dutch in gold trade faded away with the arrival of the British (Hilson, 2002).

Gold exports from the Gold Coast between 1471 and 1750 amounted to about 11,200,000 oz, with average annual exports of about 40,000 oz, and an estimated value of about £51.7 million (Junner, 1935).[4] Toward the end of the sixteenth century, however, the slave trade began to dominate European trading activities on the West Coast of Africa, and gold exports declined. Despite the decline in gold trade, it still generated substantial revenue for Dutch and English firms, estimated at about £200,000 annually (Hilson, 2002).

Overall, gold trade prior to the colonization of Ghana largely benefited the Europeans while the natives only received cheap manufactured goods in exchange for large quantities of gold (Allen, 1958; Carmichael, 1993; Hilson, 2002). The unfair trade prevented the country from realizing the full benefits of the 13.7 million ounces of gold exported between 1471 and 1850 (Junner, 1935). This unbalanced trade was largely due to the lack of regulation of gold trade before colonization and the fact that local leaders lacked effective capacity to gainfully negotiate the terms of gold trade with the Europeans.

Colonial Era (1844–1957): Institutionalization of Alienation of Indigenous Communities in Gold Mining

The Bond of 1844 signed between British Commander W. H. Hill and chiefs from the coastal and forest zones of Ghana marked the official annexation of Ghana (then known as the Gold Coast) as a colony of Great Britain. It also marked the emergence of the gold industry. Colonial

[4] The monetary values of gold exports presented here are only estimates, because gold was exchanged against European goods.

mining policy focused on five key issues (Tsikata, 1997): establishing an administrative and legal system that facilitates mining operations; ensuring the security of mineral rights; effective settlement of potential problems between mining companies and local communities; generating revenue for the colonial government through export duties and income tax; and contributing to self-sufficiency of the British Empire. Thus, colonial mining policy was largely geared toward protecting the interests of the British Empire, with no specific attempt to ensure that the Ghanaian people living in mining areas benefited from the proceeds of gold trade.

The introduction of colonial mining policy, coupled with announcements of newly discovered gold ores in Tarkwa, Abosso, and Bibiani in the Western part of the Gold Coast induced an influx of European capital into the mining industry starting in 1880. However, the lack of motorable roads and railway lines resulted in high mining costs, and the absence of an appropriate legal framework to protect concessions complicated the relationships between mining firms and the native population. As a result, some European mining firms were forced to close (Allen, 1958; Hilson, 2002).

To improve England's benefits from gold trade, the colonial administration enacted the first law to regulate the mining sector, the Concessions Ordinance in 1900. The law aimed to secure land entitlements for European firms as their mining concessions. The enactment of this law was followed by improvements in infrastructure, which facilitated the transport of gold from the countryside to the coast for onward export to England. By 1901, the railway had reached Tarkwa from Sekondi, and it later reached Obuasi in 1903 and Prestea by 1910 (Allen, 1958).

These developments in the Gold Coast coupled with reports by engineers from the Transvaal region of South Africa indicating that the reefs in the Tarkwa goldfields were similar to or even of higher grade than the deposits in Johannesburg, ignited interest in the gold industry. In addition, the end of the Anglo-Ashanti wars (of 1823–1900) signaled an era of peace and led to an increase in gold mining by European firms toward the end of the nineteenth century and the start of the twentieth century. Between 1881 and 1882, European firms purchased more than 70 mining concessions, the most important by the Ashanti Goldfields Company (now called AngloGold Ashanti) which secured about 25,000 hectares of mining land in Obuasi in 1890. Subsequently, the country witnessed a massive increase in gold production from 5,223 ounces in 1901 to over 400,000 ounces per annum by the end of 1914. The First

World War, however, caused a reduction in gold production, down to about 167,115 ounces per annum by 1929. Gold production picked up again, increasing to over 336,065 ounces by the end of 1934, partly a result of England's decision to go off the gold standard, leading to an increase in gold price, which induced an increase in gold production (Fig. 3.2).

While the mining industry yielded high profits for foreign firms, few benefits accrued to local communities, as the colonial mining policy focused on generating revenue for the colonial administration and the British Empire. Although the natives were employed in mining, and despite large corporate profits from mining, native workers were severely underpaid and lived in poor conditions. This discouraged Ghanaians from working for European firms, prompting the colonial government to enact the *Mercury Ordinance* of 1932 that made it illegal for Ghanaians to access mercury, thus cutting them off from gold mining. It is important to note that this law came into force at the back of the *Concessions Ordinance* which prevented natives from mining lands that had been allocated to European mining firms. With the *Concessions Ordinance* and the *Mercury Ordinance*, the local population was definitively pushed out of an industry that they had controlled for several centuries. Europeans thus became the main beneficiaries of gold exploitation, repatriating most profits from gold trade. This foreign dominance of the gold industry has endured until today.

After the boom of the 1920s and 1930s, gold mining began to decline after the First World War, partly because of the unwillingness of the natives to work for European mining companies and partly because of the Second World War (Hilson, 2002). By 1951, gold production had declined to about 590,475 ounces in 1951 from its peak of 885,712 ounces in 1941 (Fig. 3.2). In fact, out of the 50 mining companies operating in the country in the 1930s, only 11 were still in operation with deteriorated mines in the 1950s. The companies were denied loans and grants from the government to revive their operations (Acquah, 1995), and most were forced to reduce their operations, and some had to close completely. After the country gained independence in 1957, the conditions in the gold mining industry deteriorated.

"Years of Mismanagement and Undercapitalization"[5] *(1957–1983)*

The decline of the gold industry after World War II was partly due to the lack of support from the central government, coupled with poor transport infrastructure in mining areas. In addition, around the same time, South Africa had developed strong gold mining capacity with better infrastructure, which caused a shift of foreign direct investment from Ghana's ailing mines to the booming mining industry in South Africa.

To resolve the problem of low investment and productivity in the gold sector, a Commission of Enquiry was established in 1958 to examine the terms of various mining agreements, the profitability of mines, and to assess unexploited mining concessions (Tsikata, 1997). The Commission made the following recommendations: the Government of Ghana should take over mineral rights from communities; royalties paid by mining firms should be a percentage of corporate profits; the government should be the regulator of the industry; the government should establish state monopoly over the export of gold[6] (Tsikata, 1997). Based on these recommendations, the government established the State Mining Corporation in 1961 and by 1966, it had acquired all mining companies in the country (except the Ashanti Goldfields in Obuasi)[7] (Jackson, 1992). It is important to note that all the gold mining firms that were acquired by the State Mining Corporation were ailing firms whose foreign owners were about to pull out; they were in fact nationalized to prevent a sure collapse (Afrifa Taylor, 2006). The government enacted the Minerals Act (Act 123) in 1962 to further strengthen its control over the mining industry. Act 123 was similar to the Land Bills of 1894 and 1897 which gave the sole authority of granting concessions to the British Governor of the Gold Coast (Ilegbune, 1976).

While government's interventions in the gold sector contributed to an increase in gold production between 1951 and 1960, the trend was not sustained, and by 1970 gold production had declined by over 21% relative to the previous decade (Fig. 3.2). Developments in the gold

[5] Quotation from Hilson and Hilson (2017).

[6] The Precious Mineral Marketing Company (PMMC) regulates the purchase of gold produced by small mining firms as well as its exports. For large-scale firms, the PMMC focuses on grading, assaying, valuing, and processing precious minerals.

[7] The State Mining Corporation later acquired equity shares in Ashanti Gold Fields (Acquah, 1995).

mining industry during this period affected the overall performance of the economy. In 1966, for example, GDP growth declined by 4% as gold production declined by 16.7%. The decline in gold production resulted in substantial losses for the State Mining Corporation amounting to 6.75 million Cedis in 1970 alone (Leith & Söderling, 2003).

In 1972, the government issued the Mining Operations Decree (NRCD 132, 1972), which gave the government 55% shares of all mining companies and demanded the payment of "fair compensation" to the government based on 55% of each company's total assets (Hilson, 2002). The decision exacerbated the already precarious position of mining companies and made it more difficult to make a profit. Gold mining was further adversely affected by a severe shortage of foreign exchange to import key inputs (Antwi, 1991). As a result, gold production started a steady decline and by 1983, it was less than 35% of the quantity recorded in 1960 (Minerals Commission, 2014).

During the 26 years of independence—from 1957 to 1983, the gold mining industry experienced a general decline in production and low profitability. A report by the Minerals Commission (2014) attributed it to high government taxes and levies coupled with the implementation of strict foreign exchange controls, which affected the repatriation of profits and access to foreign exchange for the replacement of old equipment. The sector also suffered from uncoordinated and unclear fiscal and legal regimes as well as high front-end charges. For instance, royalty was levied at 6%, in addition to a mineral duty of 5% to 10% and an export levy of about US$3 per ounce of gold exports exceeding 100,000 ounces. The mining industry also suffered from an exodus of skilled labor due to difficult economic conditions in the country. Hilson and Hilson (2017) characterized the period as "years of mismanagement and undercapitalization."

Revival of the Gold Industry Under the Economic Recovery Program (1984–2000)

The two decades after independence were characterized by government domination in economic activities. Due to corruption, economic mismanagement, and shortage of foreign exchange, the country recorded negative growth rates and rising inflation, which reached 123% by the end of 1982.

To revive the economy, the Provisional National Defense Council (PNDC) government together with the International Monetary Fund (IMF) implemented the Economic Recovery Program (ERP) and the Structural Adjustment Program (SAP) from 1983 to 1991 aimed at reversing the economic decline by realigning the exchange rates and implementing reforms in the productive sectors to enhance exports (Government of Ghana, 1998; Issahaku, 2000). The implementation of the ERP and SAP resulted in the liberalization of almost all sectors of the economy, including the financial sector and foreign exchange markets. As one of the key areas of focus of the ERP and SAP was to increase the government's access to foreign exchange, mining was identified as a key sector to achieve this objective (Akabzaa & Darimani, 2001). Thus, the government undertook reforms and enacted new laws aimed at liberalizing the gold sector to make it more attractive for foreign investors. Bilateral and multilateral financial institutions, including the IMF and the International Finance Corporation facilitated loans to some mining firms to finance their expansion and rehabilitation. Ailing mining companies were put on management contracts to help improve their profitability and financial sustainability.

The SAP reforms led to a systematic reduction of the government's involvement in productive sectors, including the mining industry. Thus, the government sold its shares in gold mining firms to private investors. It reduced its shares in Ashanti Goldfield Corporation (Now AngloGold Ashanti) from 55% to 19% by the end of 1998. Foreign firms that were initially given management contracts during the implementation of the SAP were allowed to eventually acquire mining firms in their trust. Goldfields South Africa, which had a contract to manage the Tarkwa mine from 1993 to 1994, eventually purchased it in 1995 (Akabzaa & Darimani, 2001). Similarly, Johannesburg Consolidated Investments, which managed the Prestea mine on a contract between 1995 and 1996, purchased it in 1997. Several state-owned enterprises were privatized through the divestiture program. These reforms ultimately contributed to the revival of the gold mining industry.

The changes in the mining laws helped to attract over US$900 million in investments in the mining sector between 1983 and 1993. While it is difficult to access data on the amount of FDI that goes directly into gold mining, it is estimated that about 95% of FDI in the mining industry in Ghana largely goes to the gold mining sector (Bloch & Owusu, 2012). During the liberalization period, Ashanti Goldfields alone underwent

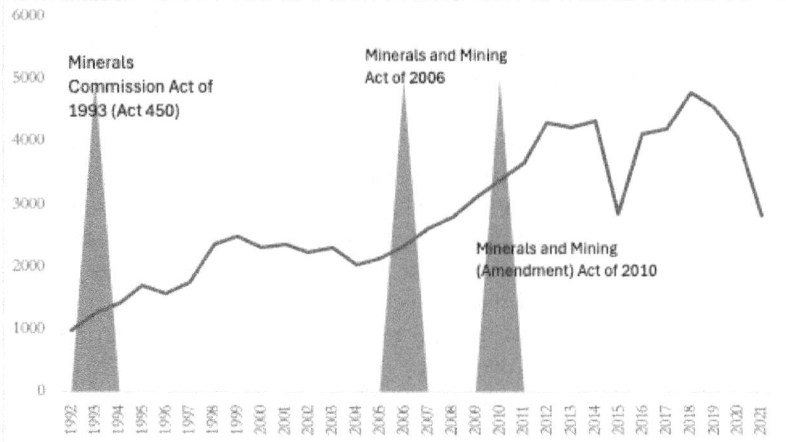

Fig. 3.3 Gold production in Ghana in the post-structural adjustment era (1992–2021, '000 ounces) (*Source* Authors' construction using data from Ghana Minerals Commission)

rehabilitation and expansion worth more than US$700 million. Given the number of new start-ups of gold mines during this period, it is likely that most investments in the mining sector went into the gold sector (Addy, 1998). Between 1983 and 1998 the mining industry received foreign investments to the tune of US$4 billion (Hilson, 2002), including US$90 million for the Mining Sector Rehabilitation Project in 1989 (World Bank, 1995). The regulatory reforms in the gold sector stimulated a gradual increase in gold production, mainly due to increased foreign investments in the mining industry.(Fig. 3.3).

Small-Scale Gold Mining Production

While the attention has primarily focused on large-scale gold mining, small-scale gold mining is a substantial segment of the gold sector in terms of gold production and employment. Between 2010 and 2021, Ghana produced 49.2 million ounces of gold, with over 67% being produced by foreign-owned large-scale mining firms. The remaining 15,978,548 ounces or 33% was produced by small-scale mining firms that are largely owned by Ghanaians. The share of small-scale mining firms rose consistently, peaking at 43% in 2018. However, in the context of the government's fight against illegal mining (popularly known as *galamsey*), production by legally registered small-scale mining firms declined, partly due to the inability of officials in charge of "operation vanguard" (the main operation to stop illegal mining activities) to differentiate between legal and illegal small-scale gold miners. The share of small-scale mining declined from 43% to 31% by the end of 2020 (Fig. 3.4). Experts from the Chamber of Mines brought to our attention the introduction of a 3% withholding tax on gold output as a potential factor of the decline in ASGM production in 2020. They also noted a ban on small-scale gold production in 2018.[8]

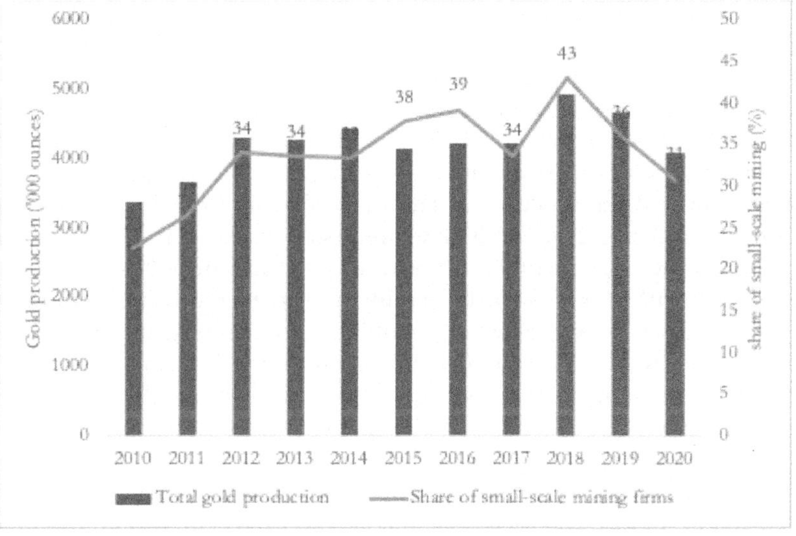

Fig. 3.4 Gold production in Ghana and share of small-scale mining firms, 2010–2020 (*Source* Authors' construction using data from the Minerals Commission)

[8] Information obtained by the authors during meeting during fieldwork in Ghana in January and October 2023.

Management of the Gold Mining Sector

Over the years the government enacted a series of legal instruments to regulate the gold mining industry with the aim of maximizing the country's benefits from mining. One of such initiatives was the establishment of the Minerals Commission of Ghana under the Minerals Commission Law (PNDCL.154) of 1986, which was later replaced with the Minerals Commission Act (Act 450) of 1993. The Commission coordinates and develops mining policies and monitors their implementation by other government agencies.

The legal and regulatory framework of Ghana's mining industry was largely influenced by the country's economic situation between 1983 and 1992. Like most sectors, the mining sector was on the verge of collapsing, prompting the need to attract more external capital. Thus, under the liberalization agenda of the Structural Adjustment Program of 1986, mining laws and regulations were enacted to make Ghana's mining sector more attractive to foreign investors.

The Minerals Commission Law of 1986 was established with the goal of reducing the number of State agencies responsible for granting mining concessions in Ghana. This was later amended in 1993 by the Minerals Commission Act (Act 450). The Commission also had the responsibility to monitor the implementation of various government policies on mining and bodies with linkages to the mining sector, to receive, examine, and negotiate leases as well as various public agreements related to mining, and report to the Parliament. The enactment of the Minerals Commission Act reduced bureaucratic constraints to the acquisition and operation of mining licenses, notably by establishing a one-stop investment center for mineral resources.

As part of the 1986 Structural Adjustment Program, the Government of Ghana developed the country's first and probably the first consolidated mining regulation in Africa, the Minerals and Mining Law (PNDCL 153), which includes various financial incentives aimed at attracting foreign direct investment, including the following (Rutherford & Ofori-Mensah, 2011):

- Exemption of mining firms from duties on machinery, plants, and accessories imported for mining.
- Exemption of mining firms' staff from income tax related to furnished accommodation at the mine site.

- Tax free quota for outward remittances by expatriate staff of mining firms.
- Exemption of mining firms from the alien employment tax under the Selective Alien Employment Tax Decree, 1973 (NRCD 201).[9]
- Granting to mining firms the deferment of the payment of registration and stamp duties up to five years.

In addition to these incentives, the law also provided for a reduction in corporate income tax and other fiscal allowances to reduce the tax liability of mining firms (Akabzaa & Darimani, 2001). Corporate income tax was reduced from 55% in 1975 to 45% in 1986 and later to 35% by the end of 1994. The capital allowance was increased from 20% and 15% in the first and second years of operation in 1975 to 75% and 50%, respectively, in 1986. The royalty payment rate was also reviewed to establish a sliding scale between 3% and 12% (Rutherford & Ofori-Mensah, 2011). Although the Mining Law officially allowed the government to secure up to 30% stake in mining firms, in practice the government kept its interest at around 10%.

The incentives embedded in the Minerals and Mining Law stimulated inflows of equity shares into existing firms and in the exploration of new gold mines. Foreign direct investment inflows into the mining sector continued to increase at the start of the twenty-first century, driven by the increase in demand for gold in the world market as investors looked for alternative means to store their wealth in the context of loose monetary policy, the talks of Greece exiting the European Union, the elevated sovereign debt of several advanced economies, and the need for emerging markets to diversify portfolios away from major currencies (Ghana Chamber of Mines, 2013).

The implementation of the Minerals and Mining Law was lauded by the International Council on Mining and Metals (ICMM) and the World Bank for improving the performance of the gold industry, with production increasing by 800% between 1992 and 2007. Analysts noted, however, that Ghana failed to derive the full benefits of the growing participation of multinational companies and the influx of foreign direct investment in the mining sector (Hilson & Maconachie, 2008). Although

[9] The alien employment tax is a special tax imposed on expatriate workers in the private sector.

mining firms produced over US$5.2 billion worth of gold between 1990 and 2002, the Bank of Ghana's reports indicate that the government received only US$68.6 million (1.3%) in royalties and US$18.7 million (0.35%) in corporate income tax (Bank of Ghana, 2003, as cited by Hilson & Nyame, 2006). Clearly, the mining laws made gold mining more lucrative for foreign investors than for the country.

In addition to reducing corporate tax liabilities, the mining laws also allowed mining firms to retain most of the foreign exchange earned from gold exports in their home countries or anywhere in offshore bank accounts, arguably to pay for the import of equipment, spare parts and other materials, and to cover expatriate workers' dividends and remittances (Campbell, 2009). Most of the gold produced in Ghana between 1990 and 2000 was sold directly to refineries in Switzerland and the revenue accruing from such sales was held up in bank accounts there (Akabzaa & Darimani, 2001). The ratios of foreign exchange retentions vary substantially by firm, from a low of 45% (Associated Goldfields) to a high of 95% (Goldfields Gh Ltd) (Akabzaa & Darimani, 2001).[10] It is not clear whether these large disparities reflect actual variations in the cost structure (foreign vs. domestic expenditures), or simply variations in negotiation capabilities across firms.

Because of the long duration of mining agreements, and the binding nature of the clauses, mining firms continue to benefit from the privilege of holding substantial portions of foreign exchange earnings from gold exports abroad. This feature of mining contracts has prevented the country from realizing the full benefits of its mineral resources. The actual amount of gold export earnings repatriated in Ghana varies substantially each year; it has been as low as 44% in 2016, with a peak of 74% in 2021 (Fig. 3.5). Clearly, the regulatory framework undermines the contribution of gold mining to the country's foreign exchange reserves and reduces the spillover effects of gold exploitation on the rest of the economy, implying that the potential of the country's endowment in gold has never been realized. In other words, the country is punching below its weight in leveraging its endowment in gold. Hence, even though gold contributes about 41% of Ghana's total exports (average over 2016–2020), its contribution to GDP is only 2%–6%.

[10] These ratios refer to the 1990–2000 period. A detailed table is provided in Cantah and Ndikumana (2023). At the time of writing, the authors have not been able to access information on the rules on the repatriation of export earnings for the post-2000 period.

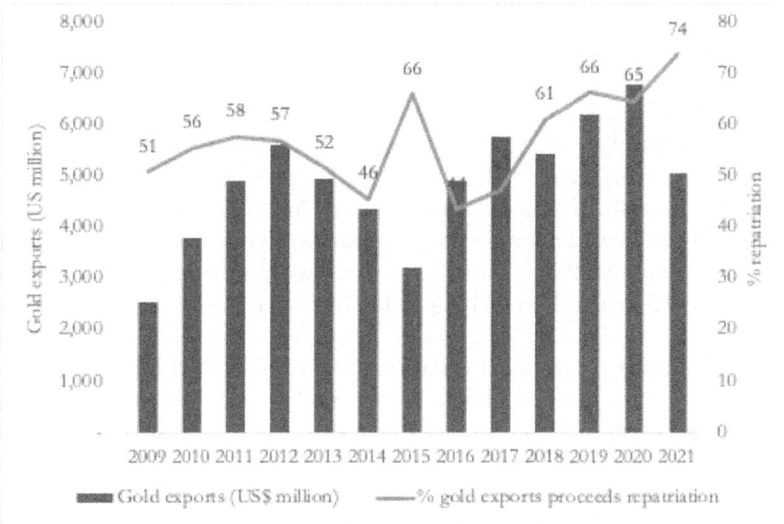

Fig. 3.5 Repatriation of foreign exchange earnings from gold exports in Ghana[11] (*Source* Authors' construction using data from the Bank of Ghana)

Despite the inability of Ghana to derive the full benefits from FDI into the mining sector, other resource-rich African countries (including DR Congo, Niger, etc.) emulated the legal and institutional framework established by Ghana through the Mineral Commission Act and the Minerals and Mining Law with all the generous incentives to attract foreign firms into their mining industries. Thus, the adoption of Ghana's mining regulatory framework by other countries seems to have reduced Ghana's competitiveness in terms of attracting FDI into the mining sector. The government therefore amended the Minerals and Mining Law of 1986 and replaced it with the Minerals and Mining Act of 2006 (Act, 703), with the aim of adjusting the clauses that seem to have made Ghana less competitive in attracting FDI while maintaining all fiscal incentives contained in it. The 2006 Act restricts the government's participation in mining firms to a maximum of 10% stake, one-third of the initial ceiling

[11] The percentage of export proceeds repatriation is simply the ratio of total foreign earnings repatriated by total gold exports obtained from the Bank of Ghana.

of 30%. The amendment repealed the Additional Profit Tax[12] which was imposed by the PNDCL 122 (1985) and reduced the range of royalty payment rates from 3–12% to 3–6%.

As companies systematically tend to pay the lower rate in any given range, the government replaced the range of royalty rates with a fixed royalty rate of 5% in the 2010 Budget Statement with the enactment of the Minerals and Mining (Amendment) Act of 2010 (Act 794). This change did not have an immediate impact on existing large-scale mining firms due to the stability clauses in existing mining agreements, which lasted up to 15 years. Thus, changes in the law affected only new mining firms.

As part of efforts to increase national benefits from the booming gold sector in the early 1990s, the government legalized small-scale mining through the Small-Scale Gold Mining Law (PNDCL 218, 1989), which was amended by the 2006 Minerals and Mining Act (Act 703). The law made small-scale mining a domain reserved only to Ghanaians and exempted small-scale miners from income tax and royalties for the first three years of operation. However, the law introduced important restrictions. First, while large-scale mining firms are authorized to sell their gold wherever they choose, small-scale miners can only sell their gold to authorized buyers, namely, the Precious Minerals Marketing Company. Second, the law gives small-scale miners a maximum five-year license that can only be renewed when various government agencies have verified that the small-scale miner has followed all established procedures.

The difficulty in acquiring a small-scale mining license and the inability of small-scale mining entities to sell their gold freely have fostered illegal small-scale mining and illegal export of gold (Adu-Baffour et al., 2021). In a symposium on illegal gold mining in January 2018, the President of Ghana pointed out discrepancies in gold trade statistics between Ghana and the United Arab Emirates (UAE), which came to the attention of the government after a visit by a Senior Minister to the UAE. While the UAE recorded US$7 billion worth of gold imports from Ghana in 2017, Ghana's official records showed only US$2 billion of gold exports to the UAE (Nwokolo, 2019). The statistical discrepancies in gold exports and imports are examined in the last section of this chapter.

[12] This law imposed a 25% extra tax on profits over a certain level (like a windfall profit) (Rutherford and Ofori-Mensah, 2011).

The main laws governing the mining are presented chronologically in Table 3.1.

Table 3.1 Major mining laws in Ghana since 1900

Law	*Date*	*Key elements and objectives*
Concessions Ordinance	1900	To secure land entitlements for European firms as their concessions for mining activities
Mercury Ordinance	1932	Made it illegal for the natives to have access to mercury (the raw material used in the extraction of gold)
Minerals Act (Act 123)	1962	To enhance Government control over the mining industry. It also made all mineral resources in Ghana the property of the Government of Ghana
Mining Operations Decree (NRCD 132)	1972	Set Government's shares of 50% in all mining firms in Ghana
PNDCL 154	1986	Providing one-stop investment center for all mining related investments to reduce the burden of bureaucratic processes associated with the acquisition and operationalization of mining licenses
Minerals and Mining Law (PNDCL 153)	1986	Ghana's first consolidated mining code which provided a range of incentives to attract foreign investors into Ghana
PNDCL 218	1989	Legalizing small-scale gold mining activities
Minerals Commission Act (Act 450)	1993	Replacing the Minerals Commission Law (PNDCL.154) that initially established the Minerals Commission
Minerals and Mining Act 703	2006	To address the lack of competitiveness of Ghana in attracting FDI to the mining sector
Minerals and Mining (Amendment) Act of 2010 (Act 794)	2010	Amendment to the 2006 Minerals and Mining Act 703

Source Authors' compilation from government records

Dominance of Foreign Companies in the Gold Sector

Between 1957 and 1983, Ghana's mining industry was largely dominated by state mining companies. Liberalization under the Economic Recovery Program and the Structural Adjustment Program in the 1980s resulted in a shift from state-led mining to private-sector-led mining dominated by large foreign firms. Today Ghana's mining industry is dominated by firms that originate from Australia, Canada, South Africa, the United States, and more recently from China (United States International Trade Administration, 2022). It is important to note, however, that by the mineral laws of the country, the Government of Ghana is automatically entitled to 10% of equity interest in every mining firm without any form of financial contribution or commitment by the government.

Table 3.2 presents the nationality and ownership structure of gold mining firms. Goldfields Ghana Limited, AngloGold Ashanti, and Newmont Ghana Limited, which are all foreign-owned, operate at least two different mining concessions in the country. Only two large-scale gold mining companies are Ghanaian-owned, namely Adamus Resources Ltd and Prestea Sankofa Gold Ltd.

Abosso Goldfields Limited (AGL) is owned by Goldfields Limited, a South African-based mining firm. Goldfields Limited owns about 71% shares in AGL, while IAMGold, an American firm based in Ontario owns 18.9% of the shares in AGL with the remaining 10% owned by the Government of Ghana. Although AGL has operated in the country since 1882, Goldfields Limited obtained a mining lease in 1995 and began operation in 1997. AGL accounts for 9.4% of total gold produced by large-scale mining firms in the country. Goldfields Ghana Limited also has mining leases in Damang and Takwa in the Western Region of Ghana. Goldfields owns 90% of the shares in each of the two mining concessions while the Government of Ghana owns the rest. These two gold mines accounted for about 19% of total gold production in 2021. Apart from these mining concessions which are wholly owned by Goldfields Ghana Limited, it is also joint owner of Asanko Gold Ghana Limited, a mining firm with a concession at Manso Adubia in the Ashanti region. It jointly owns this concession with Galiano Gold, a US-based gold mining firm. The Government of Ghana owns 10% of the total shares while each of the two firms own 45% of the shares. Asanko Gold Ghana Limited accounts for a little over 9% of total gold produced in 2021. Thus, including all its

Table 3.2 Nationality and ownership of large-scale gold mining firms in Ghana

Firm	*Company's nationality (country of majority shareholder)*	*Ownership (private or public)*
Abosso Goldfields Ltd	South Africa	Public
Adamus Resources Ltd	Ghana	Private
AngloGold Ashanti (Ghana) Ltd	South Africa	Public
AngloGold Ashanti (Iduapriem) Ltd	South Africa	Public
Asanko Gold Ghana Ltd	Canada	Public
Azumah Resources Ltd	Australia	Private
Chirano Gold Mine Ltd	Canada	Public
Gold Fields Ghana Ltd	South Africa	Public
FGR Bogoso Prestea Ltd	Britain	Private
Golden Star (Wassa) Ltd	China	Public
Newmont Ghana Gold Ltd	America	Public
Newmont Golden Ridge Ltd	America	Public
Perseus Mining (Gh)Ltd	Australia	Public
Prestea Sankofa Gold Ltd	Ghana	Private

Source Authors' compilation from various sources

four mining concessions (including the one jointly owned with Galiano Gold), Goldfields accounted for over 36% of total gold produced in 2021.

Other important players in Ghana's mining industry are Newmont Ghana Gold Limited and Newmont Golden Ridge Limited, both owned by Newmont Limited, an American-based mining firm. The two companies accounted for about 18% and 14% of total gold production in 2021, respectively. Together, Goldfields and Newmont account for nearly 70% of total gold production by large-scale mining firms.

Although AngloGold Ashanti used to be a major player in gold mining, the closure of the Obuasi gold mine in 2014 reduced its share significantly. Despite the resumption of production in 2019, the firm is yet to reach its pre-closure production levels up to today. Apart from the Obuasi mine, AngloGold also operates in Iduapriem in the Western Region (a mining concession formerly owned by Ghanaian-Australian Goldfields Limited). Production of gold by South African Companies—Abosso Goldfields Limited, AngloGold Ashanti (Ghana) Limited, AngloGold Ashanti (Iduapriem) Limited, and Gold Fields Ghana Limited—accounted for about 40% of total gold production in 2021. This is followed by American-owned Newmont Ghana Limited with about 33% of total gold produced, while Ghanaian-owned mining firms account for just 2%. The shares of other countries are as follows: Canada (13.2%), China (5.8%), Australia (5.5%), and the United Kingdom (1%). The data clearly shows that Ghana's mining industry is firmly in the hands of foreign firms.

Taxation of Gold Mining

The fiscal regime governing the mining industry in Ghana is quite generous, with an explicit objective of attracting private investors into the sector (Ayee et al., 2011). For example, until 2010 mining firms paid the minimum royalty of 3% of gross revenue, and until 2012 they paid the same corporate tax rate of 25%, much below the average of 40% in the mining industry across countries (Price Waterhouse Coopers, 2010).

The depreciation rule which is embedded in mining agreements has been quite generous as well. While it is reasonable to provide accelerated depreciation on the capitalized value of prospection, exploration and development costs, Ghana has extended this rule to all assets including buildings, machinery, and equipment (Ayee et al., 2011). Furthermore, the fiscal regime provides generous income tax exemptions on furnished accommodations to company staff on site as well as concessionary tax rates for overtime income. The leniency of the fiscal regime implies that even when gold prices reach record highs, the contribution of gold mining to tax revenue does not increase proportionally. The generous depreciation laws together with other incentives were expected to attract foreign direct investment into the mining industry in a competition with other resource-rich African countries. Whether this has worked in practice remains an empirical question worth investigating.

Corporate Profit Tax and Royalty in the Mining Sector

Corporate profit tax and royalty are the two main revenue generation instruments used in the gold mining industry in Ghana under the concession model. Whereas profit tax flows directly into government revenue streams, royalties are primarily meant to compensate local communities that host mining operations. Prior to 2010, the effective royalties paid by mining firms were largely based on the profitability of their operations, as measured by the operating ratio, which is the ratio of the operating margin (obtained by subtracting operational costs from total revenue) to total revenues. When the operating ratio was less than 30%, the royalty was set at 3%. Thus, mining firms took advantage of this specific loophole by inflating operational costs to maintain their effective royalty payment at 3%, half the maximum of the 6% provided in the Minerals and Mining Act of 2006 (Ofori-Mensah & Rutherford, 2011).

Operational costs include current expenditures (which include the cost of transporting, processing, and sale of gold) as well as capital allowances and interest payments for the year. The inclusion of capital allowances and interest payments significantly increased costs, reducing the profit margin below the 30% threshold for the payment of 3% royalty. Furthermore, mining firms were allowed to carry forward excessive operating costs into future years, which substantially reduced government revenue from royalties. This practice enabled mining firms to remain below the 30% threshold even during periods of high gold prices (Ayee et al., 2011).[13] The continued exploitation of loopholes in the Mining Act meant that no gold mining firm in the country effectively paid any royalty above 3%. This was the main motivation for the amendments of the Mining Act in 2010 which fixed royalties at a flat rate of 5% of total revenue earned from gold production. The amendments eliminated the uncertainty associated with the payment of royalties and made the process relatively more transparent. The existence of stabilization clauses in mining agreements means that this change did not affect mining firms that were operating before the amendment[14] (Ofori-Mensah & Rutherford, 2011).

Mining firms receive additional concessions such as accelerated depreciation which allows for a rate of 80% of assets in the first year, then 50% in the subsequent years. Moreover, 5% of the cost base of the firm is added to its recorded value of assets during the second year prior to any depreciation allowance in the year (Ayee et al., 2011). This means that investors could effectively recover up to 105% of their investment costs. To reduce potential losses from the loopholes in the mining tax regime, in 2012 the government raised the corporate income tax rate for mining

[13] The authors were informed by experts from the Chamber of Mines that the carry-forward of losses is an economy-wide practice.

[14] In an interview in April 2022, an official of Ghana's Minerals Commission informed the authors that the Minerals Law is expected to be amended to reduce the duration of the stabilization clause to just five years. At the time of writing, no information on when that amendment is likely to happen was available to the authors.

firms from 25% to 35% and imposed a uniform capital allowance rate of 20% on mining assets based on the straight-line amortization method for a period of five years (Minerals Commission, 2012).

Mining firms also receive additional tax incentives for employing fresh graduates from a Ghanaian university: tax deductions of 10%, 30%, and 50% of fresh graduates' salaries and wages when fresh graduates comprise up to 1%, more than 1% but less than 5%, and more than 5% of the workforce, respectively.

Furthermore, mining firms benefit from a concessionary rate for customs duties on plant and equipment that are imported exclusively for the purpose of mining subject to approval by the Ministry of Finance. It is important to note that royalties paid by mining firms are tax deductible. Moreover, mining firms are entitled to retain a portion of export proceeds in foreign accounts to pay for imported inputs.

In addition to these general tax incentives that apply to all firms in the gold mining industry, per the 2006 Minerals and Mining Act (Act 703), the government signs specific agreements with individual mining firms under special circumstances.[15] For instance, in 2018 the government provided incentives and concessions to induce AngloGold Ashanti Ghana (AGAG) to reopen its operations in Obuasi after it closed in 2014; the operations resumed in 2019. AGAG received a reduction of corporate income tax from 35% to 32.5%, a cut in withholding tax from 10% to 8% over the concession period which is expected to end in 2027, a waiver of import duties for all goods (including plants and machinery), a refund of value added tax (VAT), and special arrangements for the payment of royalties, which were pegged against the movement of gold prices rather than the firm's gross revenue as indicated in the amended Mining Act of 2010. The royalty rate varies from 3% for gold prices up to $1300 per ounce to 5% above $2000 per ounce (Government of Ghana, 2017).[16]

Ghana and other resource-rich countries across Africa engage in tax competition to give foreign investors the best tax deals to attract them into the mining sector. Analysts argue, however, that there is no need for such generous fiscal concessions in the natural resource sector where it is almost certain that investment will occur. For example, Otoo (2019)

[15] A minimum threshold of $500 million of investment is required for a firm to qualify for these tax incentives.

[16] Gold prices as determined by the London Bullion Market Association.

maintains that multinational mining corporations would only mine gold where there is gold, hence there is no need for large tax incentives to attract them. A study by Andoh and Cantah (2020) on tax obligations and foreign direct investment revealed that investors tend not to care about the amount of tax they pay when profitability is as high as is the case in the mining sector.

Apart from the tax incentives enjoyed by mining firms, the government loses tax revenue from discrepancies in the reporting of gold production and export values. This puts a heavy premium on the technical capacity of government agencies in charge of overseeing gold production and export processes, notably Customs, Excise, and Preventive Services (CEPS) and the Precious Minerals Marketing Company (PMMC).[17] In an interview with CEPS officers, Ayee et al. (2011) found out that these officers were not present in the bullion rooms of gold mining firms to authenticate the shipment documents; they are contacted to validate the records only at the time of sealing the boxes for export. Interestingly, mining firms get the value of gold from refineries outside Ghana (notably in South Africa) to determine royalty payments. This complicates the independent verification of the weight and quality of exported gold, making it difficult for the Large Taxpayer Office of the Ghana Revenue Authority to monitor production figures and assess profit tax and royalty liabilities. Another challenge is the inability of the Large Taxpayer Office to verify the accuracy of the cost of mining operations, cashflow, and market prices reported by firms, while these items are essential for the assessment of profit tax.

The loopholes in the tax administration system and certain provisions of the mining agreements signed between the government with mining firms have prevented Ghana from reaping the expected benefits from mining activities. A study by Albertin et al. (2021) revealed that payments of royalties and corporate taxes constituted about 40% of total payments from the mining sector. The study found that in Ghana, taxes on mining companies' goods and trade (i.e., exercise tax, customs duties, and exports taxes) were less than 15% of total payments from the mining industry, making it one of the lowest earnings in terms of taxes on goods from the mining sector in Africa (Albertin et al., 2021). About 38% of total

[17] The Precious Minerals Marketing Company (PMMC) is the authorized body, legally permitted to grade, assay, value, process, buy, and sell precious minerals and to issue mining licenses in Ghana.

payments to the government came from state participation as a shareholder in various mining companies. The evidence suggests that over time Ghana has recorded the lowest ratio of mining revenue to GDP in Sub-Saharan Africa at less than one percent on average over 2010–2016. Average mining revenue as a percentage of the government's total revenue was below 3% during the same period, which was one of the lowest recorded in Sub-Saharan Africa (Albertin et al., 2021).

Contribution of Gold Mining to the Ghanaian Economy

Gold mining accounts for about 95% of Ghana's mineral revenue (United States International Trade Administration, 2022), underscoring the potential importance of the mining sector for the country's economic development. But how has gold mining performed in practice? This section seeks to shed light on this question by examining evidence on the contribution of gold mining to employment, exports, government revenue, and GDP over the recent decades.

Employment in the Gold Sector

Gold mining contributes very little to employment, and most of the employment is created in the informal and small-scale gold mining subsector. It is estimated that the mining sector accounts for about 1% of total employment in Ghana, with about 120,000 people, although some government documents put the figure at 500,000 (Baah-Boateng, 2018). The small-scale mining industry employs over 73% of workers in the gold sector. It is important to note that most workers in the informal sector are in vulnerable employment as they do not have any form of contract and can be laid off at the firm's will without any form of severance compensation.

Large-scale mining firms employed about 15,427 workers between 2010 and 2020—of which 98% are Ghanaian—with employment peaking in 2020 at 35,000 (Chamber of Mines data). Historical data shows a strong correlation between employment in the large-scale mining industry and gold prices in the world market. When world prices of gold increase, firms in the large-scale mining sector tend to employ more workers to increase their production and cash in on the rising market prices to increase their profitability.

Contribution of Gold Mining to Exports

Over the last decade, large-scale mining firms have accounted for over 75% of total gold exports from Ghana (Table 3.3). Interestingly, the share of small-scale mining firms in total gold exports is relatively lower than their share in total production. Whereas small-scale mining firms accounted for over 31% of total gold production, their share in total exports was 24.6%. This difference could be attributed to two main factors. First, there may be a reporting lag between end-year production and export values. Second, small-scale mining firms may not sell all the gold produced to the Precious Mineral Marketing Company (PMMC) and other licensed gold buying companies as required by law, but through informal, unrecorded, and probably illicit channels.

Over the last two decades, gold exports have been an important contributor to Ghana's export despite the discovery and production of oil. Between 2010 and 2020 gold exports accounted for close to 40% of Ghana's total export earnings, reaching 47% in 2020 (Fig. 3.6). The high share of gold in total exports puts the country in a vulnerable position, as a reduction in gold production or prices has negative effects on its foreign exchange earnings and external balances.

Table 3.3 Gold production and exports from Ghana over 2010–2020 (million US$)

Year	*Exports by LSF (in US$ million)*	*Exports by SSF (US$ million)*	*Total export (US$ million)*	*Share of SSF in exports (percent)*
2010	3179.7	623.8	3803.5	16.4
2011	3057.7	1855.2	4912.9	37.8
2012	4394.2	1249.1	5643.3	22.1
2013	3956.4	1009.3	4965.7	20.3
2014	3867.0	521.1	4388.1	11.9
2015	2978.7	233.9	3212.6	7.3
2016	3200.1	1719.4	4919.5	35.0
2017	3533.6	2252.5	5786.2	38.9
2018	3546.7	1889.0	5435.7	34.8
2019	3843.7	2385.8	6229.5	38.3
2020	4956.0	1862.2	6818.1	27.3
2021	4794.1	289.1	5083.2	5.7

Source Authors' compilation using data from Minerals Commission and the Bank of Ghana
Note LSF = large-scale mining firms; SSF = small-scale mining firms

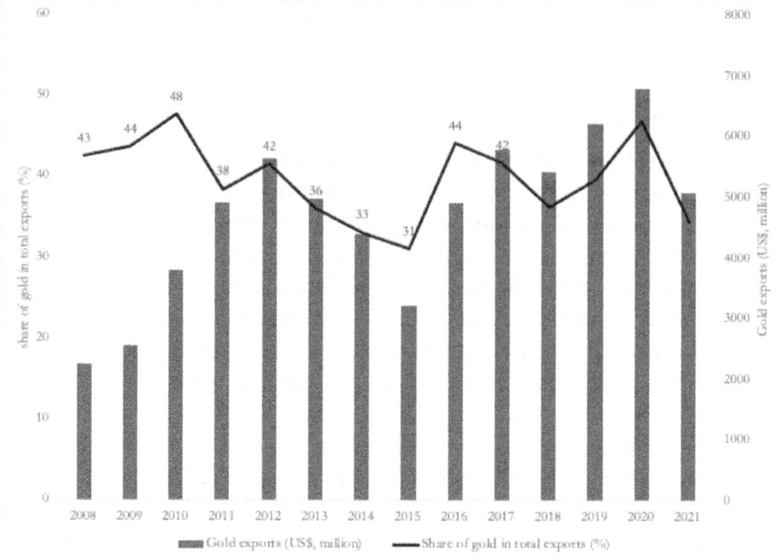

Fig. 3.6 Contribution of gold to total exports in Ghana, 2010–2020 (*Source* Authors' construction using data from the Bank of Ghana)

In analyzing the data on gold trade, it is important to note that there is a major difference between the value of gold exports and the amount of the country's earnings in foreign exchange from gold trade. Gold exports are dominated by large-scale mining firms which enjoy agreements that entitle them to keep portions of gold export revenue in foreign bank accounts. There is, therefore, some disconnect between gold exports and additions to the country's stock of foreign exchange reserves. Moreover, the domination of the sector by foreign-owned firms puts the country in a vulnerable position when a firm decides to wind up its operations in the country.

Contribution of Gold Mining to GDP

Over the last decade, gold mining contributed an average of 6.8% to GDP, 58.8% to mining and quarrying, and 20.6% to industry over 2013–2021, with a peak of 8% in 2014 (Table 3.4). Clearly, gold mining has the potential to significantly contribute to the Ghanaian economy.

Table 3.4 Contribution of gold mining to GDP in Ghana

	Contribution of gold to GDP (percent)	*Share of gold to mining and quarrying value added (percent)*	*Contribution of gold to industry value added (percent)*
2013	7.1	54.1	19.8
2014	8.0	51.6	21.4
2015	6.5	64.0	19.2
2016	7.1	85.4	23.7
2017	6.4	59.6	19.9
2018	7.1	51.8	21.2
2019	7.0	49.4	21.1
2020	7.6	67.3	24.0
2021	4.5	45.9	15.1
Average	6.8	58.8	20.6

Source Authors' compilation using data from Ghana Statistical Service

Data from Ghana Chamber of Mines indicate that the mining sector contributed 17.4% of total government revenue over 2010–2020, with the highest ratio recorded in 2011 at 27.6% of total revenue (Table 3.5). Most of the revenue is raised from corporate taxes, which on average account for over 48% of total taxes paid by the mining industry. Mineral royalties accounted for an average of 28 percent of total tax revenue from the mining industry.

The leniency of the mining tax regime, through generous individual firm agreements, compromises the country's ability to achieve its potential in terms of tax revenue mobilization from the mining sector. This is exacerbated by the fact that besides foregone tax revenue through tax incentives, the country also fails to leverage its gold endowment to mobilize foreign exchange earnings as part of the export revenues are held offshore by the foreign-owned large-scale mining firms that dominate the gold sector.

On the "Gold Trail": Investigating the Opaque Gold Export Statistics

This section examines gold trade statistics with a view to shed light on the extent of export misinvoicing, which is an important channel of capital flight. The analysis begins with a comparison of the trend of gold exports

Table 3.5 Contribution of mining to tax revenue in Ghana (million Ghana Cedis), 1990–2020

	Corporate tax	*Mineral royalties*	*PAYE*	*Total mining tax*	*Total revenue (GRA)*	*Share of mining revenue in total revenue (%)*
1990	0.3	0.2		0.5	5.3	8.9
1991	0.1	0.3		0.4	6.2	6.3
1992	0.1	0.5		0.5	7.5	6.7
1993	0.4	0.8	0.3	1.5	11.3	12.8
1994	0.7	1.3	0.5	2.5	16.7	14.9
1995	2.0	2.1	0.8	4.9	27.6	17.9
1996	0.9	3.6	1.7	6.2	42.5	14.5
1997	1.0	3.5	2.5	7.0	60.6	11.5
1998	1.5	5.0	3.1	9.5	78.5	12.1
1999	3.1	4.9	2.8	10.8	90.2	11.9
2000	1.6	11.9	5.9	19.4	140.9	13.8
2001	2.5	12.7	7.6	23.3	195.0	11.9
2002	2.4	15.4	10.2	30.5	275.8	11.1
2003	6.8	19.4	14.1	42.0	382.4	11.0
2004	10.0	21.6	13.4	48.7	533.3	9.1
2005	27.0	23.6	19.4	72.3	644.6	11.2
2006	40.4	31.6	21.7	74.8	733.4	10.2
2007	47.4	40.9	34.6	123.0	901.2	13.7
2008	73.6	59.0	47.1	180.0	1222.3	14.7
2009	124.6	90.4	103.1	319.0	1731.6	18.4
2010	241.6	144.7	132.5	519.7	2441.3	21.3
2011	649.9	222.0	161.8	1034.2	3746.0	27.6
2012	893.8	359.4	207.5	1461.2	7461.2	19.6
2013	518.6	364.7	220.1	1104.1	5900.1	18.7
2014	441.2	470.4	259.5	1172.1	7622.6	15.4
2015	463.1	137.7	404.7	1354.4	9091.5	14.9
2016	697.0	550.7	399.9	1648.2	10,425.1	15.8
2017	970.0	702.4	488.0	2298.5	19,637.8	11.7
2018	1199.6	705.3	457.2	2499.7	24,442.9	10.2
2019	2269.8	1006.7	736.3	4013.4	21,838.4	18.4
2020	2139.2	1391.2	641.9	4172.9	23,022.9	18.1

Source Authors' compilation using data from Ghana Revenue Authority
Note PAYE = Pay as You Earn income tax; GRA = Ghana Revenue Authority

as recorded by Ghana relative to gold imports from Ghana as recorded by its trading partners. This is followed by a statistical estimation of gold export misinvoicing by incorporating the cost of insurance and freight (c.i.f.) in comparing gold exports and imports, focusing on the most important trading partners.

Disparities in Gold Trade Statistics

The analysis of Ghana's gold trade statistics reveals substantial discrepancies between the value of exports as recorded by Ghana and the value of imports as recorded by Ghana's trading partners in the United Nations' Comtrade database. The data plotted in Fig. 3.7 show a large gap from 2004 to 2014, suggesting, quite oddly, that Ghana sold more gold than its partners bought from it! This is counterintuitive given that the recorded value of the partners' imports includes the cost of freight insurance (c.i.f.) while Ghana's exports are recorded on a free on board (f.o.b.) basis. This suggests that some partners under-report or simply do not report the gold coming from Ghana, which is inconsistent with established international conventions on trade statistics recording. According to these conventions, when Ghana records a transaction as an export to a particular partner, that partner is expected to report it as an import from Ghana, which may be re-exported later and recorded as such. Note that the series on Ghana's gold exports from the Bank of Ghana (Balance of Payments) and those from Comtrade are similar, except for 2012 where the latter show a higher value.

Further exploration of the data reveals that the opaque node of the gold trade chain is the Ghana-South Africa connection. As can be seen in Fig. 3.8, when South Africa is excluded from the set of partners as both an export destination and an importer, even when there are differences, they are in the expected direction whereby partners' imports are larger than Ghana's exports due to the cost of insurance and freight, as is clear over the period 2012–2016. This indicates that South Africa is not recording gold coming from Ghana as gold imports.

The observed discrepancies whereby the reported exports by Ghana exceed the reported imports by partners are even more intriguing when we consider the process of valuation of gold exports by the Ghanaian tax

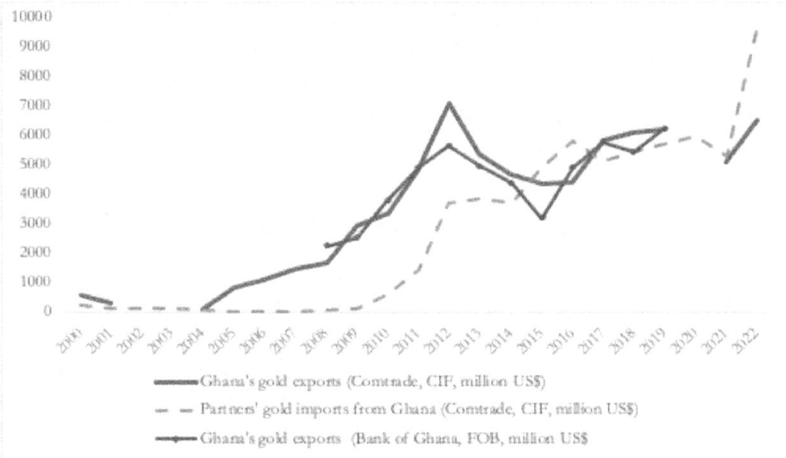

Fig. 3.7 Ghana's gold exports as recorded by Ghana vs. its partners (million $) (*Source* Author's construction using data from Comtrade and Bank of Ghana databases)

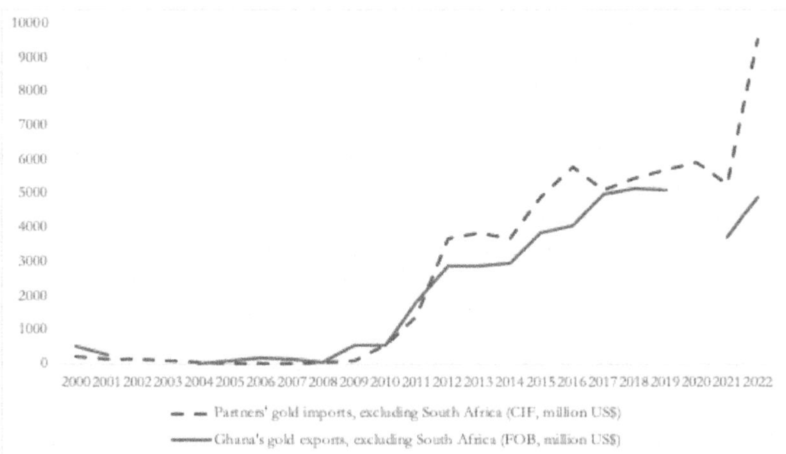

Fig. 3.8 Ghana's gold exports: total and excluding South Africa (million US$) (*Source* Authors' construction using data from Comtrade database)

authorities and the Chamber of Mines.[18] Gold export statistics reflect the value of gold at the point of sale in Ghana, typically to a refining company, such as Rand Refinery of South Africa. The value of the gold bars at that stage—gold doré—is[19] a percentage (normally 85–90%) of the value of the gold bullion at the exit of the refinery. While the final value of the gold is assessed, updated, and recorded for tax purposes, the export statistics are not revised upward to incorporate the value addition from refining. We would therefore expect that the value of imports recorded by the partners, which include the cost of insurance and freight, would be larger than the value of exports recorded by Ghana. Therefore, situations where the reported values of Ghana's gold exports exceed the reported values of partners' imports are at odds with the normal value chain in the gold industry.

Important questions emerge from these observations. The first is how is gold from Ghana treated in South Africa's trade statistics? The second is what is the destination of the gold from Ghana that goes to South Africa? The price of Ghana's gold at its destination determines the actual world market value of Ghanaian gold. It is the basis on which we can assess whether the price paid at the exit from Ghana is a fair value of its gold in terms of tax base valuation and remuneration of labor and capital used in the exploitation of gold in the country. Transparency over the entire gold value chain is essential for determining whether each player in the chain is receiving a fair value in the trade, and specifically whether Ghana is obtaining a fair market price for its gold. These issues deserve further consideration.

Estimates of Trade Misinvoicing

The discrepancies in gold trade statistics presented above call for further examination of potential export misinvoicing as a mechanism of capital flight. There is gold export underinvoicing when the c.i.f.-augmented

[18] This description draws from information received from the authors' consultations with officials in the Chamber of Mines.

[19] *Gold doré* is "a bar of newly Mined Gold metal alloy, generally originating from extensive processing of ores and smelting at mines to a high concentration (normally of 85%–90% purity)." To reach commercial quality such gold must be refined through chlorination and electrolysis. Source: London Bullion Market (LBM): https://www.lbma.org.uk/publications/responsible-gold-guidance-v9/definitions.

value of gold exports recorded by Ghana is significantly less than the value of gold imports as reported by Ghana's trading partners in the Comtrade database. We obtain the c.i.f. factor from the OECD's International Transport and Insurance Costs of Merchandise Trade (ITIC) online database, using HS categories 7108, 7109, and 7112. We apply the methodology developed by Ndikumana and Boyce (2022)[20] to estimate gold export misinvoicing using data from Comtrade over the period from 2000 to 2022.

Relative to Ghana's trading partner j in year t, gold export misinvoicing DX is estimated as follows:

$$DX_{jt} = M_{jt} - cif_{jt} * X_{jt} \tag{3.1}$$

where M_{jt} represents gold imports by Ghana's trading partner j as recorded by partner j , X_{jt} is Ghana's gold exports to partner j as recorded by Ghana, and cif_{jt} is the cost of insurance and freight ratio recorded by the partner according to the ITIC database. A positive value for DX represents export underinvoicing implying capital flight; a negative DX suggests export overinvoicing which is a peculiar and rare situation that is unlikely to apply to the case of Ghana.

The literature has identified three main motives of export misinvoicing, namely financial motives, circumventing foreign exchange controls, and reducing administrative burdens (Buehn & Eichler, 2011; Buehn & Farzanegan, 2012; Kellenberg & Levinson, 2016; Patnaik et al., 2012; Storti & de Grauwe, 2012). All three motives are quite likely in the case of gold exports from Ghana. Unlike cocoa, gold is produced and exported by private companies and is therefore less monitored by the government. Temptations and opportunities for export underinvoicing to obtain undeclared foreign exchange earnings are therefore more likely in the gold sector than in the cocoa sector.

The analysis focuses on Ghana's top four gold trading partners, which account for nearly all Ghanaian gold exports. If we exclude years where reporting is not matched, the four countries still represent 97% of total gold exports by Ghana. The leading destinations of Ghanaian gold are South Africa and Switzerland, which account for 39.7% and 34.6% of total

[20] Also see Ndikumana and Boyce (2010).

gold exports, respectively. Next are India (16.9%) and the United Arab Emirates (13.3%).[21]

According to the results presented in Table 3.6, the dominant scenario is apparent export overinvoicing driven by the Ghana-South Africa connection. In practice, export overinvoicing occurs in rare situations where exporters have financial incentives to over-declare the value of their exports. One case is when the government provides substantial fiscal incentives to promote exports. In this scenario, an exporter would weigh whether the benefits from the export promotion incentives exceed the value of the extra foreign exchange which they would have to surrender to the central bank. No such export promotion scheme has ever existed for gold in Ghana. So, this cannot explain the discrepancies in the statistics of gold trade with South Africa. The discrepancies therefore reflect under-declaration on the partner side, primarily in the case of South Africa.

The results show that Ghanaian gold exports to the United Arab Emirates are underinvoiced by a cumulative total of $9.7 billion over the 23-year period. Underinvoicing of gold exports to the Emirates has been documented in other studies (Lewis et al., 2019). This is a matter of concern considering the emergence of the UAE as a dominant destination of gold exports from Africa. Exports to India are also underinvoiced by a cumulative $1.2 billion over 2000–2022.

At the aggregate level, gold exports are underinvoiced by a cumulative $5.4 billion over 2000–2022 if we exclude South Africa. Gold trade between Ghana and South Africa remains a "black box" in terms of export statistics. The $5.4 billion could very well be an underestimation of the true extent of overall gold export underinvoicing. Therefore, the contribution of gold export misinvoicing as a channel of capital flight merits further investigation. In particular, the treatment of movements of gold from Ghana to South Africa is intriguing and worth further examination.

[21] The shares are similar to those in the Trade Vulnerability Report published by the Ghana Statistical Service (2023 edition), although the report shows higher shares for Switzerland than those from the Comtrade data reported here in the table.

Table 3.6 Estimated misinvoicing of gold exports from Ghana over 2000–2022 (billion, constant 2022 US$)

Partner	*Matched years only*			*All years*		*Shares in total exports (percentage)*	
	Export misinvoicing	*Ghana's exports*	*Partner's imports*	*Ghana's exports*	*Partner's imports*	*All years*	*Matched years only*
India	1.2	15.0	17.1	15.0	18.0	16.9	16.9
South Africa	−32.6	30.6	0.05	35.1	0.05	39.7	34.6
Switzerland	−1.1	23.0	22.8	24.0	26.1	27.2	26.0
United Arab Emirates	9.7	11.8	22.0	11.8	23.8	13.3	13.3
Top 4 partners	−22.9	80.3	61.8	85.9	68.0	97.1	90.8
World	−27.2	88.4	65.1	88.4	72.2	100.0	100.0
World excluding South Africa	5.4	57.9	65.0	53.3	72.1	60.3	65.4

Source Authors' computation using data from Comtrade

Conclusion

The analysis in this chapter indicates that since its beginning, gold mining has been entirely dominated by foreign actors, resulting in biased distribution of the gains from the sector in favor of foreign investors. In the pre-colonial and colonial eras, the indigenous populations were explicitly prohibited from any gainful business in gold exploitation. Unknown amounts of gold (who was counting?) were bought by European traders in exchange for low-value manufactured goods handed to the native populations. In the modern era, foreign companies still dominate gold mining, perpetuating an unequal exchange that benefits foreign corporations to the detriment of the Ghanaian nation.

The evidence presented in this chapter clearly demonstrates the critical importance of the industrial organization and fiscal regime that govern a resource sector for its impact on the economy. In this perspective, the regime governing the gold sector differs significantly from that of the cocoa sector. As discussed in the next chapter, in the case of the cocoa sector, the government agency COCOBOD has control over the commercialization and export of cocoa. This enables the government to set the producer price to promote farmers' wellbeing, and to control and repatriate foreign exchange earnings from cocoa exports. In contrast, the gold sector is dominated by foreign companies and the mining agreements they sign with the government enable them to keep fractions of the foreign exchange earnings abroad, at a rate that is determined on a company-by-company basis, varying between 25% and 95%. The absence of a standardized foreign exchange repatriation requirement enables gold mining companies to game the system to minimize the foreign exchange earnings that come back to Ghana.

In the case of artisanal and small-scale gold mining, which is dominated by Ghanaians, there is no regulation of the price paid to producers. The bulk of the value of gold is captured at higher levels in the trade to the detriment of local populations. In this context, the new Ghana Gold Board Bill is much welcome, indeed overdue. It is expected that the establishment of the Ghana Gold Board (GoldBod) will enhance the country's benefits in terms of domestic value addition in the gold sector, foreign exchange inflows and reserve accumulation thanks to better management and monitoring of gold exports.

Gold trade statistics are quite opaque, with gaps between the values recorded by Ghana as gold exports and the amounts recorded as imports by its partners. However, gold exports to South Africa represent a peculiar case where Ghana records a large value of exports while South Africa records virtually no gold imports from Ghana. This is particularly important given that South African companies account for a substantial share of gold exports (about 40%) and that South Africa hosts a major gold refinery. This calls for further investigation to understand how Ghanaian gold is recorded in South Africa's books, and then how that gold, once refined, is recorded when exiting South Africa in terms of origin, value and destination. This further strengthens the need for further investigation of the Ghana-South Africa gold trade. At the aggregate level, gold exports are underinvoiced by a cumulative \$5.4 billion over the 2000–2022 period. This represents capital flight, which is a major drain on the country's capital that undermines its efforts to meet its development financing requirements.

Overall, the country's benefits from gold mining are much below potential because of the organizational structure of the sector, the lenient fiscal regime that governs the gold sector, and the lack of transparency in gold trade. The dominance of the gold sector by foreign companies, weak regulation, a generous fiscal regime maintaining low effective taxation[22] and enabling foreign companies to retain abroad substantial portions of foreign exchange earnings from exports, and wide disparities in gold export statistics are major factors that limit the country's gains from gold exploitation. Investigating all these issues and taking appropriate corrective measures will be essential for increasing the country's benefits from gold exploitation.

References

Acquah, P. C. (1995). *Natural resources management and sustainable development: The case of the gold sector in Ghana*. Geneva: United Nations Conference on Trade and Development.

Addy, S. N. (1998). Ghana: Revival of the Mineral Sector. *Resources Policy, 24*(4), 229–239.

Adu-Baffour, F., Daum, T., & Birner, R. (2021). Governance Challenges of Small-Scale Gold Mining in Ghana: Insights from a Process Net-Map Study. *Land Use Policy, 102,* Article 105271.

Afrifa Taylor, A. (2006). An Economic History of the Ashanti Goldfields Corporation, 1895–2004: Land, Labour, Capital and Enterprise (Doctoral dissertation). London School of Economics and Political Science.

Akabzaa, T., & Darimani, A. (2001). Impact of Mining Sector Investment in Ghana: A Study of the Tarkwa Mining Region. *Third World Network, 11*(2), 47–61.

Albertin, M. G., Yontcheva, B., & Devlin, D. (2021). *Tax Avoidance in Sub-Saharan Africa's Mining Sector* (Departmental Paper DP/2021/022). International Monetary Fund, African Fiscal Affairs Department.

Allen, G. K. (1958). Gold Mining in Ghana. *African Affairs, 57*(228), 221–240.

Andoh, F. K., & Cantah, W. G. (2020). Foreign Direct Investment in Sub-Saharan Africa: Is Tax Obligation Still an Issue? *Global Business Review, 23*(5), 1236–1251.

[22] Commenting on the draft of the working paper from which evolved this chapter, the experts from the Chamber of Mines claimed that the effective taxation regime in the mining sector exceeds 60%, and that the proportion of forex repatriated in practice averages 70%. As of the time of writing, we have not been able to obtain data that generate these average ratios.

Antwi, L. H. (1991). The contribution of Gold Mining to the Economic Recovery Programme of Ghana. *Cambourne School of Mines Journal, 91*, 51–57.

Aryee, B. N. (2001). Ghana's Mining Sector: Its Contribution to the National Economy. *Resources Policy, 27*(2), 61–75.

Ayee, J., Søreide, T., Shukla, G. P., & Le, T. M. (2011). *Political Economy of the Mining Sector in Ghana* (Policy Research Working Paper No. 5730). The World Bank.

Baah-Boateng, W. (2018, April 23–24). *Job Creation in the Mining Sector: Evidence from Ghana* [Conference presentation]. United Nations Conference on Trade and Development (UNCTAD) 8th Global Commodities Forum, Geneva, Switzerland.

Bank of Ghana (2003). 2002 Annual Report, Accra.

Bloch, R., & Owusu, G. (2012). Linkages in Ghana's Gold Mining Industry: Challenging the Enclave Thesis. *Resources Policy, 37*(4), 434–442.

Boakye, O. B. (2020a). *Beggared Nation: An Economic History of Ghana, 1946–1976*. PhD dissertation, Stanford University.

Boakye, S. (2020b). The Role of the Extractive Sector in Ghana's Comparatively Low Public Sector Revenue Mobilization (Occasional Paper 24). Institute for Fiscal Studies.

Buehn, A., & Farzanegan, M. R. (2012). Smuggling Around the World: Evidence From a Structural Equation Model. *Applied Economics, 44*(23), 3047–3064.

Buehn, A., & Eichler, S. (2011). Trade Misinvoicing: The Dark Side of World Trade. *World Economy, 34*(8), 1263–1287.

Campbell, B. (2009, May 5–7). *Regulation of the Extractive Sector: Issues Raised by the Revision of Mining Regimes in Africa* [Conference presentation]. Conference on Rethinking Extractive Industry: Regulation, Dispossession, and Emerging Claims, York University, Toronto, ON, Canada.

Carmichael, J. (1993). *African Eldorado: Ghana from Gold Coast to Independence*. Duckworth.

Ghana Chamber of Mines. (2013). *Performance of the Mining Industry 2012*. The Ghana Chamber of Mines.

Ghana Statistical Service. (2023). *Ghana 2022 Trade Vulnerability Report*. Ghana Statistical Service.

Gocking, R. S. (2005). Ghana (Republic of) (Gold Coast): Colonial Period: Administration. In K. Shillington (Ed.), *Encyclopedia of African History* (pp. 569–570). Fitzroy Dearborn.

Government of Ghana. (2017). Tax concession agreement between the Government of the Republic of Ghana and AngloGold Ashanti (Ghana) Limited. Ministry of Finance. https://www.mincom.gov.gh/wp-content/uploads/2021/06/AGA-Final-Tax-Concession-Agreement-MOF.pdf

Government of Ghana. (1998). *Ghana—Enhanced Structural Adjustment Facility, Economic and Financial Policy Framework Paper, 1998–2000*. Government of Ghana in collaboration with staff of the IMF and the World Bank. https://www.imf.org/external/np/pfp/ghana/ghana0.htm

Hilson, G. (2002). Harvesting Mineral Riches: 1000 Years of Gold Mining in Ghana. *Resources Policy, 28*(1–2), 13–26.

Hilson, G., & Nyame, F. (2006). Gold mining in Ghana's forest reserves: a report on the current debate. *Area, 38*(2), 175–185.

Hilson, G., & Maconachie, R. (2008). "Good governance" and the Extractive Industries in Sub-Saharan Africa. *Mineral Processing and Extractive Metallurgy Review, 30*(1), 52–100.

Hilson, G., Hilson, A., Maconachie, R., McQuilken, J., & Goumandakoye, H. (2017). Artisanal and small-scale mining (ASM) in sub-Saharan Africa: Re-conceptualizing formalization and 'illegal'activity. *Geoforum, 83*, 80–90.

Ilegbune, C. U. (1976). Concessions Scramble and Land Alienation in British Southern Ghana, 1885–1915 1. *African Studies Review, 19*(3), 17–32.

Issahaku, A. N. (2000). The Political Economy of Economic Reform in Ghana: Implications for Sustainable Development. *Journal of Sustainable Development in Africa, 2*(1), 13–27.

Jackson, R. (1992). New Mines for Old Gold: Ghana's Changing Mining Industry. *Geography, 77*(2), 175–178.

Junner, N. R. (1935). Gold in the Gold Coast. Ghana Geological Survey. *Memoir, 4*(5), 20.

Kellenberg, D., & Levinson, A. (2016). *Misreporting Trade: Tariff Evasion, Corruption, and Auditing Standards* (Working Paper No. 22593). National Bureau of Economic Research.

Kimble, D. (1963). *A Political History of Ghana: The Rise of Gold Coast Nationalism, 1850–1928*. Clarendon Press.

Leith, J. C., & Söderling, L. (2003). Ghana-long term growth, atrophy and stunted recovery. *Nordiska Afrikainstitutet*.

Lewis, D., McNeill, R., & Shabalala, Z. (2019). Gold Worth Billions Smuggled out of Africa: High Prices Are Luring Africans into Prospecting for Gold. But Huge Volumes Are Smuggled out through the Middle East. *Reuters*, 24 April.

Minerals Commission. (2012). *Fiscal Regime for the Mining Industry*. Ghana Minerals Commission.

Ndikumana, L., & Boyce, J. K. (2010). Measurement of capital flight: Methodology and results for Sub-Saharan African Countries. *African Development Review , 22*(4), 471–481.

Ndikumana, L., & Boyce, J. K. (2022). Capital Flight from Angola, Côte d'Ivoire, and South Africa: An Overview. In L. Ndikumana & J. K. Boyce (Eds.), *On the Trail of Capital Flight from Africa: The Takers and the Enablers* (pp. 11–44). Oxford University Press.

NRCD 132 (1972). Mining Operations (Government Participation) Decree.

Nwokolo, M. N. (2019). *Ghana's Battle with Illegal Small-Scale Mining*. London School of Economics, Blog. https://blogs.lse.ac.uk/africaatlse/2019/07/15/ghana-illegal-asm-artisanal-mining/

Ofori-Mensah, M., & Rutherford, L. (2011). *Ghana's Mining Code: In Whose Interest?* Institute of Economic Affairs.

Ofosu-Mensah, A. E. (2013). Traditional Gold Mining in the Akan States of Ghana. In *Proceedings of XV Balkan Mineral Processing Congress* (pp. 1265–1269). University of Mining and Geology "St. Ivan Rilski" Publishing House.

Otoo, K. N. (2019). *Tackling tax incentives, Ghana. Public Services International* (The Global Union Federation of Workers in Public Services).

Patnaik, I., Gupta, A. S., & Shah, A. (2012). Determinants of Trade Misinvoicing. *Open Economies Review, 23*(5), 891–910.

PNDCL 122 (1985). Additional Profit Tax Law, 1985.

PNDCL 218 (1989). Small-Scale Gold mining law, 1989.

Price Waterhouse Coopers. (2010). *Total Tax Contribution: A Study of the Economic Contribution Mining Companies Make to Public Finances*. Price Waterhouse Coopers.

Rutherford, L., & Ofori-Mensah, M. (2011). Ghana's Mining Code: In Whose Interest? *Governance Newsletter, 17*(4), 1–18.

Storti, C. C., & de Grauwe, P. (Eds.). (2012). *Illicit Trade and the Global Economy*. MIT Press.

Tsikata, F. S. (1997). The Vicissitudes of Mineral Policy in Ghana. *Resources Policy, 23*(1–2), 9–14.

World Bank. (1995). *Republic of Ghana, Mining Sector Development and Environmental Project: Staff Appraisal Report* (Report No. 13881-GH). World Bank, Industry and Energy Operations, West Central Africa Department.

CHAPTER 4

Cocoa in Ghana, the "Political Crop": State Control Matters

Léonce Ndikumana and Kwame Adjei-Mantey

Introduction

Cocoa is not like any other crop in Ghana. The government keeps it "close to its chest," with heavy involvement in the organization of the sector, from setting producer prices to organizing the purchase and export of cocoa beans (see, among others, Kolavalli & Vigneri, 2017). In fact, cocoa is so important that it is referred to as "a political crop"; one that can make or break political regimes, as in February 1966 when the government succumbed to popular pressure following its attempt to cut the producer price of cocoa to save the ailing Cocoa Marketing Board (CMB). The operations in the cocoa sector are controlled by the Ghana Cocoa Board (COCOBOD) which commissions licensed buying companies (LBCs) that collect cocoa from the farmgate and sell conditioned beans to its warehouses where they are prepared for sale to cocoa processing companies.

Ghana is the second largest producer and exporter of cocoa behind its neighbor Côte d'Ivoire, with the two contributing more than 60% of the world's cocoa exports. Cocoa plays an important role in the Ghanaian economy, employing 3.2 million people, representing 33% of the labor force. It is the third leading export product accounting for 19% of total

L. Ndikumana, *Capital Flight from Cameroon, Ghana, and Zambia*, https://doi.org/10.1007/978-3-032-22770-6_4

exports, after gold (35%) and crude oil (27%). However, its relative position has declined in recent decades following the start of oil exploitation. Nonetheless, cocoa remains a strategic crop in many dimensions.

A recurrent theme among operators in the cocoa sector is that cocoa trade is less subject to capital flight than other natural resources.[1] This claim seems to be at least partly supported by evidence on research on illicit financial flows associated with trade of primary commodities (see Ahene-Codjoe et al., 2022 for the case of Ghana; and more elaborate discussions in Bonanomi et al., 2024) and the analysis of export misinvoicing in this chapter compared to gold (Chapter 3 of this volume). Capital flight is indeed an important issue for Ghana as it is for most African countries. The latest estimates suggest that the country has lost $85.7 billion through capital flight from 1970 to 2022. The phenomenon exploded since the turn of the century, with a total of $44.6 billion in capital flight between 2010 and 2022.

The expectation that the cocoa sector is less vulnerable to capital flight than other natural resource sectors is inspired by state regulation and the special organizational structure of the cocoa sector whereby COCOBOD controls exports of cocoa beans and repatriates the proceeds of exports through the Bank of Ghana. Note, however, that the export of processed cocoa products, which is handled by private companies, operates under separate rules. While national companies are required to repatriate their foreign exchange earnings from exports of cocoa products, foreign-owned companies are not required to do so. This is important as foreign companies dominate the cocoa processing segment of the sector, implying that the distribution of the benefits from cocoa processing is biased in favor of foreign companies.

The cocoa sector in Ghana differs significantly from the gold sector, which is fully liberalized, privately run, and dominated by foreign companies (Chapter 3). Statistical analysis reveals systematic inconsistencies in gold export statistics, pointing to both export underinvoicing and unmatched exports, especially for gold registered as being exported to South Africa. The cocoa sector in Ghana also differs significantly from that in Côte d'Ivoire, which is fully privatized and dominated by foreign

[1] Opinion expressed by operators in the cocoa sectors during our meeting with representatives of LBCs and COCOBOD officials during fieldwork in January 2023.

corporations, and where trade statistics exhibit substantial discrepancies pointing to export underinvoicing as a conduit of capital flight (Merckaert, 2022).

This chapter examines the extent to which the cocoa sector may be exposed to or protected from capital flight by exploring its industrial organization with an emphasis on the nature of the main actors and the fiscal regime that governs operations along the entire cocoa value chain from production to exports. This chapter begins with a review of the long history of cocoa planting in Ghana and the various phases of the evolution of cocoa production over time. It then presents the institutional framework and the industrial organization of the sector with an emphasis on the fiscal regime governing the sector. This is followed by an analysis of the contribution of the sector to foreign exchange earnings and poverty reduction. The analysis is supported by data collected from various government sources and first-hand information and insights gained from meetings with various stakeholders, as well as visits to cocoa farms in the Central region in January 2023. The paper examines whether the cocoa sector is exposed to capital flight by analyzing bilateral cocoa trade statistics between Ghana and its trading partners, using data from Comtrade, in search of evidence of export misinvoicing as a channel of capital flight. Over 2000–2022, total export misinvoicing of cocoa beans and cocoa products amounted to $12 billion out of $59 billion of partners' imports. The corresponding amount of export misinvoicing of cocoa beans is $7.3 billion out of $47.8 billion of exports. The discrepancies between Ghana's recorded exports and its partners' imports are much lower than in the case of gold exports, where a large fraction of Ghana's gold exports cannot be traced in the records of partners' imports. The comparison of gold and cocoa sectors has important implications for the regulation of natural resource sectors to maximize the benefits for the country.

History of Cocoa Production in Ghana

In 1879, entrepreneur Tetteh Quarshie arrived in Ghana, carrying cocoa pods from Fernando Po in Equatorial Guinea and built a plantation at Akuapem Mampong (Hill, 1963). Today cocoa is grown in the forest districts of Ashanti, Bono, Bono East, Ahafo, Eastern, Volta, Central, Western North, and Western regions, covering between 1.6 million and 2 million hectares (FAOSTAT, 2016; Fig. 4.1).

Fig. 4.1 Cocoa growing regions in Ghana (*Source* Authors' design with assistance from Didier Wayoro)

Cocoa production in Ghana has gone through four phases (Kolavalli & Vigneri, 2011): exponential growth from 1888 to 1937; stagnation before and following independence (1938–1964); a downturn from 1965 to 1982; and recovery and expansion corresponding with the launch of the Economic Recovery Program in 1983. These phases are discussed below and the long-term trend of cocoa production is presented in Fig. 4.2.

Following the introduction of cocoa by commercial producers from the eastern part of Ghana, cocoa production grew rapidly as farmers migrated and purchased land in other cocoa growing areas. The "cocoa rush" propelled Ghana to the status of the world's leading cocoa producer during the 1910–1914 period. Export of cocoa began during this phase, with two bags of cocoa beans shipped out of the country in 1891 (Manu, 1989). Thereafter, cocoa exports increased rapidly and accounted for half

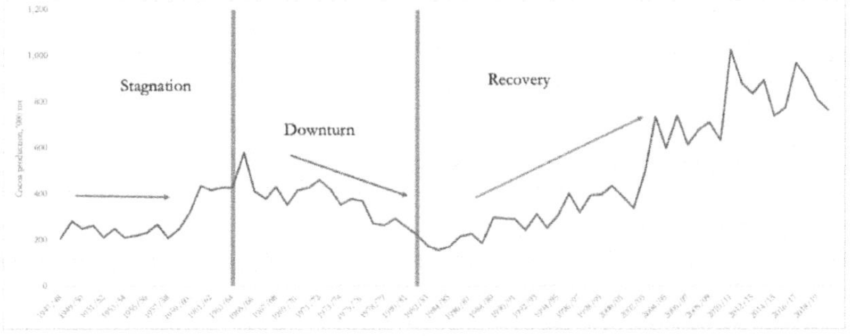

Fig. 4.2 Production of cocoa beans in Ghana from 1947 to 2020 (thousand metric tons) (*Source* Authors' construction using data from COCOBOD and other official sources)

of global production by 1935 (Manu, 1989). The rapid expansion of cocoa production during this phase was mainly due to the opening of new plantations and expansion of existing ones throughout cocoa growing districts. Cocoa emerged as a potential contributor to export-led growth with the development of a "capitalist cocoa growing community," while it also generated spillover and linkage effects across the economy (Berry, 2018; Hill, 1963).

From 1938, cocoa production slowed down, as pests and diseases wreaked havoc on the sector, compounded by a decline in international cocoa prices. The government encountered considerable financial difficulties, with the financial resources of the Cocoa Marketing Board (CMB) nearly depleted, and it was forced to cut cocoa producer prices, a move that proved to be politically costly. In February 1966, the government was overthrown, the state of the cocoa industry worsened, and the economy suffered a downturn marked by high inflation.

From 1965, cocoa production was further undermined by the crash in world cocoa prices exacerbated by the aging of cocoa trees and diseases, which rendered cocoa growing unappealing to farmers (Amanor, 2010). This period also witnessed substantial smuggling of cocoa across borders, with an estimated 20% of Ghana's cocoa smuggled to Côte d'Ivoire between 1970 and 1980 (Stryker et al., 1990). To revitalize the cocoa industry, the government implemented new policies including financial incentives to cocoa growers, ushering in a new era of recovery and a second expansion phase starting in 1983 (Kolavalli & Vigneri, 2011).

The cocoa sector began to improve starting in 1983 thanks to the Cocoa Rehabilitation Project under the Economic Recovery Program (ERP) (Kolavalli & Vigneri, 2017). In particular, the government increased the producer price, making cocoa growing lucrative relative to other crops, and discouraging cocoa smuggling. Farmers were also granted some compensation for removing and replacing disease-infested cocoa plants. These measures coupled with the introduction of higher-yield cocoa trees, led to an increase in cocoa production to 400,000 tons by 1996, accelerating further from 2001. This boost in production was also driven by high global market prices during that period, as well as the deployment of various interventions by COCOBOD such as the cocoa mass spraying program and fertilizer subsidies (Vigneri & Santos, 2008).

An important factor behind the observed trends and fluctuations in cocoa production was the change in the size of harvested area, which responded to a combination of factors, including a reduction in producer prices, pests, and diseases, as well as aging plants. From 1965 to 1982, cocoa production declined by a cumulative 51.3%, as the size of the harvested area shrunk by 50.8%, while yields declined by only 1%. From 1983, cocoa production accelerated, and by 2004 it had risen by a cumulative 264%. The upward trend has generally continued until recent times, albeit with marked cyclical variations, which are typical for cocoa production. The post-1983 production expansion has been driven by an increase in both harvested area and yield. As the size of the harvested area rose by 122.2% from 1983 to 2004, yields also increased by 63.8% during the same period. Interestingly, cocoa yields have moved in tandem with those of other major agricultural products.

Cocoa production in the 2020/21 season hit a record of 1,047,000 tons, a 34.8% increase over the previous season's output (Ministry of Finance Budget for 2022). For the 2021/22 crop season, production was predicted to reach 900,000 tons, but actual production turned out to be only 683,000 tons due to unfavorable weather conditions and the activities of illegal mining (Ministry of Finance Budget for 2023). Production declined further to 656,140 tons in the 2022/2023 crop season.

Industrial Organization of the Cocoa Sector

The Main Operators

The operators in the cocoa value chain can be classified into main actors and supporting actors (Abbadi et al., 2019). The main actors are those contributing directly to the production, processing, transportation, and marketing of cocoa and cocoa products. This includes farmers, private input suppliers, licensed buying companies (LBCs), haulers, Cocoa Marketing Company (CMC), processors, and retailers of cocoa products. Supporting actors do not participate directly in production, processing, transport, and retailing, but rather provide various types of services in the form of research, extension, quality control, finance and insurance, and disaster management. They include cocoa research institutions, COCOBOD's Quality Control Company (QCC), farmers' groups, Non-Governmental Organizations (NGOs), and formal and informal finance and insurance companies. See Monastyrnaya et al. (2016) for details on the functions of each actor.

Ghana Cocoa Board (COCOBOD)

Founded in 1947, the Ghana Cocoa Marketing Board was renamed the Ghana Cocoa Board (COCOBOD) in 1984 (Ghana Cocoa Board Act 1984, PNDCL 81). In 2020, the COCOBOD Act was amended to transfer the oversight of COCOBOD and its activities from the Ministry of Finance to the Ministry of Food and Agriculture; it was transferred back to the Ministry of Finance in early 2025. COCOBOD has two subsidiary companies, namely Cocoa Marketing Company Limited (CMC), which engages in the sale and marketing of cocoa beans, and Quality Control Company (QCC), which oversees and enforces quality standards for cocoa beans.

COCOBOD's mandate includes the following functions:

- Control pests and diseases affecting cocoa, coffee, and shea nut plants.
- Assist in the development of the cocoa, coffee, and shea nut industries of Ghana.

- Undertake and encourage the processing of cocoa, coffee, shea nut, and cocoa waste with the aim of adding value for export and local consumption.
- Undertake, promote, and encourage scientific research aimed at improving the quality of cocoa, coffee, shea nut, and other tropical crops.
- Regulate the internal marketing of cocoa, coffee, and shea nut. Secure the most favorable arrangements for the purchase, grading and sealing, certification, sale and export of cocoa, coffee, and shea nut.
- Purchase, market, and export cocoa and cocoa products graded under the Cocoa Industry Regulation and Consolidation Decree, 1968 NLCD 278.

The functions of COCOBOD are classified into two main areas, specifically pre-harvest and post-harvest—and they are performed by its specialized divisions. The pre-harvest functions are carried out by the Cocoa Research Institute of Ghana (CRIG), the Seed Production Division (SPD), and the Cocoa Health and Extension Division (CHED). The post-harvest functions consist of setting and enforcing quality control standards that farmers must observe to produce and supply high-quality cocoa beans to COCOBOD through the Licensed Buying Companies (LBCs). They are performed by Quality Control Company Limited (QCCL) and CMC Limited. Foreign companies may obtain a license to operate as LBCs, provided they meet COCOBOD's requirements as stipulated in the 2015 Regulation and Guidelines for the internal marketing of cocoa.

Licensed Buying Companies (LBCs)

COCOBOD commissions Licensed Buying Companies (LBCs) to buy cocoa beans from farmers, check the quality of the cocoa beans, package them, and deliver them to its warehouses where they are subjected to further quality testing. Except for the Produce Buying Company Limited (PBC), which is a private company in which the government owns shares, all other LBCs are fully privately owned, and the majority are owned by Ghanaians. According to COCOBOD's 2018 annual report, there were 48 LBCs registered to operate in Ghana at that time.

Despite the large number of companies, the cocoa purchase business is quite concentrated, with the four largest LBCs accounting for over 57% of total beans purchased in a season. The largest LBCs are Olam Ghana Limited with a market share of nearly 17%, PBC with 16%, Agroecom Ghana Ltd (AGL) capturing 12.4%, and Nyonkopa Cocoa Buyers Ltd (NCBL) with about 12%.

Produce Buying Company Limited (PBC)

PBC is the largest and only LBC in which the government owns shares. It was incorporated in November 1981 as a wholly state-owned enterprise and a subsidiary of COCOBOD, changed into a public limited liability company in 1999, and subsequently listed on the Ghana Stock Exchange (GSE) in May 2000. PBC is primarily responsible for the purchase of cocoa beans, coffee, shea nuts, and shea butter, transportation and storage of these products in its warehouses and subsequent sale to COCOBOD. The main shareholders are Social Security and National Insurance Trust (SSNIT) with 38.1% and the Ministry of Finance with 36.7%. Minor shareholders are African Tiger Mutual Fund Ltd, NTHC/Institutional Investor Consortium, SCBN/Mauritius Re Altree Custody Services Ltd, PBC Employees/Commission Agents, and others.

Cocoa Processing Companies

Cocoa processing companies transform cocoa beans into finished and semi-finished products for domestic consumption and exports, such as chocolate, cocoa butter, cocoa powder, cocoa beverages, and cocoa liquor. Cocoa processing is open to both local and foreign companies. Foreign firms engaged in cocoa processing in Ghana include Barry Callebaut Ghana, a subsidiary of the Swiss multinational; Cargill Ghana, part of the American multinational; and Olam Cocoa Ghana, part of the Olam group. National processing companies include the Cocoa Processing Company (CPC), Plot Enterprise Ghana Ltd., and Afrotropic Cocoa Processing Ltd. The CPC was established in 1965, incorporated in 1981 as a limited liability and wholly state-owned company, and it was publicly listed on the Ghana Stock Exchange (GSE) in 2003. The listing on the GSE allowed private individuals and corporate entities to acquire shares in the company. However, the state has commanding majority in the company with COCOBOD and the government of Ghana together owning about 83% of the shares. The CPC produces the famed "Golden Tree" chocolates and other cocoa products. Raw cocoa beans make the bulk of cocoa exports, indicating that there is room for greater cocoa processing in Ghana to maximize the benefits from the "political crop."

Cocoa Purchase and Export Processes

COCOBOD has the exclusive authority to regulate cocoa purchasing processes and to export cocoa beans. It purchases cocoa beans directly from farmers, a function that it also delegates to licensed buying companies (LBCs). The procedures for storage and exporting of cocoa beans are stipulated in the 1968 Cocoa Industry Regulation and Consolidation Decree (NLCD 278) and the 1968 Cocoa Industry Regulations (L.I. 598), which spell out cocoa quality standards, the rules regarding the handling and inspection of the quality of cocoa beans, as well as how and where cocoa should be stored. Paragraph 2 of N.L.C.D. 278 states that "no person other than a grower of cocoa who is transporting his cocoa from the land on which it was grown to his premises for the purpose of fermenting and drying, shall transport cocoa which has not been thoroughly dried." Paragraph 3 states that "No person shall export or cause or permit to be exported or attempt to export any cocoa unless and until the same has been inspected by an inspector who shall have affixed to each bag a seal and grade-mark" (N.L.C.D 1968).

LBCs that wish to enter the cocoa purchasing business must obtain a purchase license and comply with criteria set up by COCOBOD regarding their organizational structure, operational strategy, and financial strength. In addition, applicants are required to demonstrate that they have access to adequate well-ventilated warehousing duly approved and certified by QCC. They must also abide by requirements concerning the type of packaging bags, grading and sealing procedures, minimum capacity of the sheds, and disinfection of sheds. The applications are reviewed by the Cocoa Sector Marketing Committee (CSMC), consisting of representatives of cocoa farmers, Licensed Buying Companies (LBCs), cocoa hauliers, QCC, CMC, COCOBOD, the Institute of Statistical Social and Economic Research of the University of Ghana, the Bank of Ghana, and the Ministry of Finance. The committee is chaired by the Minister of Food and Agriculture.

At the start of each cocoa season COCOBOD provides LBCs with seed funds to purchase cocoa beans from farmers. LBCs must submit to

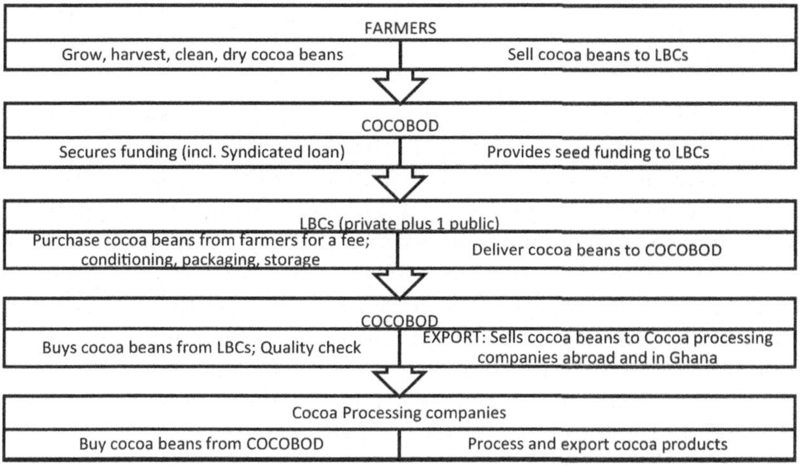

Fig. 4.3 Value chain and division of labor in Ghana's cocoa industry (*Source* Designed by the authors)

COCOBOD an advance performance bond in the form of a bank guarantee to ensure the recovery of the seed funds. The cocoa beans purchased by LBCs from farmers are temporarily stored in their warehouses and later moved to district cocoa depots where quality is rechecked by QCC officers. Next, cocoa beans are graded and sealed with each cocoa bag tagged with a seal indicating the quality of the cocoa and the station identification number. The cocoa beans are then transported to CMC's warehouses where QCC officers undertake further quality checks. The graded and sealed bags of cocoa beans are transported to the port where they are received by the CMC and final checks are done to ascertain quality by QCC before final export.

A flow chart summarizing the division of labor among various actors involved in the cocoa sector is presented in Fig. 4.3.

Financing Cocoa Operations

The operations of purchasing, transporting, conditioning, and storing cocoa beans are financed by a combination of seed funds raised by COCOBOD on the international market and LBCs' own internal funds and loans. Since 1992/93 COCOBOD has been raising funds through one-year syndicated loan agreements with foreign and local financial institutions, which are backed by cocoa sale contracts with its cocoa buyers.

The syndicated loan is expected to provide sufficient funding to cover the purchase of all cocoa produced in the season. However, in some years, the syndicated loan has covered only a fraction of the cocoa purchase, the lowest being in 2020 at 66% (Fig. 4.4).[2] Some of the cocoa purchase is covered by LBCs' own funds and borrowing from banks locally or abroad (in the case of foreign-affiliated LBCs). LBCs have expressed concern that the seed funds are often disbursed late, forcing them to use other sources to pay for the cocoa at the farmgate, as they must honor their commitments vis-à-vis the farmers to secure reliable delivery of cocoa every season.[3,4] Given that all LBCs must pay the same price to farmers, and therefore cannot compete based on the crop price, they must entice farmers on other dimensions, including by paying swiftly upon delivery of cocoa beans. Therefore, delays in the disbursement of seed funds by COCOBOD can be costly for the LBCs, especially in terms of their reputation vis-à-vis the farmers.

COCOBOD's Financial Performance as a Company

COCOBOD has recorded poor financial performance, with significant operating deficits, even though it operates as a monopoly with exclusive rights to purchase and export cocoa beans. So, why is it unable to generate a profit in the cocoa business? Monopolies typically leverage their privileged position in a sector to earn above-normal profits. COCOBOD is an institutionalized monopoly, set up for the explicit purpose of serving the government's goal of managing a sector deemed too strategic to be fully liberalized. In that sense, maybe the performance assessment

[2] Note that the seed funds may turn around a few times before they are recovered. Therefore, a given amount of funds can be used to purchase a much larger amount of cocoa during the season. It is therefore normal that the value of the seed fund distributed by COCOBOD is less than the total volume of cocoa beans purchased in a season.

[3] Information obtained from meetings with managers of LBCs.

[4] Note that, according to COCOBOD, seed funds are a privilege not a right for LBCs. When an LBC prepares its business plan to apply for a license, it does not include seed funds from COCOBOD as a source of financing for its activities. LBCs are supposed to raise their own funds to purchase cocoa beans. COCOBOD grants seed funds to LBCs to enable them to pay the farmers promptly.

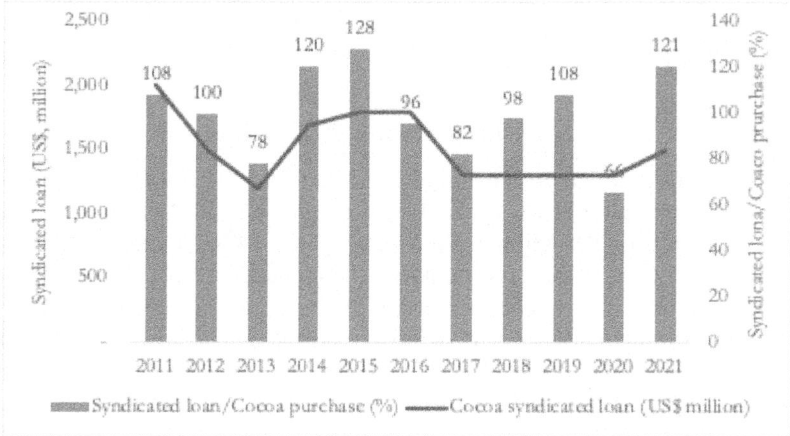

Fig. 4.4 Cocoa syndicated loan: Value and coverage of cocoa beans purchase in Ghana (*Source* Authors' construction using data from the Bank of Ghana)

yardstick should not be limited to monetary profit. What would be the yardstick then? The performance metric for COCOBOD is multidimensional; it includes the regulation of cocoa trade so that it is transparent, notably to keep cocoa smuggling and export misinvoicing to a minimum; the provision of training and technical support to farmers to improve productivity and combat crop diseases; and the promotion of the well-being of cocoa farmers by ensuring a "living producer price," providing support services on the farms, investing in infrastructure, and providing social services such as scholarships for farmers' high school children.[5]

A key advantage of the centralized organizational structure of the cocoa sector is that the proceeds of export of cocoa beans by COCOBOD and cocoa products by Ghanaian-owned companies are fully repatriated into the country. This is different from the gold sector which is dominated by foreign companies that enjoy special arrangements that entitle them to retain substantial fractions of their export proceeds abroad (Chapter 3). Those are all very important outcomes, and they must feature in the

[5] COCOBOD runs a Cocoa Scholarship Award Scheme that provides scholarships for second cycle school, benefiting about 7,500 students per year for the 3-year stream or 10,000 students for the 4-year stream. Source: https://cocobod.gh/social-responsibility-category/cocobod-child-education-support.

assessment of the performance of COCOBOD as a statutory monopoly in the cocoa sector.

Cocoa Price Setting Mechanism

The price of cocoa at the farmgate is determined by the Producer Price Review Committee (PPRC), which was created in 1983 (Kolavalli et al., 2012). Chaired by the Ministry of Finance,[6] the PPRC includes representatives from COCOBOD, the Bank of Ghana, farmers, LBCs, and haulers. Per government policy, cocoa farmers must receive no less than 70% of the international market price of cocoa beans on an annual basis. The technical committee of the PPRC undertakes the price setting exercise based on projections of FOB cocoa prices in US$, the exchange rate of the cedi to the US dollar, and the crop size in the following incoming crop year (Vigneri & Kolavalli, 2017). The PPRC also considers expected cocoa prices in the neighboring countries to discourage smuggling. The cocoa producer price is announced just before the opening of the main cropping season in October.

Figure 4.5 presents the trend of the ratio of the domestic producer price to the world market cocoa price. While the government's goal is to guarantee a stable producer price of at least 70% of the world cocoa price, the actual ratio fluctuates substantially; it was as low as 48% in 2007, and as high as 98% in 2011. The variation in the ratio is due to fluctuations in the world price, imperfect information about other factors considered in setting the producer price, notably movements in the GH¢/ US$ exchange rate, and the government's commitment to not cut the producer price.

The year 2011 was unique in that the domestic price nearly equaled the world price. This situation was caused by a sharp fall in the world market price relative to 2010 partly due to increased global supply of cocoa, while the government could not cut the farmgate price. In response, the government reduced the export tax on cocoa to support the domestic price in the interest of farmers, effectively reducing the government's expected revenue (Budget statement, 2012).

[6] Since this year (2025), the oversight of COCOBOD has been transferred from the Ministry of Agriculture to the Ministry of Finance. The latter therefore oversees the PPRC.

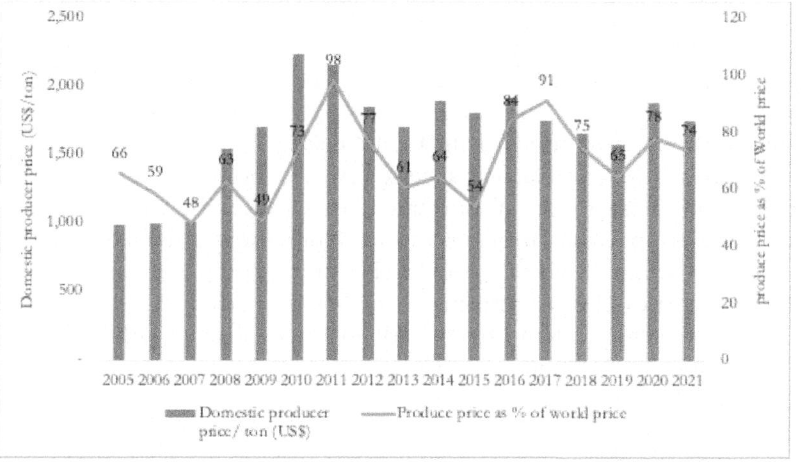

Fig. 4.5 World market price and domestic producer price of cocoa in Ghana (*Source* Authors' construction using data from the International Cocoa Organization (world market price) and the Ministry of Finance (domestic producer price). GHC prices are converted into US$ prices using the average annual exchange rate of the cedi[7])

Challenges Faced by Operators in the Cocoa Sector in Ghana

Private companies operating in the cocoa sector in Ghana face several challenges related to the cyclical nature of the crop, the centralized regulation of the sector, uncertainties, and costs related to the domestic economic environment as well as the vagaries of global cocoa markets. For LBCs, an important challenge is inherent to the centralized control of price setting mechanism, which forces LBCs to devise non-price means to secure their supply of cocoa beans, notably by establishing credibility of timely payment. In addition, LBCs offer various services to farmers, including credit, support to farmers' cooperatives with education and sensitization, and geo-mapping of farms to determine input needs and land potential to increase productivity. LBCs may also engage in other

[7] Note that while the world cocoa price includes the cost of insurance and freight (CIF), the farmgate price is on a free-on-board basis. Therefore, part of the difference is accounted for by the CIF.

activities related to corporate social responsibility, including promoting environmental sustainability.

Another challenge faced by LBCs is securing adequate financing to purchase cocoa beans and cover other operating expenses. LBCs rely significantly on seed funds from COCOBOD, leading to high debt to equity ratios in their balance sheets.[8] An important problem cited by LBCs is the delay in the disbursement of seed funds, which constrains their ability to pay the farmers on time. While foreign-owned LBCs may be able to secure funding from their parent companies abroad, such financing creates currency mismatch problems as they must pay farmers in cedis, collect payments from COCOBOD in cedis, while servicing foreign-currency denominated loans.

For all LBCs, borrowing from domestic banks is costly given the high lending interest rates and their limited profit margins. The agriculture sector generally receives a very small share of domestic bank credit partly due to banks' high-risk perception vis-à-vis the sector (Nkurunziza et al., 2016; Ndikumana et al. 2023). The lion's share of bank credit goes to the service sector, especially commerce and finance, and it has been rising over time. Over 2020–2022, 31% of total bank credit in Ghana was allocated to the services sector. The commerce and finance subsector received 18.7% of the loans, followed by manufacturing (11.5%) and construction (10.2%). Agriculture received a meager 3.7% of total loans while mining and quarrying received 2.3%.

To alleviate the financing constraints faced by local LBCs, COCOBOD has now restricted its supply of seed funds to domestically owned LBCs. However, foreign-owned companies believe that such a practice creates an uneven playing field in favor of domestic companies. Foreign-owned LBCs find this ironic given that they are often approached to make advance payments of cocoa beans to help COCOBOD bridge its cash shortages.[9]

[8] However, note that LBCs are expected to mobilize their own funds and that the seed funds are granted by COCOBOD to ensure prompt payment to farmers.

[9] Insights from meeting with managers of private LBCs in Ghana in January 2023.

Contribution of the Cocoa Sector to the Ghanaian Economy

Exports and Foreign Exchange Earnings from Cocoa

Cocoa has the potential to be an important contributor to foreign exchange earnings through three key channels, namely exports of cocoa beans and products, external financing of cocoa purchase through syndicated loans, and foreign direct investment inflows into the sector. A key distinguishing feature of the cocoa sector from other export-oriented sectors, such as gold, is that exports of cocoa beans are fully controlled by COCOBOD; therefore, export proceeds are fully repatriated to the country through the Bank of Ghana. National private cocoa processing companies are also obligated to repatriate all the proceeds of exports of processed cocoa products, while foreign-owned companies are exempt from such obligation. This is different from the gold sector where development agreements include specific negotiated ratios of gold exports earnings that must be repatriated to Ghana. It is important to note, however, that while private companies control all exports of gold produced in the country, in the case of cocoa, the government has full control of the exports of cocoa beans, with private companies controlling the export of semi-processed and processed cocoa products. Therefore, requiring gold companies to repatriate at least a fraction of their export proceeds is the only way to guarantee that the country receives some foreign exchange from gold exports.

In 2021, Ghana exported $2.8 billion worth of cocoa beans and products, which represented 19% of total exports. This placed cocoa in third position after gold (35%) and crude oil (27%). The share of cocoa in total exports has declined steadily over time, especially at the beginning of the 2010s with the discovery of oil (Fig. 4.6). Between 2009 and 2021, the share declined by a full 13% points from 32% to 19%.

In addition to exports, the cocoa sector brings in foreign exchange reserves through the syndicated loan contracted by COCOBOD annually. Over the past five years up to the 2021/2022 crop year, the loan brought in an average of $1.3 billion in foreign exchange annually, with variations in the amount reflecting fluctuations in the size of annual cocoa production. The syndicated loan stood at $1.1 billion in 2022, down from $1.5 billion in 2021.

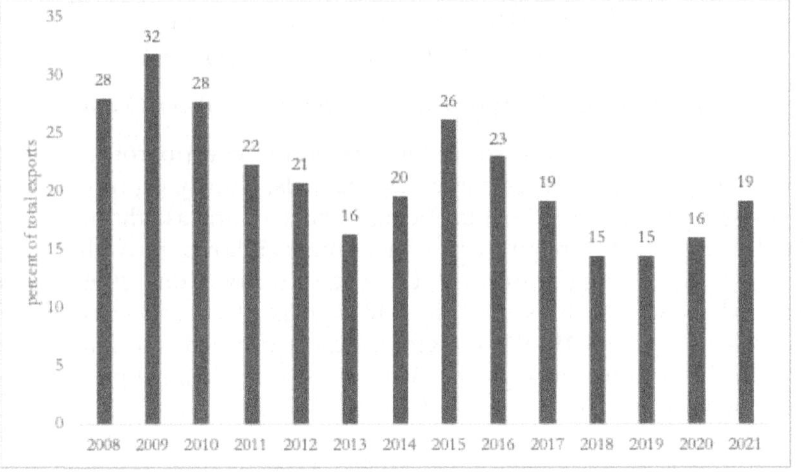

Fig. 4.6 Share of cocoa beans and cocoa products in Ghana's total exports (percent) (*Source* Authors' computation using data from the Balance of Payments Statistics, Bank of Ghana)

The last source of foreign exchange inflows into the country associated with the cocoa sector is foreign direct investment. While we could not obtain data on FDI destined specifically for the cocoa sector, an examination of the distribution of FDI across sectors suggests that the share of the cocoa sector is likely to be very small. The entire agriculture, forestry, and fishing sector receives less than 1% of total FDI inflows to Ghana (data from the Bank of Ghana). Most foreign direct investments go to the mining and quarrying sector which captures 68% of total inflows, with finance and insurance coming at a distant second place with 14%. The limited amount of foreign investment in the cocoa sector is partly a result of the dominance of the government in the sector, a strategic decision that carries costs as well as benefits.

Cocoa and Poverty Reduction

Cocoa is a source of livelihood for households that are directly involved in planting cocoa as well as those that are employed at the various stages of the cocoa value chain. The cocoa sector, therefore, has a high potential for contributing to the fight against poverty. It can be a source of wealth creation through the development of local entrepreneurship along the cocoa value chain, as well as activities that are related directly or indirectly to the sector through spillover effects. The actual contribution of cocoa to poverty reduction and wealth creation ultimately depends on production and productivity at the farm level, access to financing for farmers and other operators in the sector, crop prices, and the overall economic environment as it influences the purchasing power of revenue from cocoa as well as the cost of living of those involved in the cocoa sector.

Data on the actual contribution of cocoa to poverty reduction and wealth creation is quite scarce. But an approximate picture can be gleaned from the limited information we were able to obtain from various sources. A 2007 study found that poverty among cocoa farmers had declined from 60% in 1991/92 to 23.9% in 2005/2006 (World Bank, 2007). Amankrah (2008) also found evidence of a reduction in poverty associated with cocoa farming activities and the provision of social amenities by the government in cocoa growing areas. While it is difficult to isolate the impact of cocoa on poverty, the evidence shows that on average poverty tends to be lower in cocoa growing areas compared to non-growing areas as indicated in the 2016/17 Ghana Living Standards Survey (GLSS 7; Table 4.1 and Fig. 4.7).[10]

Several historical and structural factors account for the stark disparity in poverty incidence between Ghana's northern regions and the other regions. One major historical factor of these disparities is colonial legacy. During the colonial era, Ghana's northern regions suffered marginalization, while southern regions, which are richer in natural resources such as gold, cocoa, and timber, were the focus of the colonial administration's economic program. This resulted in the underdevelopment of the Northern regions' infrastructure, lack of educational opportunities, limited access to markets, and less favorable economic prospects (Shepherd et al., 2004). Even in the post-colonial era, the northern areas have received less investment in infrastructure development, resulting in poor healthcare services, low access to electricity, and inadequate road networks. Despite efforts to close the infrastructure gap, there hasn't been a coordinated plan to balance growth and living standards across regions.

[10] It is worth noting that rural roads and other types of infrastructure are in higher supply and better quality in cocoa-growing areas than in non-cocoa growing areas. This might also contribute to overall better economic environment and lower poverty in cocoa growing areas.

Table 4.1 Cocoa farming and poverty incidence in Ghana by region, 2016/2017

Region	*Poverty incidence (%)*	*Volume of cocoa beans purchased by COCOBOD (tons) 2019/2020 year*
Ashanti	11.6	165,830
Eastern	12.6	89,131
Volta*	37.3	5383
Central	13.8	85,526
Western*	21.1	332,647
Brong Ahafo*	26.8	88,460
Non-cocoa growing regions		
Upper West	70.9	–
Upper East	54.8	–
Northern*	61.1	–
Greater Accra	2.5	–

Source Ghana Living Standard Survey 2016/2017 and COCOBOD
**Note* Under the new administrative map, Brong Ahafo has been split into three regions: Ahafo, Bono, and Bono East; Western was split into two regions: Western and Western North; Volta was split into two regions: Volta and Oti; and Northern was split into three regions: Northern, North East and Savannah

Secondly, geographical factors partly explain the higher levels of poverty in the North. Compared to the South, the North is characterized by a more arid climate and less fertile land, which makes agriculture more difficult and less productive (Fagariba et al., 2018)). The North experiences frequent droughts, which cause crop failures and deepen food insecurity and poverty. Furthermore, the northern areas have historically had limited access to high-quality education, resulting in higher illiteracy. In 2013, the adult literacy rate was 30.6% in Northern Region, 36.6% in Upper East, and 38% in Upper West, compared to the national average of about 60%, and 79.1% in Greater Accra and 63.1% in Ashanti Region (GSS, 2014). Lastly, in contrast to the southern areas, which are more industrialized and have a better environment for food and cash crop agriculture, the northern regions offer fewer economic opportunities. Cash crops like cocoa tend to do better in the southern areas, enhancing the

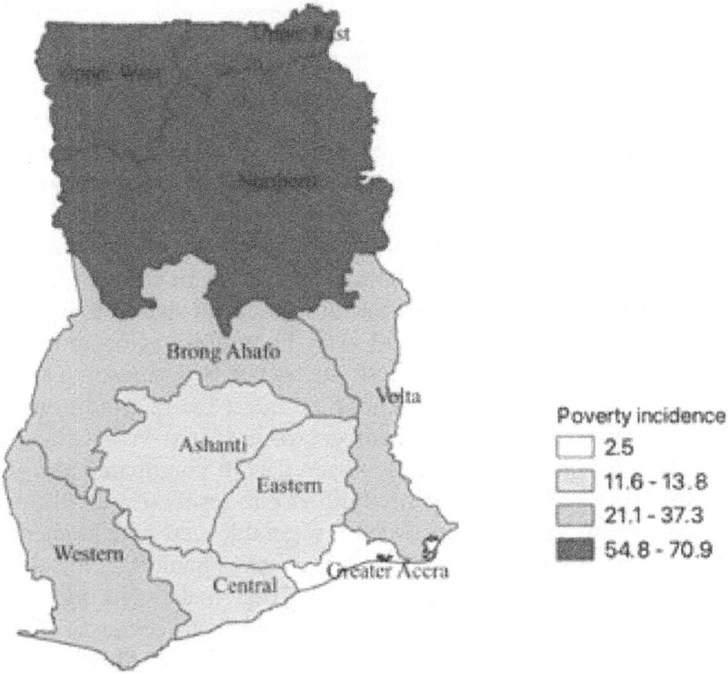

Fig. 4.7 Poverty incidence in Ghana by region (*Source* Authors' design with assistance from Didier Wayoro.[11] **Note* Under the new administrative map, Brong Ahafo has been split into three regions: Ahafo, Bono, and Bono East; Western was split into two regions: Western and Western North; Volta was split into two regions: Volta and Oti; and Northern was split into three regions: Northern, North East and Savannah)

comparative advantage of the south.[12] The combination of colonial legacy of marginalization, structural and geographical disadvantages, and lack of mitigating policies contribute to keeping the northern regions behind

[11] The map shows the 10 regions (as opposed to the new 16 regions) according to which the survey data was collected.

[12] The northern regions have potential for cultivation of cotton, rice, and shea nut, but these have received less attention than cocoa.

in terms of social and economic development, hence the higher poverty rates.

What Would the Cocoa Farmer Say?

To get a real-life sense of the contribution of cocoa to the wellbeing of farming households, we visited farms in Nyankrom near the town of Swedru in the Central region of Ghana in January 2023. Cocoa cultivation is the main activity for farmers in Nyankrom. One of our hosts grows cocoa on an eight-acre land and produces an average of eight bags of fresh cocoa beans per season. The male head of household shared that working on cocoa occupies all his time—and even his nights, as he must "keep one eye open" watching over his fresh cocoa beans drying on a wooden stand outside his house. The household's modest living conditions illustrate the low income generated from growing cocoa. While the family has been able to build a small house covered with corrugated aluminum sheets, it does not have much of anything else in terms of valuable assets. Subsistence farming (banana, cocoa yam, vegetables, etc.) helps the family to supplement the monetary revenue from cocoa. Thankfully, the children can receive scholarships from COCOBOD if they make it to high school.

So, how much does our host household earn from cocoa farming? At the 2022–2023 season cocoa price of GHC 800/bag,[13] the 8 bags that is produced annually would have generated GHC 6,400, which is 46% of the 2021 per capita GDP. This means that to earn the national average per capita GDP from growing cocoa, our host farmer in Nyankrom would have to more than double either productivity or the area planted (to 17.5 acres), both of which are impossible to achieve. If our host farmer is representative of the average cocoa farming household, it means that poverty remains a real threat for cocoa growers in Ghana.

This example seems to represent the lower bound of the earning prospects of a cocoa farmer given the low yield reported by the farmer. Estimates of cocoa yields vary substantially by source, region (quality of the soil), type of land tenure, and even gender of the owner. As can be seen in Table 4.2, the yield varies from 1 bag to 2.3 bags per acre. The estimates suggest that to earn the average GDP per capita, a farmer would

[13] The beans in a bag of cocoa weigh 62.5 kg. The empty bag adds about 1 kg, and a sample for the three quality checks adds another 0.5 kg to bring the gross weight to 64 kg.

have to engage a minimum of 8 acres at the highest productivity and up to 20 acres at the lowest productivity.

The disparities in cocoa yields suggest that there is room for improvement with appropriate policy levers, especially increased investments in quality input, enhanced care for the cocoa trees, and increased technical support to farmers. Such investments can yield substantial benefits both at the household level and at the national level.

"Counting the Beans": Investigation of Cocoa Export Misinvoicing and Smuggling

In this section, we assess the degree of exposure of the cocoa sector to capital flight by estimating cocoa export misinvoicing and possible smuggling of cocoa into Côte d'Ivoire, Burkina Faso, and Togo. While there are other channels of capital flight, export misinvoicing of primary commodities constitutes an important mechanism of capital flight that plagues resource-rich countries in Africa. The analysis is based on a comparison of mirror trade data between Ghana and its trading partners following the established methodology in the literature (Ndikumana & Boyce, 2022). The section begins by comparing export data from various sources to examine possible inconsistencies across sources, which is a preliminary indicator of possible export misinvoicing. This is followed by formal estimation of cocoa export misinvoicing focusing on the ten leading trading partners.

Inconsistency in Cocoa Exports Data

The data on cocoa exports exhibit inconsistencies in levels and trends across sources as can be seen in Fig. 4.8 which presents data from COCOBOD, the Balance of Payments (from the Bank of Ghana) and Comtrade. The differences may arise for various reasons, including whether the data refers to just cocoa beans alone or includes processed cocoa products, reporting delays and various statistical errors. Specifically, COCOBOD exports only include cocoa beans, while the other series include cocoa beans and processed cocoa products. This explains the differences between the values reported in the Balance of Payments and those reported by COCOBOD. Further below, we assess whether the observed statistical differences could be due to export misinvoicing

Table 4.2 Estimates of cocoa yields by land tenure rights and gender of the farm owner in Ghana

	Yield per hectare (kg)	*Yield per acre (kg)*	*Yield per acre (bags)*	*Income per acre in cedis*	*Income per acre in current US$*	*Cocoa income per acre as a percent of per capita GDP 2021*	*Acres needed to earn income equivalent to per capita GDP*
				at 800 cedis/ bag	*at 10GHC/US$ (2023 rate)*	*Per capita GDP: 13983GHC*	
By land tenure type							
*Abunu**	214.9	87.0	1.4	1113.7	111.1	7.9%	12.6
*Abusa***	157.5	63.8	1.0	816.2	81.6	5.8%	17.1
Owner	139	56.3	0.9	720.3	72.0	5.1%	19.4
By rights to land							
Full rights	327.3	132.5	2.1	1696.1	169.6	12.1%	8.2
Partial rights	233.6	94.6	1.5	1210.6	121.1	8.7%	11.6
By gender							
Female	334	135.2	2.2	1730.9	173.1	12.4%	8.1
Male	360.3	145.9	2.3	1967.1	186.7	13.3%	7.5
Farmer visited in Nyankrom			1	800	80	5.7%	17.5

Source Report on Land Tenure & Cocoa Production in Ghana A CRIG/WCF Collaborative Survey, February 2017, Nana Kofi Acquah/LANDMAPP

Notes 1 bag = 62.5 kg; 1 ha = 2.47 acres. Acres needed to earn per capita GDP in 2021 are obtained by dividing GDP per capita (13,983GHC) by income per acre in GHC. Total earnings by the farmer in Nyankrom on 8 acres = 8 × 800 GHC = 6400 GHC = 46% of 13,983 GHC (2021 per capita income)

*Under the ***Abunu*** land tenure system, a piece of land is given to a farmer and crops are shared equally between the farmer and landowner. The ***Abunu*** system is used for perennial crops or tree crop production

**Under the *Abusa* land tenure system, the farm is divided into three: two-thirds go to the farmer and one-third to the landowner. The *Abusa* system is often used in the case of annual crop production

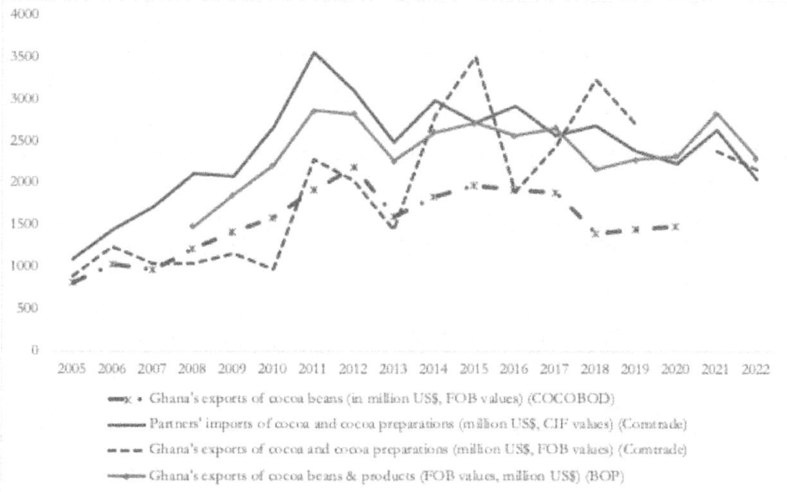

Fig. 4.8 Ghana's cocoa exports and partners' imports by source (million US$) (*Sources* Authors' construction using data from COCOBOD, the Bank of Ghana, and Comtrade)

by using Comtrade as the common source for data on Ghana's exports and its partners' imports, accounting for the cost of insurance and freight.

Estimation Methodology

Cocoa export underinvoicing refers to situations where the value of cocoa exports recorded by Ghana, augmented by the cost of insurance and freight, is significantly below the value of cocoa imports (CIF value) as reported by Ghana's trading partners in the Comtrade database. To estimate cocoa export misinvoicing we use the methodology developed by Ndikumana and Boyce (2022)[14] with data from Comtrade over the period 2000–2022 reported under categories HS 1801–1806.

Considering Ghana's trading partner j in year t, cocoa export misinvoicing DX is estimated as follows:

$$DX_{jt} = M_{jt} - cif_{jt} * X_{jt} \quad (4.1)$$

[14] Also see Ndikumana and Boyce (2010).

M_{jt} represents cocoa imports by Ghana's trading partner j as recorded by partner j, X_{jt} is Ghana's cocoa exports to partner j in year t as recorded in Ghana's data in Comtrade, and cif_{jt} is the cost of insurance and freight for cocoa exports from Ghana to country j.[15] A positive value of DX indicates export underinvoicing, reflecting capital flight, while a negative value would indicate export overinvoicing, which is a rare scenario.

Export misinvoicing may be motivated by three factors: financial gains; circumventing foreign exchange controls; and reducing administrative burdens (Buehn & Eichler, 2011; Buehn and Farzanegan, 2012; Patnaik et al., 2012; Storti & de Grauwe, 2012). In the case of Ghana, these motives do not apply to cocoa beans because the entity that has the monopoly of exporting the beans is a government-owned organization (COCOBOD), which has no incentives of minimizing taxation and evading exchange controls. Under this specific industrial organization, discrepancies between Ghana's recorded exports and partners' recorded imports of cocoa beans would reflect statistical inconsistencies, possibly due to reporting delays, inaccurate c.i.f. estimates[16] and other statistical errors, as well as smuggling of cocoa beans between Ghana and its neighbors. The smuggling of cocoa beans would generate apparent export underinvoicing if the importer is able to identify the cocoa beans as originating from Ghana while the transaction does not appear in Ghana's trade statistics as the cocoa crossed borders illicitly.

The standard motives for export misinvoicing may apply to the case of cocoa products, which are exported by private cocoa processing companies. For this reason, we present estimates of export misinvoicing for total exports of cocoa and cocoa products, as well as results for export misinvoicing of cocoa beans separately, which represent 81% of total cocoa exports.

Estimates of Export Misinvoicing of Cocoa Beans and Cocoa Products

The analysis focuses on the top ten leading partners in terms of shares in total exports (Table 4.3). The leading buyer of Ghanaian cocoa and cocoa products is the Netherlands, accounting for 27% of Ghana's total

[15] The cost of insurance and freight is obtained from the "OECD's International Transport and Insurance Costs of merchandise trade" (ITIC) database.

[16] We requested actual c.i.f. figures from COCOBOD. We did not receive them until the time of writing.

exports. It is followed by Malaysia (10% of total exports), and farther behind by the United States (7.2%), Belgium (6.5%), and the United Kingdom (6.2%).

The comparison of Ghana's exports and its partners' imports reveals relatively low discrepancies. Nonetheless, some cocoa export underinvoicing is detected for cocoa sold to France ($2.2 billion), the United Kingdom ($1.5 billion), and Germany ($1 billion), while apparent overinvoicing is observed in the case of trade with Belgium ($1 billion) and Malaysia ($880 million). Overall, trade with the rest of the world exhibits apparent export underinvoicing to the tune of $12 billion out of the $59 billion of total exports. Relative to the volume of exports, the estimated export misinvoicing of cocoa and cocoa products is limited. This contrasts with the case of neighboring Côte d'Ivoire where cocoa trade exhibits substantial discrepancies pointing to both export underinvoicing as well as export overinvoicing connected with transit through trading hubs (Merckaert, 2022). The case of the cocoa sector in Ghana also differs markedly from the gold sector which exhibits large discrepancies in the export data, pointing to both export underinvoicing and export underinvoicing (Chapter 3 in this volume).

The Case of Cocoa Beans

The geographical distribution of the destination of cocoa beans exports is similar to that of total cocoa exports, with the Netherlands and Malaysia as leading importers (Table 4.4). The pattern of export misinvoicing is also similar, with underinvoicing of cocoa beans destined for France ($2.2 billion) and the United Kingdom ($1.4 billion). There is overinvoicing of cocoa beans destined to the Netherlands ($1.5 billion), Belgium ($865 million), and Malaysia ($855 million). Overall misinvoicing of cocoa beans is much smaller than that of cocoa and cocoa products, estimated at $7.3 billion over the period 2000–2022. In a nutshell the discrepancies in mirror trade statistics are substantially lower for cocoa beans than overall cocoa exports, which is a result of the control of exports of cocoa beans by COCOBOD. Even the observed discrepancies in the cocoa beans trade statistics cannot be explained by the usual motives of export misinvoicing as they do not apply to a product managed by a state-owned company.

Table 4.3 Estimated export misinvoicing of cocoa beans and cocoa preparations from Ghana, total over 2000–2022 (million, constant 2022 US$)

Partner	*Matched years only*			*All years*		*Partner's share (%)*	
	Export misinvoicing	*Ghana's exports*	*Partner's imports*	*Ghana's exports*	*Partner's imports*	*Share in Ghana's exports to World*	*Share in Partners' imports*
Belgium	−1070.2	2850.1	2003.2	2850.1	2098.0	6.5	3.3
France	2203.9	2200.6	4575.3	2200.6	4894.5	5.0	7.8
Germany	1002.7	2292.1	3472.9	2292.1	3703.1	5.2	5.9
Japan	528.3	2238.7	2967.2	2238.7	3202.2	5.1	5.1
Malaysia	−880.4	4401.7	3933.0	4401.7	4123.8	10.0	6.5
Netherlands	−81.4	11,915.3	12,759.8	11,915.3	13,468.8	27.1	21.3
Spain	−186.2	1755.6	1705.6	1755.6	1852.4	4.0	2.9
Türkiye	812.0	1526.8	2459.9	1526.8	2731.7	3.5	4.3
United Kingdom	1555.4	2714.1	4485.3	2714.1	4697.1	6.2	7.4
United States	621.8	3172.7	3964.4	3172.7	4233.9	7.2	6.7
World	12,047.5	44,040.3	59,550.4	44,040.3	63,106.4	100.0	100.0

Source Authors' computation using data from Comtrade

Table 4.4 Estimated export misinvoicing of cocoa beans* from Ghana, total over 2000–2022 (million, constant 2022 US$)

Partner	*Matched years only*			*All years*		*Partner's share*	
	Export misinvoicing	*Ghana's exports*	*Partner's imports*	*Ghana's exports*	*Partner's imports*	*Share in Ghana's exports to the World (percent)*	*Share in Partners' imports (percent)*
Belgium	−865.6	2609.8	1927.6	2609.8	2020.3	7.3	5.7
France	2205.0	1425.8	3730.0	1425.8	3937.4	4.0	11.1
Germany	638.8	1473.3	2214.6	1473.3	2331.4	4.1	6.6
Japan	446.2	2102.2	2719.1	2102.2	2937.2	5.9	8.3
Malaysia	−855.2	4313.3	3826.5	4313.3	4005.6	12.1	11.3
Netherlands	−1524.4	9142.0	8255.2	9142.0	8628.2	25.7	24.3
Spain	−419.9	1301.4	971.4	1301.4	1071.2	3.7	3.0
Türkiye	391.9	1438.2	1931.6	1438.2	2185.8	4.0	6.1
United Kingdom	1444.8	2386.8	4002.2	2386.8	4188.3	6.7	11.8
United States	472.8	2349.5	2904.2	2349.5	3084.8	6.6	8.7
Total (cocoa beans only)	7330.6	35,566.9	45,371.9	35,566.9	47,791.8	100.0	134.4
Share of total cocoa & processed products	61%	81%	76%	81%	76%		

* *Note* The statistics in this table cover cocoa beans only (HS 1801) and do not include cocoa preparations

How About Cross-Border Cocoa Smuggling?

Smuggling of cocoa across borders from or into Ghana can be attributed to several factors that can be categorized into structural, policy, and other domestic and global factors. The key structural factor is the seamless nature of the borders between Ghana and its neighbors, where no deterrent physical barrier such as a river or lake separates Ghana from Côte d'Ivoire, Togo, and Burkina Faso. This makes it particularly difficult to monitor the movement of cocoa between Ghana and its neighbors. In fact, in some areas, cocoa farms straddle the border between Ghana and Côte d'Ivoire, making it difficult to enforce the "rule of origin" for cocoa from those areas. The seamless nature of the borders implies that farmers can sell their crop in either country depending on the differential in producer prices and convenience and timeliness of the payment procedures.

A key policy factor driving cocoa smuggling is the disparity in price setting mechanisms. While the producer price is determined by the Producer Price Review Committee in Ghana, it is market determined in Côte d'Ivoire. This implies possible price differences between Ghana and its neighbors, which induce smuggling into or out of Ghana depending on the direction of the price differential. An empirical study by Jebuni-Dotsey (2023) found that the real price differential between Ghana and its neighbors induces smuggling, especially in the cocoa growing regions bordering Côte d'Ivoire and Togo. The study estimated that 1% higher price abroad leads to between 0.11% and 0.53% losses in cocoa sales for Ghana. The study found that the intensity of cocoa smuggling has trended down recently as the gaps in real prices have narrowed. Another policy factor of cocoa smuggling is the exchange rate, as it influences the purchasing power of the farmer's and trader's earnings in each country.

Measuring cocoa smuggling is difficult given that it is a clandestine and illicit activity. To provide a glance at the extent of cocoa smuggling we compare the value of Ghana's exports to neighboring countries as reported by Ghana and the value of imports of Ghana's cocoa reported by its neighbors in the Comtrade database. Obviously, this is an imperfect approach given that the very purpose of smuggling is to avoid recording on either side of the border. Moreover, when cocoa is eventually exported, there is no clear means of identifying its true origin in the importer's statistics. In other words, when a company in Côte d'Ivoire purchases cocoa that was smuggled from Ghana, it has no effective means of distinguishing it from locally produced cocoa. The Ghanaian cocoa beans may therefore get out of Côte d'Ivoire with a Côte d'Ivoire label. A similar scenario happens on the Ghana side where smuggled Ivorian cocoa is mixed with Ghanaian cocoa at the export station.

The analysis of cocoa export statistics in Comtrade shows very little trade with Ghana's neighbors. Cocoa exports to Burkina Faso, Côte d'Ivoire, and Togo reported in Comtrade database represent less than 0.1% of total cocoa exports. The discrepancies in bilateral trade statistics are also very small. Considering the period 2000–2021, regardless of matched reporting, Ghana's exports to Burkina Faso, Côte d'Ivoire, and Togo amounted to $25 million (constant 2022 US$), and these three partners' imports totaled $22.6 million. The results suggest that there is limited systematic smuggling of cocoa across Ghana's borders.

Conclusion

The special place of cocoa in Ghana as a "political crop" is exhibited in the scrutiny exerted by the government over the operations from the plantations to the export counter. The cocoa sector is an important source of livelihood for millions of Ghanaians who draw income directly from growing cocoa and indirectly from employment along the cocoa value chain and from businesses that benefit from the sector's spillover effects. While there is no good data to isolate the direct impact of cocoa on household revenue, the limited information available suggests that it is relatively modest.

This chapter sought to investigate the role of the cocoa sector in the Ghanaian economy and to specifically examine whether and to what extent it is exposed to capital flight, notably through export underinvoicing. While there are some discrepancies in the export data across various sources, the results from standard analysis of trade statistics show that cocoa export misinvoicing is relatively limited. In that sense, the cocoa sector in Ghana is indeed very different from the one in Côte d'Ivoire (Merckaert, 2022). It is also very different from the gold sector in Ghana where there is substantial gold export misinvoicing and systemic opacity in gold trade statistics (Chapter 3 in this book). These outcomes are a result of the ownership structure—domestic vs. foreign, private vs. public—and the extent of government regulation of the sector throughout the entire value chain. The analysis indicates that government regulation of the cocoa sector in Ghana is associated with lower risk of capital flight through export misinvoicing. Government involvement in the cocoa sector is also associated with substantial welfare gains, especially in terms of predictability and stability of the cocoa producer price, support to cocoa farmers through scholarships for their children, and ensuring repatriation of foreign exchange earnings from exports of cocoa beans that are managed by COCOBOD, which is an elusive goal for other resource-rich African countries where extractive sectors are fully liberalized and privatized. The evidence implies that the organizational structure and regulatory regime of the extractive sector play an important role in maximizing the country's benefits from resource exploitation, and particularly in reducing the exposure to capital flight.

References

Abbadi, S., Senadza, B., Lieuw-Kie-Song, M., & Abebe, H. (2019). *Assessing the Employment Effects of Processing Cocoa in Ghana*. Strengthen Publication Series.

Ahene-Codjoe, A. A., Alu, A. A., & Mehrotra, R. (2022). Abnormal Pricing in International Commodity Trading: Evidence from Ghana. *International Economics, 172*, 331–348.

Amankrah, K. D. (2008). *Assessing Poverty Situations: A Case Study of Cocoa Farming Households in the Asikuma-Odoben Brakwa District of the Central Region* [Bachelor's thesis, University of Cape Coast].

Amanor, K.S. (2010). Family Values, Land Sales and Agricultural Commodification in South-Eastern Ghana. *Africa, 80*(1), 104–125. doi:10.3366/E0001972009001284.

Berry, S. (2018). Migrant Cocoa Farmers of Southern Ghana: A Study in Rural Capitalism. *Journal of Peasant Studies, 45*(7), 1539–1547.

Bonanomi, E. B., Brugger, F., Carbonnier, G., Dzanku, F. M., & Insisienmay, S. (2024). *Missing Dollars: Illicit Financial Flows from Commodity Trade* (International Development Policy Series No. 17). Brill. (International Development Policy Series no. 17. Geneva Graduate Institute of International and Development Studies.)

Buehn, A., & Eichler, S. (2011). Trade misinvoicing: The dark side of world trade. *World Economy, 34*(8), 1263–87.

Buehn, A., & Farzanegan, M. R. (2012). Smuggling around the world: Evidence from a structural equation model. *Applied Economics, 44*(23), 3047–64.

Fagariba, C. J., Song, S., & Baoro, S. K. G. S. (2018). Climate Change Adaptation Strategies and Constraints in Northern Ghana: Evidence of Farmers in Sissala West District. *Sustainability, 10*(5), 1484.

FAOSTAT. (2016). *FAO Statistical Yearbook*. Food and Agricultural Organization of the United Nations, Rome, Italy.

Ghana Statistical Service. (2014). *Ghana Living Standards Survey Round 6. Main Report*. Accra, Ghana.

Hill, P. (1963). *The Migrant Cocoa Farmers of Southern Ghana. A Study in Rural Capitalism*. Cambridge University Press.

Jebuni-Dotsey, S. (2023). Price incentives and supply Response in Cocoa-a Case of Border Regions of Ghana. *Journal of Sustainable Development, 16*(3), 1–17.

Kolavalli, S., Vigneri, M., Maamah, H., & Poku, J. (2012). *The Partially Liberalized Cocoa Sector in Ghana: Producer Price Determination, Quality Control, and Service Provision* (IFPRI Discussion Paper No. 1213). International Food Policy Research Institute.

Kolavalli, S., & Vigneri, M. (2011). Cocoa in Ghana: Shaping the Success of an Economy. In P. Chuhan-Pole & M. Angwafo (Eds.), *Yes, Africa Can: Success Stories from a Dynamic Continent* (pp. 201–217). The World Bank.

Kolavalli, S., & Vigneri, M. (2017). *The Cocoa Coast: The Board-Managed Cocoa Sector in Ghana*. International Food Policy Research Institute.

Manu, S.Y. (1989). *The Golden Cocoa Pod*. Accra, Ghana, Sedco Publishing Limited.

Merckaert, J. (2022). Côte d'Ivoire: Bitter Chocolate. In L. Ndikumana & J. K. Boyce (Eds.), *On the Trail of Capital Flight from Africa: The Takers and the Enablers* (pp. 99–148). Oxford University Press.

Monastyrnaya, E., Joerin, J., Dawoe, E., & Six, J. (2016). *Assessing the Resilience of the Cocoa Value Chain in Ghana* (Case Study Report). Sustainable Agroecosystems Group, Swiss Federal Institute of Technology Zurich.

Ndikumana, L., & Boyce, J. K. (2022). Capital Flight From Angola, Côte d'Ivoire, and South Africa: An Overview. In L. Ndikumana & J. K. Boyce (Eds.), *On the Trail of Capital Flight From Africa: The Takers and the Enablers* (pp. 10–36). Oxford University Press.

Ndikumana, L., & Boyce, J. K. (2010). Measurement of Capital Flight: Methodology and Results for Sub-Saharan African Countries. *African Development Review, 22*(4), 471–481.

Ndikumana, L., Naidoo, K., & Perez, F. (2023). Can National Development Banks Help Alleviate the Shortage of Patient Investment Capital in Africa? Evidence from Bank-Level Panel Data. *Journal of African Development, 24*(1), 1–42.

Nkurunziza, J., Ndikumana, L., & Nyamoya, P. (2016). The Financial Sector in Burundi: An Investigation of Its Efficiency in Resource Mobilization and Allocation. In E. Sebastian, S. Johnson, & D. N. Weil (Eds.), *African Successes,*

Volume III: Modernization and Development (pp. 103–156). Chicago University Press.

Patnaik, I., Gupta, A. S., & Shah, A. (2012). Determinants of trade misinvoicing. *Open Economies Review, 23*(5), 891–910.

Republic of Ghana (2012). *Budget Statement and Economic Policy of the Government of Ghana for the 2012.* Accra, Ghana: Ministry of Finance and Economic Planning. Accessed on 24 April 2026, https://mofep.gov.gh/sites/default/files/budget-statements/2012_budget.pdf

Shepherd, A., Gyimah-Boadi, E., Gariba, S., Plagerson, S., & Musa, A. W. (2004). *Bridging the North South Divide in Ghana? Background Paper for the 2005 World Development Report*. The World Bank.

Storti, C. C., & de Grauwe , P. (Eds.) (2012). *Illicit Trade and the Global Economy.* Cambridge, MA: MIT Press.

Stryker, J., Dumeau, E., Wohl, J., Haymond, P., Cook, A. and Coon, K. (1990). *Trade, exchange rate, and agricultural pricing policies in Ghana*. World Bank comparative studies—The political economy of agricultural pricing policy. The World Bank.

Vigneri, M., & Santos, P. (2008). What Does *Liberalization Without Price Competition Achieve? The Case of Cocoa Marketing in Rural Ghana* (IFPRI-GSSP Background Paper No. 14). International Food Policy Research Institute.

Vigneri, M., & Kolavalli, S. (2017). *Growth Through Pricing Policy: The Case of Cocoa in Ghana* (Background Paper for UNCTAD-FAO Commodities and Development Report). UNCTAD.

World Bank. (2007). *World Development Report: Agriculture for Development*. World Bank.

CHAPTER 5

The State, Corporations, or the People: Who Benefits From Mining in Zambia?

Léonce Ndikumana, Dale Mudenda, and Bilen Gurara

> Before the beginning of colonial rule, smelters and blacksmiths were "wealthy and influential" members of their societies... For the products of their crafts, they received high rewards from the chiefs and ordinary citizens. However, with the coming of colonial rule, the imported goods such as knives, hoes and axes provided a very strong competition to the local products... Gradually the imports won the competition. Smelting was proscribed and became punishable offence (Musambachime, 2016, pp. 316–317).
>
> It was Zambia's good fortune to be "born with a copper spoon in its mouth", although for much of the 45 years since independence in 1964, natural resource dependence has been more of a curse than a blessing (Adam & Simpasa, 2010, p. 85).[1]

[1] This was a lamentation by Kenneth Kaunda, Zambia's first president, in the 1980s when the economy collapsed.

L. Ndikumana, *Capital Flight from Cameroon, Ghana, and Zambia*, https://doi.org/10.1007/978-3-032-22770-6_5

Introduction

Zambia is best known for its vast endowment in mineral resources, which attracted foreign investors and traders since the start of the nineteenth century, and maybe even earlier (Cunningham, 1981; Musambachime, 2016). Foreign interest in Zambia's minerals persists today. Zambia is the ninth largest producer of copper in the world, with about 760 thousand tons in 2023, second in Africa behind the Democratic Republic of Congo (USGS).[2] The country also has a wide range of other minerals in various quantities, including strategic products such as cobalt, lithium, nickel, and gemstones, which are highly demanded in the context of global clean energy transition.

Long before Western traders set foot on the Zambian soil, indigenous populations earned a living by making various tools and ornamental objects from surface-level artisanal mining (Chitonge, 2021; Cunningham, 1981; Musambachime, 2016; Robinson, 1933).[3] The entry of Europeans in the sector marked the end of domestic control of mineral resources, as the sector was captured to serve the interests of foreign companies and the colonial British regime, while the natives were formally banned from engaging in mining. After independence in 1964, the new national leadership sought to regain control over the mining sector, which it considered to be a key driver of economic growth. Hence, the government of President Kenneth Kaunda (in power from 1964 to 1991) embarked on a nationalization and Zambianization agenda—or "the big decision" (Martin, 1972), transferring the control of mines to state-owned enterprises and setting up regulatory agencies to manage the sector. Moreover, the mission of mining was expanded to include the provision of welfare services to citizens, referred to as the "cradle to grave" model.

The state-led mining development model encountered severe challenges, including underinvestment in expansion and maintenance, leading to stagnation and decline in production and chronic losses by mining houses. By the 1980s it was clear that the model had failed, and reform and re-privatization became inevitable. The trend of production and

[2] USGS, Copper - Mineral Commodity Summaries 2024, https://pubs.usgs.gov/periodicals/mcs2024/mcs2024-copper.pdf.

[3] Also see Sikamo et al. (2016) and Roberts (1976).

exports has reflected changes in policy regimes in addition to developments in global demand and prices of minerals. The failure to transform and diversify the structure of the economy away from mining has exposed and continues to expose the Zambian economy to the vagaries of global commodity markets with severe consequences for its macroeconomic balances and economic growth. As the data presented in this chapter shows, international copper price volatility is a key driver of production, employment, government revenue, exports, and foreign exchange earnings.

A key driver of the country's benefits from mining is the fiscal regime whose objective is to maximize government revenue while creating an environment that attracts private investment. With a sector that is dominated by private foreign companies, the main instruments of revenue generation are the royalties embedded in the mining agreements and earnings from government minority shareholdings in the mining companies. Despite various reforms initiated in the post-independence era that aimed at increasing revenue generation, the main structure of the fiscal regime has not changed, and the concession model has yielded suboptimal results over time. The regime has been regarded as relatively lenient compared to international standards among mineral producers (Adam & Simpasa, 2010; Adam et al., 2014a, b).

Zambia has struggled to leverage its mineral endowment to ride the commodity booms which are expected to increase foreign exchange inflows through both expansion of export volumes as wells a foreign direct investment. Instead, the country has continued to nurse chronic fiscal and trade deficits, and it accumulated a heavy debt burden whose servicing drains the limited hard-earned income from mineral exports. Zambia was the first developing country to declare debt default amidst the COVID-19 crisis, forcing the government to seek assistance from creditors to alleviate the debt burden through restructuring. The shortage of foreign exchange reserves and the volatility of capital inflows continue to put pressure on the national currency, exemplifying the difficulties associated with being a "copper currency."

Mineral resource exploitation is expected to generate wealth and help to elevate the living standards of the population. This has not happened in the case of Zambia. To the extent that wealth has been generated, it remains heavily concentrated in the hands of the very tiny fraction of the population at the top of the wealth ladder. Some of the wealth is stashed in offshore secrecy jurisdictions, as it results from capital flight notably through export misinvoicing, transfer pricing, and other manipulations of trade and financial transactions (see Chapter 2 for estimates of capital flight). The contribution of mining to the Zambian people's well-being remains inadequate. This chapter presents evidence that suggests that while regions with mining activity appear to have relatively lower incidence of poverty, overall, improvement in poverty reduction is inadequate and slow. The chapter aims to explore the various factors behind the weak performance of the mining sector in Zambia since independence, with a view to shed light on strategies to improve the sector's performance going forward.

Becoming a Mining Economy

Zambia is a mining economy, and it has been so long before its encounter with European traders in the eighteenth century (Chitonge, 2021; Ndulo, 1977; Robinson, 1933). The capture of its mining sector by the Europeans in the pre-colonial era marked the beginning of the end of the country's control over its natural resources. Below we trace the evolution of mining over time starting from the pre-colonial era.

Mining in the Pre-colonial and Colonial Times

From time immemorial, local populations in the territory that became today, Zambia engaged in mining using primitive technologies, mainly harvesting surface-level mineral deposits. The Portuguese were the first Europeans to set foot in the territory in the eighteenth century, as they were attracted by gold trade. They established a mission at Zumbo at the confluence of Luangwa and Zambezi rivers. In addition to gold, the Portuguese gradually extended trade to copper and ivory. From the Zumbo mission, they exported over 300 tons of copper annually. Naturally, as the Europeans monopolized the mining industry this created resentment among local populations who were sidelined in their own territories. In the 1800s, local tribes destroyed the Portuguese stronghold, which disrupted mineral trade (Ndulo, 1977).

Prospection and commercialization of minerals in Zambia began during the late 1800s and gained pace after the partition of Africa at the Berlin Congress in 1884 that granted to the British crown the control of most of the Southern African region up to the Congolese border. In turn, Britain granted power to the British South African Company (BSAC) to annex and administer the territories situated North of the Limpopo on its behalf (Mudenda & Bardouille, 1988).[4] The BSAC signed treaties with local chiefdoms that granted them protection while prohibiting chiefs from signing similar agreements with competing companies.[5] Through these treaties, the chiefs ceded mineral rights to the BSAC, marking the beginning of the surrender of control of mining to foreign corporations, which endures until today in Zambia. The BSAC retained the mineral rights even after the country became a British protectorate in 1924; therefore, the colonial government had no control over income from copper mining (Chitonge, 2021, p. 132). Between 1923 and 1940 the BSAC earned twice as much as the estimated £2.4 million tax revenue received by the colonial government (Chitonge, 2021, citing Baldwin (1966) and Roberts (1982)).

BSAC-led investments in exploration led to the discovery of various minerals including lead and zinc deposits at Broken Hill (modern day Kabwe), which were opened between 1905 and 1910, and subsequent development of Bwana Mkubwa Copper Mine in 1910–1912 (Reeves, 1963). However, except for the Broken Hill mine, these mining operations were closed before the outbreak of the First World War (1912–1918) due to financial difficulties, as they relied on simple technology that proved expensive and could not generate sufficient economies of scale.

As a policy response, the colonial government began to award large-scale mining rights only to large mining companies with a strong financial bottom line such as Anglo-American Corporation (AAC) Group and the Rhodesian Selection Trust (RST) Group owned by American Metal Climax Inc (Mudenda & Bardouille, 1988). These companies focused on exploration of minerals with high economic value, leading to the discovery of large high grade copper deposits at Luanshya, Nkana, Mufulira, and Nchanga. Between 1931 and 1936, the RST commissioned four major copper mines, namely Luanshya (Roan Antelope) in 1931, Nkana (Rhokana) in 1932, Mufulira in 1933, and Nchanga in 1936 (Table 5.1). The AAC formed Nkana Mines, Nchanga and took over the Kabwe mines. AAC became the largest shareholder in the mining industry by buying shares in RST before World War II.

[4] The BSAC's rule was terminated in 1924 and the British government assumed responsibility.

[5] Examples of treaties were with King Lewanika of modern-day Zambia, Mzilikazi, and Lobengula of modern-day Zimbabwe.

Table 5.1 Pre-independence ownership of copper mines in Zambia

Name of the mine	*Year opened*	*Ownership*
Bancroft Mines Ltd	1953	AAC
Nchanga Consolidated Copper Mines Ltd	1936	AAC
Nkana (Rhokana) Corporation Ltd	1932	AAC
Redevelopment of Kansanshi Copper Mine	1953	AAC
Chibuluma Mines Ltd	1951	RST
Mufulira Copper Mines Ltd	1933	RST
Roan Antelope Copper Mines Ltd	1931	RST
Baluba Mine	1952	RST
Chambishi Copper Mine	1962	RST

Source Mudenda and Bardouille (1988)

With the involvement of large foreign mining companies, Zambia emerged as a major producer of copper in the world. Its global share of copper exports rose from 10% in the 1930s and 1940s to 15 percent in 1959, trailing the United States, Russia, Chile, and the Democratic Republic of Congo (Adam et al., 2014a, b). Minerals accounted for 95% of total exports, and formal employment in the mining sector reached 50% of total formal employment in 1963.

During the mining modernization and expansion phase of 1947 and 1953, many companies supplying technological inputs to mines were established in Zambia. The AAC and RST moved their headquarters from London to Zambia. Furthermore, the AAC bought shares from BSAC and other British companies that had invested in the mining sector in Zambia (Ndulo, 1977).

Despite increasing production, the mining sector did not contribute commensurate government revenue in the pre-colonial and colonial eras for three reasons (Ndulo, 1977). First, mineral rights were owned by BSAC, which captured all the royalties. Second, because BSAC was headquartered in London for most of the period, the British government received a share of the revenue from copper in the form of taxes, which reduced taxable corporate income in Zambia. It was estimated that in 1937, mineral royalties and corporate income tax accounted for 30% of the copper produced in Zambia (Ndulo, 1986). However, only 12.5% of those revenues remained in Northern Rhodesia (Acemoglu et al., 2001). That was not just unfair trade; it was pure extortion. Third, the revenue collection and consolidation rules of the Central African Federation negatively affected revenue mobilization in Zambia. Because revenues were pooled across the three states (Malawi, Zambia, and Zimbabwe), Zambia received less than its proportional share of the revenue from mineral exploitation to the extent that the dissolution of the federation offered an opportunity for financial relief. The power structure under the federation favored Southern Rhodesia (Zimbabwe) which, coincidentally, had a larger share of white settlers (Mudenda & Bardouille, 1988). Most of the industries producing intermediate and capital goods that supplied the mines in Zambia were based in Zimbabwe.

As the independence movement gained momentum, Zambian leaders advocated for nationalizing mining rights and royalties that thus far accrued to the BSAC, arguing that the BSAC had no legal rights to the minerals. Ultimately, the BSAC ceded mineral rights and royalties to the Zambian government on the eve of independence, against monetary compensation (Ndulo, 1986).

Independence and Nationalization of Mines

Although mineral rights were owned by the Zambian government at independence in 1964, all the mines were owned by the private sector, notably RST and AAC. The new national government planned to leverage the country's large mineral endowment to boost government revenue to finance public services and investments in state-owned firms as part of the economic growth and diversification agenda. Thus, with the 1968 Mulungushi Reforms and the 1969 Matero Declaration, the Kaunda government introduced reforms that sought increased state control and "localization" of all businesses to promote its import-substitution industrialization strategy in line with the Transitional National Development Plan,[6] which was succeeded by the First National Development Plan of 1966–1971.

As part of the Mulungushi Reforms, the government announced measures aimed at nationalizing all industries in the country by acquiring majority equity holdings in major foreign-owned firms across all sectors except for some banking institutions. Thus, prospection and exploitation rights were nationalized. The government forcefully acquired 51% of the

[6] Nationalization extended from the manufacturing firms to mines. Only banks, namely Standard Chartered Bank Grindley's and Barclays Bank were not nationalized.

shares in all mining companies, which was subsequently increased to 63%. The government took hold of fifty state-owned companies and statutory boards, which it had inherited at independence, some directly from the territorial government and others created from the splinters of divided federal institutions (Craig, 1999). Key among these state-owned enterprises was the Industrial Development Corporation (INDECO), which was created by the colonial territorial government to act as a development agency, promoting private industry through finance and research. INDECO's role was to establish and promote new projects and enterprises in sectors of strategic interest where the private sector was reluctant to invest (Craig, 1999; Saasa, 1987).

The implementation of the First National Development Plan was largely financed by domestic revenue streams that Zambia inherited at independence, notably the revenue that had been transferred to the British Federal Government, which was now retained by the Zambian Government, and with the transfer of the rights of the British South Africa Company. Government revenue was boosted by high copper prices in the mid-1960s. Thus, the Government was able to quadruple total spending between 1964 and 1967 without running a budget deficit or depleting its foreign exchange reserves (Craig, 1999). In practice, during this period, the country maintained a mixed economy with considerable space for the coexistence of private, state-owned, and cooperative enterprises. In many cases, development projects were undertaken in partnership between state-owned enterprises and foreign enterprises, with state ownership being envisaged for a limited duration only.

Evolution of the Industrial Organization of the Mining Sector Through Reforms and Crises

The organization of Zambia's mining sector evolved from a purely privately owned regime before independence to state control between 1969 and 1992, and back to predominantly private ownership till today. The government's decision in 1969 to expand its ownership and control of the mining industry was motivated by several reasons (Simson, 1985). First, copper was considered a strategic product, contributing about 40% of national output, 90% of foreign exchange, and half of government revenue. Thus, the government deemed it inappropriate to leave such a strategic sector in private hands. In addition, the government sought to expand production by reinvesting profits back into the mining industry as opposed to letting foreign companies expatriate the profits. Second, the government adopted some socialist policies that sought to shift the entire economy into public ownership. Finally, prior to nationalization, the owners of private mines did little to advance domestic knowledge in mining. Thus, state ownership was considered as an instrument to promote local expertise in the mining sector.

As part of the Mulungushi Reforms, the Zambian government began to restructure its shareholding in the mines and other enterprises, using the state-owned holding company, the Industrial Development Corporation (INDECO). It took over the mines after acquiring 51% of equity using a 10-year interest-bearing bond and reorganized the mining industry into two corporations. The first involved the amalgamation of mines that belonged to Anglo-American, namely Bancroft, Nchanga, Rhokana, and Rhokana Copper refineries into one company, Nchanga Consolidated Copper Mines Ltd (NCCM). The second was the consolidation of the mines that were under RST, namely Chibuluma, Chambishi, Mufulira, and Luanshya mines to form Roan Consolidated Copper Mines Ltd (RCCM). The control of the mining enterprise shareholding acquired by the state was assigned to a new fully state-owned entity that was created in 1970, the Mining Development Corporation (MINDECO). The government also sought to create the Finance and Development Corporation (FINDECO) to take over foreign-owned banks, but the banks successfully resisted it. As an alternative the government established its own banks, such as the Zambia National Commercial Bank and the agriculture-focused Lima Bank. In 1971, the three state-owned enterprises—INDECO, MINDECO, and FINDECO—were merged into one large parastatal body, the Zambia Industrial and Mining Corporation (ZIMCO), which became one of Sub-Saharan Africa's largest holding companies.

The former mine owners, AAC and RST, remained minority shareholders and signed management contracts to continue providing managerial oversight of the operations in the mines. These management contracts empowered private investors to recruit staff, design consultancy, purchase supplies from outside the country, and market all the metals and by-products abroad (Sikamo et al., 2016; Simson, 1985).

In 1973, the Kaunda government transferred MINDECO's responsibility from managing large mining establishments to managing only small mines. An overarching parastatal, ZIMCO was created to manage the RCM, NCCM, MINDECO, and INDECO. Moreover, the government formed the Metal Marketing Corporation of Zambia (MEMACO) designed to market all the output from RCM and NCCM. Furthermore, the government prematurely redeemed the bonds issued in payment of the initial equity takeover and sought to increase its control of the mines (Simson, 1985). Moreover, management contracts with ACC and RST were canceled, making NCCM and RCM self-managed entities.

The Kaunda government further changed the ownership of mines in 1979 by increasing its equity shareholding in NCM and RCM from 51% to 60.3%, through conversion of loans extended to these companies in 1975 into equity.[7] In 1982 the government amalgamated the RCM and NCM into a single corporation—Zambia Consolidated Copper Mines Limited (ZCCM), making it the largest mining joint-venture firm in the world (Saasa, 1987). The government retained 60.3% equity holding, AAC held 27.3%, and the remaining 12.4% were held and publicly traded in London, Paris, and New York stock exchanges. The partnership granted pre-emptive rights to AACC in the event the government sold its shares to the extent of falling below 50%. The mission of ZCCM was to improve operational efficiency by cutting mining costs through centralized asset management (Craig, 2001).

In the end, the nationalization of mines and economy-wide reforms implemented from 1969 through the 1980s did not yield the expected results. During that period, the country was hit by external shocks that adversely affected the copper industry and slowed down economic growth (Musonda and Adam, 1999; Adam et al., 2014). The quadrupling of international oil prices in 1973 and 1975 caused a double whammy on the copper industry. First, the spike in oil prices inflated the cost of imported inputs in the copper industry, reducing production and profitability. Second, high oil prices dampened global economic growth, which reduced global demand for copper, resulting in a collapse of copper prices. At the same time, geological conditions in the copper mines worsened, with some mines experiencing flooding, which further reduced production.

The challenges faced by the mining industry were further exacerbated by the tenuous geopolitical environment in Southern Africa that arose

[7] The private foreign equity holders rejected the option of contributing additional capital to keep their equity share unchanged, which resulted in an increase in the government's shareholding.

from the Unilateral Declaration of Independence (UDI) in Zimbabwe and the entrenchment of apartheid in South Africa, which were opposed by neighboring states including Zambia. These regimes closed Zambia's shortest trade routes through Zimbabwe to South Africa to the Indian Ocean, increasing the cost of access to international markets. The reduction in copper prices and exports triggered a balance of payments crisis and the economy stagnated. Initially, the funds obtained from the nationalization process were used toward several social welfare projects, including investments in education and healthcare. Mineworkers and their families enjoyed a "cradle to grave" welfare policy providing services ranging from free education for mining workers' children to coverage of burial costs. The government perceived the crisis as transient and maintained its high expenditures mainly financed by commercial external borrowing. This optimism on the part of policy makers delayed the adjustments that were required to restore economic stability (Ndulo & Sakala, 1987). The governance system also lacked adequate checks and balances on the executive's appetite for excessive spending on politically motivated non-core programs.

As a result of the unfavorable global environment, investments in the mines by the government and its partners declined substantially (Craig, 2001). Copper production declined and ZCCM faced substantial financial viability problems with rising external debt. The company's liabilities rose from a third to more than half of its total assets between 1980 and 1990, forcing it to reschedule its debt obligations to remain afloat. It is estimated that ZCCM required over US$2 billion to maintain effective operations and undertake new investments, which it was unable to mobilize. With a decline in both greenfield investments and re-investments in rehabilitating existing firms, copper output and exports declined drastically.

The fall in copper production and the decline in foreign exchange inflows had adverse effects on all the sectors that depended on copper revenue for operations. To avert further economic deterioration and worsening of the balance of payments problems, with the help of the International Monetary Fund and the World Bank, the government rolled out a full Structural Adjustment Program in 1983. However, the reforms were reversed in 1987 due to social unrest. Subsequently, economic growth declined, and the country faced external debt distress (Andersson & Kayizzi-Mugerwa, 1993). To address the external imbalances and reignite economic growth, the government turned again to the IMF and secured standby facilities between 1983 and 1986. The increases in food prices and the general cost of living following the removal of subsidies incited riots, forcing the government to reinstate the subsidies in 1986.

By 1991, the reforms had done little to substantially change enterprise ownership landscape. President Frederick Chiluba was elected in 1991 on a platform of shifting from a socialist regime to a market-oriented economy with the backing of the IMF and the World Bank. Thus, the Chiluba government committed to liberalizing the economy and privatizing (or re-privatizing) state-owned enterprises, by enacting the Privatization Act in 1992. It established the Zambia Privatization Agency (today's Zambia Development Agency) to manage the process of transferring state-owned enterprises under ZIMCO into private hands; ZIMCO was closed in 1995. The privatization program encountered problems, particularly given the size of ZCCM (today's ZCCM-Investor Holdings ZCCM-IH) which had a complex structure of a genuine conglomerate.[8] The government feared the potential loss of economic control to powerful foreign investors. ZCCM faced two major financial challenges (Craig, 1999). First, due to a shortage of long-term finance required to develop new and existing ore bodies, its mines neither received adequate recapitalization nor underwent modernization since they fell under state ownership. Secondly, the lack of short-term working capital made it difficult to fund the operations in existing mines. Gross capital formation in the mining sector declined from a peak of 38% of GDP in 1978 to 7% in 1989, which was insufficient to cover the depreciation of the capital stock (Adam & Simpasa, 2011).

In 1995, the government passed the Investment Act and the Mines and Minerals Act, both aimed at creating a conducive environment to attract private investment in the mining sector. The two Acts were expected to facilitate privatization and the transfer of ZCCM assets to private hands between 1993 and 1996. Given the structural complexity of ZCCM, the government decided to unbundle it and sell its operating units separately. The negotiations for the sale of mines proved difficult in a context of declining copper prices and negative global economic outlook, leading to low demand for the mining assets. This was exacerbated by the fact that the mines were making losses, with the government losing more than a million US dollars a day.

[8] Detailed discussions of the challenges involved with the privatization of ZCCM can be found in Simutanyi (2008), Adam and Simpasa (2010), and Chitonge (2021).

The deterioration of mining assets exacerbated the urgency of privatization of the mines. Furthermore, the donor community, led by the IMF and World Bank, pressured the government to let go of its mining assets to alleviate fiscal imbalances. The government's dilemma was to find a privatization model that addressed financial viability problems while preserving the potential of the mining sector to spur long-term social and economic development. A British consulting firm, Rothschild, was hired to advise the government on strategic options for the privatization of ZCCM.

A joint government and ZCCM negotiation team represented the government during negotiations. With the unbundling of ZCCM assets, the government ended up signing separate contracts that embedded some development agreements with each mine's new owner. The first set of mines was privatized in 1997 and the process continued through the early 2000s, attracting major mining houses from Europe, Asia, and North America. The government retained minority shares in the privatized mines, which were managed by ZCCM-IH, with state participation ranging from 10% to 20% of the capital. The privatization of mines spurred an increase in investments in existing mines and stimulated the opening of new mines especially in the Northwestern province, ranging from small-scale to large-scale operations. Table 5.2 presents the ownership structure of large and medium-scale mines after the privatization process.

In 2020 and 2021 the government returned to a short-lived 100% ownership of two large mines, namely the Mopani Copper Mines and KCM after disputes whereby the government alleged that the companies were evading taxes. The Mopani copper mine was sold in 2024 to a private investor, with the government retaining 49% of shares. However, KCM was returned to its original owners. In 2024, First Quantum Minerals, domiciled in Canada was the largest investor owning several assets including the Kansanshi gold mine and Trident. Trident comprises three mining assets, namely Sentinel Mines (copper, cobalt), Enterprise Mines (nickel), and Intrepid Mines. While the government has a minority shareholding in Kansanshi Copper Mines, Trident is wholly owned by FQM.

Exploration results reveal that Zambia's endowment in natural resources may still be underestimated. In 2024, Kobold Metals, an American owned firm, found large copper and cobalt deposits in the Copperbelt province. Substantial deposits of other minerals besides copper and

Table 5.2 Ownership of large mines after privatization in Zambia

Mines	*Investor*	*Year of acquisition or commissioning*	*Corporate structure*	*Mining assets*
Kansanshi Mines	Joint venture, First Quantum Minerals Ltd (Canada 80%), ZCCM IH (20%.)	2001 to date	Listed on LSE, TSX	Kansanshi (copper, cobalt, gold)
FQM Trident	First Quantum Minerals Ltd	2010	Private equity, 100% FQM listed TSX	Sentinel (copper); Enterprise (nickel); Intrepid (copper, gold, uranium)
Konkola Copper Mines Plc	Joint venture Vedanta Resources, India (79.4%), ZCCM IH (20.6%)	2004–2021, 2024 to date	Listed on LSE	Nchanga, (copper); Konkola (copper); Nampundwe, (pyrite); Chililabombwe (copper)
Mopani Copper Mine Plc	Glencore International AG, Switzerland (73.1%), First Quantum Minerals, Canada (16.9%), ZCCM IH (10%)	2000–2021	Joint venture	Nkana, Mufulira (copper)
Mopani Copper Mine Plc	Delta—International Resources Holdings, Dubai (51.1%), ZCCM IH (48.9%)	2024 to date	Joint venture	Nkana, Mufulira
Luanshya Mines	CNMC (80%), ZCCM IH (20%)	2009 to date	Joint venture	Luanshya, Mulyanshi (copper, cobalt)
Chambishi Mines (NFC Africa Mining Co)	CNMC (90%), ZCCM IH (10%)	1998	Joint venture	Chambishi; (copper, cobalt)
Lumwana Copper	Equinox Minerals Ltd (79.4%), ZCCM IH (15%)	1999–2010	Listed ASX, TSX	Lumwana (copper, gold, uranium)

Mines	*Investor*	*Year of acquisition or commissioning*	*Corporate structure*	*Mining assets*
Lumwana	Barrick Gold Resources Corporation, Canada (100%)	1999–2010	Private listed ASX, TSX	Lumwana (copper, gold, uranium)
Bwana Mkubwa	First Quantum Minerals Ltd, Canada (79.4%), ZCCM IH (20.6%)	1997	Listed LUSE, TSX	Copper
Chambish Metals*	Eurasian Natural Resources (ENRC 80%), ZCCM IH (15%)	2009	Joint venture	Chambishi Smelter, slag dumps
Kagem Mining*	Gemfields (75%), ZCCM IH (25%)	2008	Joint venture	Emeralds
Kariba Minerals (Gems)*	ZCCM IH (100%)	1970s	SOE	Amythyst
Lubambe Copper* mines	EMR (80%), ZCCM (20%)	1997	Joint venture	Copper
Munali Nickel Mine*	Mabiza Resource Ltd (100%)	2006	Private	Munali (nickel), Mazabuka
Grizzly Mining (GM)*	100% private	1999	Private	Emeralds

Updated from Mudenda et al. (2022)
*Class B mining assets as defined by the Zambia Chamber of Mines. This information is as of March 2024

cobalt have also been uncovered, notably gold, nickel, and other precious metals. It is estimated that up to 40% of Zambia's mineral potential has not yet been geologically surveyed. Some estimates suggest that the country has 2.8 billion tons of ore ranging between 0.6% and 4% copper content (World Bank, 2011). The country's mineral potential is strategically important in the context of the growing global demand for "critical minerals' required to fuel the transition toward clean energy.

Regulation of the Mining Sector

The goal of a country's mining legislation is to create an enabling environment for exploration and development of mineral resources to ultimately improve the welfare of the people. Zambia has enacted mining legislations since the colonial era to align its laws with changing times. The first mining legislation was the Mining Ordinance of 1912, which empowered the BSAC to regulate the mining rights in Zambia. The law allowed any investor to acquire a prospecting license at a minimal fee to search for minerals in any area in Northern Rhodesia.

As indicated earlier, before independence, the Zambian leadership pressured the BSAC to surrender the mining rights and associated loyalties to the government at independence in 1964 (Ndulo, 1986). This helped set in motion the nationalization program, which was cemented by the amendment of the Constitution and a new Mines and Minerals Act enacted in 1969 allowing the government to acquire private businesses. This Act gave the President inalienable power to hold minerals rights on behalf of the Zambian people and effectively terminated all the undeveloped concessions and special grants held by private investors, mainly AAC and RST. In addition, the Act authorized the State to not only negotiate with existing mines for a majority (51%) equity holding, but also to issue licenses contingent upon productive use. Ultimately the 1969 Act gave the State control over the copper industry and the ability to direct new investments outside the Copperbelt region.

The state-led mining sector experiment proved unsuccessful, and eventually the government was forced to re-privatize the mines with the 1995 Mining and Minerals Act and subsequent amendments of the Mines and Minerals Act in 2008, 2015, 2018, 2020, and 2024. The 1995 Act was criticized for granting excessive scope for tax concessions, prompting a revision to pave the way for the Mines and Minerals Development Act (MMDA) of 2008. This Act constrained the government from entering into special development agreements with large-scale mining firms to ensure that Zambians benefit from the exploitation of minerals. It further streamlined the licensing system and clarified the procedures for mining uranium and other radioactive minerals. Small-scale mining was reserved for companies owned by Zambian citizens. However, the law did not provide explicit guidelines on how firms could transfer assets. Thus, some large-scale mining license holders could enter into third-party agreements without prior permission from the state. This flaw reduced transparency and accountability in the management and development of mineral resources.

In 2015, the 2008 Act was repealed and the Mines and Minerals Development Act No. 11 (MMDA) of 2015 was enacted, by which the ownership of minerals is vested in the presidency. The 2015 Act regulates mining rights, licenses, large-scale mining, gemstone mining, health and safety, environmental protection, geological services, royalties, and charges. It also established the Mining Appeals Tribunal. In a major shift, the Government enacted the Minerals Regulation Commission (MRC) Act of 2024 and the Geological Minerals Development Bill of 2024, repealing the 2015 Act. While the 2015 Act assigned the regulatory functions to various departments within the Ministry of Mines, the 2024 Act centralized the regulatory functions to streamline the operations in the sector. Under this new law, the Ministry of Mines is responsible for policy making, and local shareholding in mining companies is no longer mandatory.

'Mission Impossible': Demise of the State-Led Mining Development Model

At its genesis, formal mining in Zambia was the exclusive preserve of foreign capitalists, a model that was formalized with the establishment of colonial rule (Cunningham, 1981; Martin, 1972; Musambachime, 2016). At independence, the national leadership considered the country's endowment in mineral resources as a basis for consolidating economic and political independence. In a sense, minerals were seen as what Vladimir Lenin called the "commanding heights" of the economy, which needed to be controlled by the state to support the national development agenda. When President Kaunda declared nationalization of the economy in 1974, he was joining a widespread movement across the world at that time. Even today, state ownership of resource exploitation remains prevalent, as observed in oil-rich countries in the Middle East and mineral-rich countries in Latin America (Daniel et al., 2010; Radetzki, 2016). In the 1960s and early 1970s, state participation in resource exploitation was an integral part of the strategy to assert new-found sovereignty in independent nations in Africa and other regions. State participation can take various forms, the main ones being equity participation (full, free, or carried) and production sharing (McPherson, 2010).

State participation in the mining sector is an important policy lever for achieving social and economic development goals.[9] The motivation of active state involvement in the extractive industries therefore goes beyond standard financial considerations and encompasses larger goals in the realm of social development and protection of national strategic interests.

State participation in extractive industries carries important challenges that generate substantial debates, especially the classic issue of efficiency, with the premise that private enterprise and free markets achieve optimal outcomes in terms of resource use and allocation. Beyond ideological inclinations, however, practical experience over time and across countries has revealed a range of issues associated with state participation that cannot be dismissed, regardless of one's view in the debate about state vs. markets in the organization of the economy. The most important challenges relate to governance in the management of state-owned enterprises and the proceeds from resource exploitation. In practice, state-owned mining companies often face problems associated with "government interference, lack of transparency and accountability, and the extensive assignment of non-commercial tasks" (McPherson, 2010, p. 273).

Three challenges are particularly worth emphasizing. The first is the lack of independence of the managers of state-owned enterprises, which constrains their ability to set objective financial and technical goals for the firms. As managers are appointed by the government, they have limited leverage in the face of politically motivated demands, even when they compromise the company's financial sustainability. The second challenge relates to the management of the company's finances in the face of pressure from the central government's need to cover critical expenses in the context of low fiscal revenue. State-owned enterprises run the risk of becoming a fiscal arm of the government, which compromises their

[9] This is similar to the case of the cocoa management board in Ghana (COCOBOD) discussed in Chapter 4 in this book.

financial stability. The third problem is that state-owned enterprises have a regulatory mandate in the sector where they operate, thus wearing multiple hats as a profit-seeking corporation, a fiscal arm of the government, and a regulator. This makes it impossible to ensure a level playing field in the sector, which undermines competitiveness to the detriment of private operators.

These governance challenges exacerbate the effects of exogenous factors that compromise the performance of extractive industries, including the vagaries of international demand and prices of primary commodities, the variability of exchange rates and interest rates, and various shocks to the international financial markets. Indeed, the nationalization experiment in Zambia faced a range of adverse exogenous factors as soon as President Kaunda introduced it in 1974, which compromised the performance of state-owned mines. It is important to note that while nationalization of the mines transferred the ownership from foreign companies to the government, mining remained out of reach of the domestic private sector, and this remained so even after re-privatization and the liberalization of the economy in the 1990s. This means that the financing of the mining sector during the era of full state control rested solely on the shoulders of the government.

The capacity of the government to sustainably finance mining sector development rests on two pillars: an effective investment strategy and strong revenue generation capacity. An effective investment strategy involves identifying priority sectors to be targeted for public investment, and setting effective rules for accumulating, saving, and utilization of the funds generated from mineral resource exploitation. Such a strategy involves, among others, the establishment of savings vehicles such as sovereign wealth funds with explicit rules about how revenue from exports should be deposited in the fund, managed, and utilized to finance investments in the extractive industries and other targeted sectors.

The performance in revenue mobilization depends on the efficiency of the management of mining operations along the entire value chain, as well as the dynamics in the rest of the economy that affect the tax base. When state participation is in a form other than full ownership, revenue mobilization is dependent on the nature of the fiscal regime that governs the sector.

In the case of Zambia, the nationalization of mines proved to be a challenging experience due to a range of factors. We highlight three critical factors that definitively doomed the nationalization program. The first was low and unstable revenue generation from the mines, which made it difficult to sustain government investments to maintain and upgrade mining equipment. This resulted in a deterioration of productive capacity, an increase in operational costs, and a decline in the sector's international competitiveness. The second was the high financing requirements for a state-led, infrastructure-intensive, development agenda that had been premised on abundant mineral revenues. Thus, while the nationalization era was credited for commendable realizations in infrastructure, this came at the cost of financial sustainability of state-owned mining enterprises. The third factor was the low international copper prices throughout the nationalization era, which depressed the earnings from mineral exports.

Clearly, the nationalization agenda turned out to be "mission impossible," doomed by a combination of domestic structural and governance problems exacerbated by adverse external factors. The inability to finance expansion and maintenance investments in the mines was a central factor of the tribulation of the state-owned mining model. By the end of the Kaunda regime, it was clear that the scheme was unsustainable. The successor regime of Frederick Chiluba had no choice but to reverse course and embark on a (re)privatization of the mines starting in 1991.

Key Instruments of the Mining Fiscal Regime in Zambia

The mining fiscal regime includes a set of instruments in the form of taxes, royalties, dividends, and other tools that determine how the revenues from mineral exploitation are mobilized and shared between the state and mining companies. The key objective of the mining fiscal regime is to enable the government to collect a fair share of the revenue while maintaining a conducive environment for private investment in the mining sector.

The evolution of Zambia's mining fiscal regime since the colonial era has been marked by major reforms in the context of policy regime shifts, from nationalization to structural reforms of the 1980s and to re-privatization in the 1990s (see Lundstøl & Isaksen, 2018). From 1920 to 1966, the regime was dominated by mineral royalty and the rate remained relatively stable over the entire period, with the mineral royalty tax (MRT) rate set at 13.5% of the sales and adjusted by some marginal costs. The mines were also required to pay a variable corporate income tax of 37.5% of the profit up to K200,000 and 45% for profits above that threshold.

Mining companies were granted a 20-year write down of investment expenses in mines. During that period, the government collected royalty estimated at £160 million compared to £40 million from the profit tax (Saasa, 1987). Prior to independence the mines paid these taxes to BSAC, which had concessioned the mines.

In addition to tax rates, the fiscal regime also includes provisions aimed at incentivizing private investment in the mining sector through a reduction of the overall tax burden as a way of reducing production costs. These include tax deductibility of certain business expenses, capital allowance, loss carry-forward, and fiscal stability clauses in the mining agreements. Table 5.3 presents the evolution of key fiscal instruments applicable to the mining sector since independence.

The post-independence national government changed the fiscal regime in 1966 by introducing a shadow windfall export tax of 40% on copper sales, applicable when the price went above K600 per ton based on the London Metal Exchange copper price. Following nationalization, as the government became a majority shareholder between 1970 and 1980, it replaced the MRT and export tax of 40% with a 51% mineral tax on net corporate profits. This tax was deductible from the 45% corporate income tax while mines were granted a full investment write-off. However, these taxes were rarely paid as mines reported chronic losses during most of this period. The export tax of 4% was re-introduced in 1983 and raised to 13% in 1985. These taxes, together with the stringent foreign exchange policy that required exporters to surrender all their export proceeds (until this requirement was removed in 1994) and only access foreign exchange at government discretion after applying for it, adversely affected competitiveness, investment attractiveness, and ultimately the profitability of the mines.

The Zambian fiscal regime underwent significant changes during the privatization of the mining sector initiated under the Privatization Act of 1992. In addition to changes applicable to the sector, individual companies also benefited from negotiated provisions in their mining agreements. It is important to note that mining agreements were and are still not publicly disclosed. General measures included the revision of the tax regime to a netback (sales minus cost) royalty rate of 3%, and the removal of import taxes (Banda, 2020). Table 5.4 presents examples of tax provisions and other incentives embedded in the confidential development agreements signed by mining companies (Adam & Simpasa, 2011). In line with the 1995 Mines and Minerals Act, the key instruments affected

Table 5.3 Changes in Zambia's mining fiscal regime over time

	1964	*1966*	*1970*	*1983*	*1986*	*2000*	*2008*	*2009*	*2012*	*2015*	*2016*	*2022*
Royalty (%)	13.5	13.5	na	na	na	0.6	3	3	6	6–9	4–6	4–10
Export tax		40		4–8	13	na	na		10*	na	na	na
Mineral tax			51	51	51	na	na	na	na	na	na	na
Corporate income tax (%)	37.5		45	45	45	25	25–30	20–30	25–30	25–30	25–30	25–30
Variable income tax	na	na	na	na	na	na	15	15	15	15		
Windfall tax (%)	na	na	na	na	na	na	25–75	na	na	na	na	na
Tax deductibility	No	No	No	No	No	No	No	No	No	No	No	yes
Capital allowance (%)	5	5	100	100	100	100	25%	100	100	25	25	
Reference price	Yes	Yes	No	No	No	No	Yes	Yes	Yes	Yes	Yes	yes
Ring fencing	No	No	No	No	No	No	Yes	Yes	Yes	Yes	Yes	
Loss carry-forward	Yes	Yes	Yes	Yes	Yes	Yes	Yes	Yes	Yes	Yes	Yes	Yes
Tax haven owner	Yes	Yes	Yes	No	No	Yes	Yes	Yes	Yes	Yes	Yes	Yes
Government ownership of mines (%)	0	0	51	63	63	10–20	10–20	10–20	10–20	10–20	10–20	10–20
Fiscal stability	No	No	Yes	No	No	Yes	No	No	No	No	No	

*The export tax shown in 2012 was implemented in 2013

in the agreements were: (i) reduced corporate income tax rates, which for most mines was reduced to 25% compared to 35% for non-mining sectors and 40% for some service sector firms; (ii) deductibility of mineral royalty at 3% on gross proceeds; (iii) complete exemption from import duties on recurrent and capital inputs; (iv) 100% profit repatriation, with tax deductibility of interest costs and repatriated dividend income; (v) full tax deductibility of capital expenditure in the year in which it is incurred; (vi) carry-over forward of losses for 15–20 years; (vii) transfer of pension liabilities to the new state-owned ZCCM-IH; and (viii) a stability period of 15–20 years during which the agreed terms and conditions are non-renegotiable.

Most of the mining agreements allowed new mines to negotiate tax breaks to achieve early payback on their investments. The conditions in the development agreements hedged against foreign exchange controls, and some of them also required disputes to be settled by arbitrators appointed by the International Court of Arbitration rather than within the national legal system. In addition, mining agreements included provisions for subsidized electricity, which constitute a significant distortion in the energy market as the mines consume more than 50% of national power output.

The incentives contained in the mining development agreements have been perceived to be too generous and disproportionately in favor of private companies at the expense of the state. The development agreements allow mines to lock in taxation rates and other provisions for 15 to 20 years. The favorable fiscal regime reflected the government's attempt to encourage investment in the mines in the context of an unfavorable environment and its weak bargaining position due to the dilapidation of ZCCM's assets following years of underinvestment, excessive indebtedness of ZCCM, and low international copper prices. This was exacerbated by geological factors resulting in high costs of copper mining compared to other mineral-producing countries (Meller & Simpasa, 2011).

The design of the Zambian mining fiscal regime illustrates the challenges faced by the government in balancing investment incentives to stimulate economic growth and revenue mobilization to meet fiscal needs and achieve social development objectives. It appears that the balancing act worked in favor of the private sector. Development Agreements included clauses that prevented the Zambian government from benefiting from increases in mineral prices or profit windfall (Lombe & Mwakacheya, 2017). In addition to these weaknesses, a KPMG (2012, p. 1) audit

Table 5.4 Terms and conditions in a sample of Mining Development Agreements in Zambia prior to 2008

Mining company	*General terms and conditions*
Konkola Copper Mine (KCM)	• Stability period: originally 20 years for AAC, amended to 16 years following the acquisition by Vedanta four years after the initial sale • Company income tax of 25% (on net income arising from all mining activities) over the stability period • Royalty rate of 0.6% on gross revenues, except in the first 5 years where it is 0%. Throughout the stability period, royalties are deductible from corporate income tax liabilities • Customs duty of 15%, caped at US$16 million in the first year, and US$15 million per year for 4 years thereafter • Excise duty on electricity purchase of 0% • Withholding tax of 0% during the stability period, and 10% thereafter • Loss carry-forward permitted for 10 years from the date incurred • Capital expenditure deductible allowance of 100% • Price participation payment to be treated as a deductible expense for corporate income tax; royalty payments also deductible for corporate income tax • VAT on mine products charged at 0% • Facilities to be treated as single mining units for tax purposes
Mopani Copper Mines (MCM)	As in the case of KCM, except: • Stability period of 15 years • Excise duty on electricity purchase set at 10% of the amount paid to ZESCO by Copperbelt Energy Company, and only payable after the expiry of the stability period
Kansanshi Mines	• Stability period of 15 years • Royalty rate of 3% on net back value. However, actual royalty rate was scaled down to 0.6% in tandem with KCM and MCM (see GRD Minproc, 2003) • Import duty exempt for levels above 5% under Sect. 97(1) of the Mines and Minerals Act • Payment of duty on rural electrification levy at applicable rate for the duration of the stability period

(continued)

Table 5.4 (continued)

Mining company	*General terms and conditions*
Chambishi Mines	Same as for KCM and MCM, except: • Stability period of 15 years • Company income tax of 35%, but, if listed on Lusaka Stock Exchange, the rate is reduced to 30% • Royalty rate of 2% on net back value and payment deductible for income tax liability purposes
Buluba Mines	• Similar to Chambishi

Source Simpasa et al. (2013)

observed that "There are no detailed rules on transfer pricing in Zambia." This is precisely what some companies have exploited. For instance, if a company registered in Switzerland has a copper producing subsidiary in Zambia, the latter may sell copper to its Swiss-based counterpart at below-market price, and the counterpart can sell the copper at world prices as if it originated from Switzerland, netting the price differential as profit while consistently reporting losses in Zambia. Switzerland has in effect become a "major copper exporter." As Chitonge (2021, p. 145) puts it, "For mining companies, every effort is made to externalize as much money made in Zambia as is possible through any means available, including misinvoicing and outright tax evasion." This issue of mineral export misinvoicing is investigated in Chapter 6 in this book.

In 2008, in response to improved copper prices and the general investment climate, the government introduced a new tax regime (World Trade Organization, 2009). Under the new mining fiscal regime, the corporate income tax rate was increased from 25 to 30% and the MRT for companies in base metals rose from 0.6% to 3% of the gross value, while that of precious stones rose from 2 to 3%. Some taxes were re-introduced, including the withholding tax on payments of dividends, interest, royalties, payment to affiliates, and management fees at 15%. A windfall tax in the range of 25–75% for copper to be levied for prices above US$2.5 a pound was established. The proceeds from these new taxes were expected to be saved and used for priority projects. Mining companies found these taxes punitive and a backlash from the industry forced the government to remove the windfall tax in early 2009. It further increased the capital allowance from 25 to 100% and allowed hedging income to be part of the mining income tax. To address price manipulation problems, the government adopted the LME price as the reference for taxation purposes.

Following suspicions of transfer pricing by mining firms, in 2009 the government contracted the Norwegian tax auditors Grant Thornton and Econ Poyri to investigate tax avoidance and tax evasion related to the operations of the MCM, the second largest entity owned by Glencore. The audit uncovered serious breaches of OECD guidelines, including overestimation of operating costs relative to industry standards, underestimation of production volumes, and manipulation of financial statements, particularly regarding the sale price of copper. Most of the firm's output was sold to its parent company at a quarter of its market value. At the same time, Glencore was reporting losses in its operations in Zambia (Sherpa 2011; Simpasa et al., 2013). This is one illustration of price manipulations by mining companies that have robbed the country of substantial revenue from mining.

The government introduced further tax reforms in 2015. The MRT rate was increased to 20% for opencast and 8% for underground copper mines, while corporate income tax and profit taxes were re-introduced at 30% (Liebenthal & Cheelo, 2020). In the same year, the MRT rate was cut down to 9% as it was deemed too high by most mines.

New changes were introduced in 2016, with the removal of the 9% mineral royalty and the introduction of a price-based royalty of 4% when the LME price is below US$4,500 per ton, 5% when it is between US$4,500 and US$6,000, and 6% when it is above $6000 (Liebenthal & Cheelo, 2020; Manley, 2017).

Cognizant of the important role of the mining sector for the national growth strategy, the Zambian government has identified increasing copper production as a pillar of the development agenda. Specifically, the government has tailored reforms of the fiscal regime with the aim of raising copper production from the average of 788,257 mt in the period 2018 to 2022 to 3 million tons by 2031. To meet this goal, the government amended the mining fiscal regime in 2022 and 2023 and made mineral royalty tax deductible. In addition, it introduced a sliding scale for copper royalty regime applied to the incremental value based on the price.

To sum up, the mining fiscal regime in Zambia has evolved over time and has been subject to substantial reforms aimed at striking an optimal balance between stimulating investment in the sector to spur economic growth and maximizing government revenue from mineral exploitation. The question is whether that dual mandate has been achieved and to what extent. In other words, it is worth assessing the performance of the sector regarding the two objectives. The next sections seek to shed light on this complex question. Specifically, they provide an assessment of the performance of the sector in terms of output and exports, in attracting foreign direct investment, generating employment and tax revenue, and in contributing to poverty reduction.

Structural Dependence: *As Mining Goes, so Goes the Zambian Economy*

The fate of the Zambian economy has always been intricately tied to the performance of the mining sector, and the tribulations of the sector have been reflected in volatility of economic growth. So, as mining goes, so goes the Zambian economy, in the past as well as today. At the country's independence in 1964, mining represented 47% of the country's GDP and contributed as much as 53% of government revenue (Martin, 1972, p. 146).[10] The country was running a "mono-economy," with mining representing 92% of total exports. Moreover, the mining sector was fully controlled by foreign enterprises and organized to serve primarily the interests of the rest of the world rather than national development goals. The Kaunda government sought to change that legacy by attempting to make mining a real engine of improvement of the living standards of the Zambian people through reforms of the fiscal regime and the ownership structure of the mines. Today the economy remains highly dependent on mining, which in 2022 accounted for 72% of the country's exports, 44% of government revenues, and 9% of GDP (ZEITI, 2023, p. 16). The results of diversification efforts are yet to materialize, and the impact of past mineral booms on the Zambian people's living standards remains quite limited for various reasons, some of which are discussed further in subsequent sections of this chapter.

Starting at the turn of this century, in the context of consolidation of economic liberalization, the Zambian economy shifted to a regime characterized by higher investment and average GDP growth. But this shift

[10] Data from RST and Anglo American Corporation, *Mining Yearbook of Zambia*, 1970.

has been accompanied by deepening fiscal and external imbalances, with an acceleration of external debt, which in 2020 forced the government to negotiate debt restructuring to avert the debilitating effects of debt default.

From a long-term perspective, the aggregate performance of the Zambian economy as indicated by GDP per capita growth has been tightly tied to the performance of the mining sector, as can be seen in Fig. 5.1. The figure depicts the main policy reforms as well as external shocks notably the global financial crisis and recently the Covid-19 pandemic, which have influenced the trend of copper production and GDP growth.

The evolution of the mining sector was significantly marked by the policy choices of the post-independence government, especially the adoption of a socialist-oriented centrally controlled economic regime (for detailed analysis, see Fraser & Larmer, 2010) and the nationalization agenda under the Kaunda government, as described in previous sections of this chapter. Throughout the nationalization regime, copper production declined systematically. From 698,000 metric tons in the nationalization year in 1974, copper production steadily declined down to 519,000 tons at the end of Kaunda's regime in 1990. GDP per capita followed the same trend. When Kaunda took power in 1964, per capita GDP stood at $1,211 (constant 2015 US$); it had lost 27% of its value by the time Kaunda left office in 1990, settling at $890.

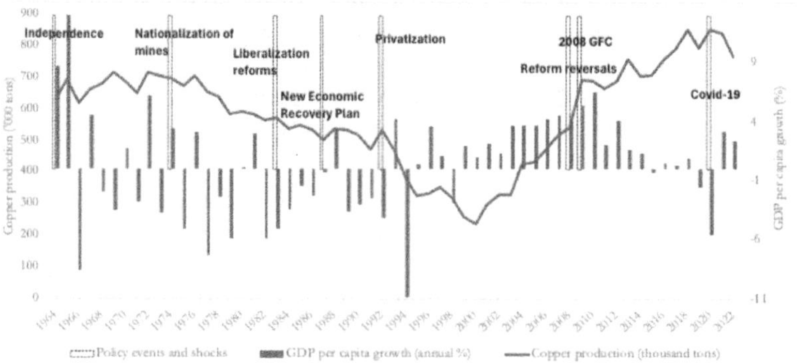

Fig. 5.1 Copper production and GDP per capita through crises and reforms in Zambia (*Source* Authors' construction using data from various sources)

The decline in mineral production and its impact on GDP growth during the Kaunda regime cannot be blamed solely on nationalization. Other policy-independent factors depressed copper production. The first was the 1970 accident at the Mufulira mine[11] that caused a major drop in production (by 100,000 tons in 1971) and forced a significant downward revision of prior plans of increasing production capacity. Moreover, structurally, it turned out that the geology of the Copperbelt was not conducive to economic exploitation of copper over 700,000 tons per year, beyond which marginal investment costs per ton would increase sharply. Most importantly, the Kaunda regime was just unlucky, facing chronically repressed international copper prices, which disincentivized private investment in mines.

Since 2000, Zambia has reaped some benefits from the combination of privatization of mines and economic liberalization supported by the IMF and the World Bank, as well as rising international copper prices. Thus, GDP growth was strong until 2014 when international mineral prices crashed. Overall, the evidence depicts the high exposure of economic growth to the performance of the mining sector, a result of the failure to diversify the economy away from primary commodities.

Mining and Elusive Economic Diversification

Since independence, consecutive governments declared that a key objective of the national development strategy was to diversify the economy and reduce its dependence on minerals, especially copper, as a driver of GDP growth and a source of employment, government revenue, and foreign exchange earnings. Economic diversification requires stimulating new investments and expansion of economic activity in other sectors, especially in manufacturing.

However, the economic diversification goal remains elusive and growth remains tributary to the performance of the mining sector, despite a steady shift in the structure of the economy with an increasing share of services. The share of mining in GDP declined from 41% in 1965 to 36% in 1970; it further declined during the "lost decade" spanning from 1980 to 1991 and continued the descent till 1999 (ZSA database). With the re-privatization of the mines and on the back of a copper price boom, the

[11] See Tembo (2019) for a history and appraisal of the Mufulira mine of September 25, 1970.

mining sector's contribution to GDP rose to an average of 13% of GDP in the period 2010–2020. The evidence shows no progress in the development of manufacturing. Overall, there has been inadequate increase in value addition in mining and very limited spillovers into other sectors.

Employment in Mining

The mining sector is expected to be a source of livelihood for the population by creating jobs directly in the mines and indirectly through spillover effects on other sectors. Over time, the contribution of mining to employment has followed a downward trend, consistent with its declining contribution to GDP in favor of services. Formal employment in the mining sector rose from an average of 40,000 between 1960 and 1965 to 57,600 (16.3% of total employment) in 1971. The Zambianization policy led to an increase in employment by government-controlled mines, peaking at 64, 800 (11.9% of total formal employment) in 1991 (Fig. 5.2). However, reforms under the Structural Adjustment Program and the privatization of the mines were accompanied by substantial job losses as new mine owners sought to reduce labor costs. Formal employment dropped to 35,040 in 2000, representing 7.4% of formal employment. Note, however, that the statistics on employment in mining need to be interpreted with caution as they often include short-term contract workers who supply material and services to mines who work in vulnerable conditions. The work in mining has become increasingly "casualized" as reflected in increasing high ratios of contract workers to directly employed workers, reaching up to 1 to 5 in the case of Kansanshi mine (Chitonge, 2021, p. 148; citing ICMM, 2014, p. 33).

The decline in the contribution of mining to job creation is a result of a gradual shift in the structure of the economy, with a transition from the primary sector straight to the service sector while manufacturing continues to stagnate. The share of services in formal employment has increased steadily from 40% in 1970 to over 70% in 2022 (ZSA statistics). This structural change raises the question of whether the jobs created in the service sector generate adequate income to sustain the livelihoods of the households. Moreover, the tradition of social service provision by the mining companies cannot be replicated by service sector firms, which are less financially equipped to support such a mission. The structural changes observed in the economy, therefore, may have significant implications for

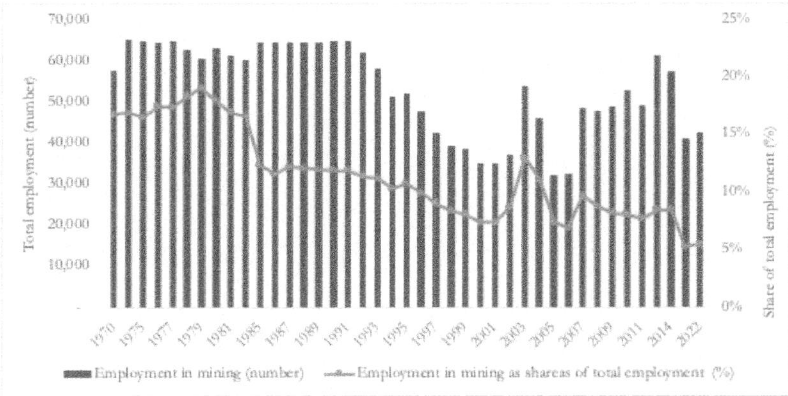

Fig. 5.2 Formal employment in mining in Zambia, 1970–2022 (*Source* Authors' construction using data from ZSA database)

social development that are often overlooked in the analysis of the performance of the mining sector and the dynamics of structural change taking place in the Zambian economy.

Mining and Government Revenue

The mining sector has always been regarded as a source for mobilizing government revenue in Zambia. Mining revenue accounted for a commanding 59% of total domestic revenue in 1965. But in 1970 it was down to 35.2%, and from 1973 (36.8%) it began a steady decline until 1986 (0.1%) (Fig. 5.3). The completion of the privatization of the mines in the early 2000s and the rebound in production and exports led to an increase in government revenue. But while investments in mining led to an increase in copper production and exports after 2002, the share of the mining in government revenue remained low. This underperformance in revenue generation is attributable to inefficiencies in the fiscal regime, notably the generosity of the incentives embedded in the mining Development Agreements granted to new private foreign mine owners (Simpasa et al., 2013).

Ultimately, revenue mobilization is a yardstick of the government's ability to leverage the country's mineral resource abundance. As Alan Whitworth points out, "With few linkages, jobs only for a relatively

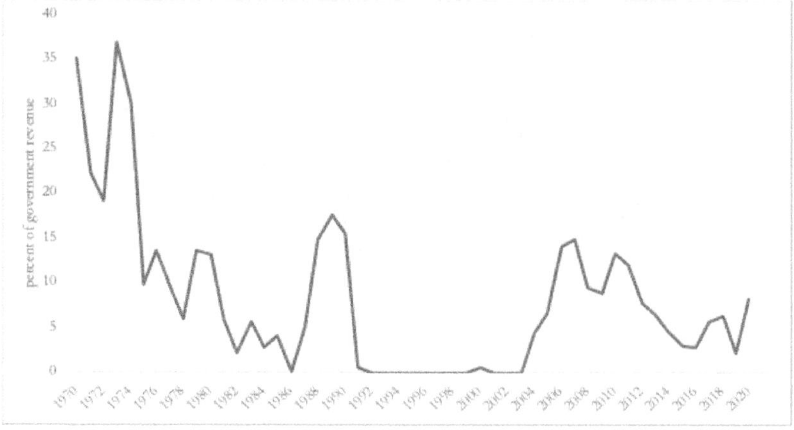

Fig. 5.3 Mining revenue as a percentage of government revenue in Zambia, 1970–2019 (*Source* Authors' construction using various CSO reports and Simpasa et al. [2013])

privileged minority and with profits accruing to mainly foreign owners, mining's greatest value to the economy is its contribution to government revenue. If productively invested, revenue from mining can benefit the entire population" (Whitworth, 2015, p. 957). Government revenue from the mining sector is critically dependent on the fiscal regime that governs the contracts between the government and private investors. In the case of Zambia, the centerpiece of the fiscal regime is mineral royalty, currently set in the range of 3–6%, which is in the mid-range of world rates. In addition, the government levies company profit tax at 30% and standard VAT at 16%.

The two main instruments for mobilizing government revenue in the mining and quarrying sector are mineral royalty and corporate income tax. In 2021, the two combined accounted for 70% of total revenue from the mining sector (Table 5.5). Mineral royalty represented 35% and company income tax brought in 34.9% of revenue from the sector. VAT comes next with withholdings on VAT representing 25.7% of total mining companies' payments in 2021. Clearly, the government's success in mobilizing domestic revenue is highly contingent on its capacity to levy royalty and corporate income tax in the mining sector.

Table 5.5 Total payments by mining companies to the Zambian Government (Kwacha, million) in 2021

	Amount (million Kwacha)	*Share of total (percent)*
Mineral royalty	12,749.3	35.1
Income tax	12,700.2	34.9
Withholding on VAT	9357.4	25.7
PAYE	2920.2	8.0
Import VAT	2281.9	6.3
Import/Customs duty	1339.6	3.7
Withholding tax	949.9	2.6
VAT	531.2	1.5
Local excise duty	195.4	0.5
Others	109.7	0.3
VAT refund	−6762.0	−18.6
Total payments	36,372.7	100

Source Zambia EITI Report 2021

It is critically important, however, to distinguish between a high share of mining in government revenue and optimality of revenue generation from mining. The dominance of mining is a result of the weakness of other sources of revenue, a reflection of the "resource curse" illustrated by the failure to diversify and transform the economy. Moreover, even as revenue from mining represents a large share of total government revenue, it is still far below the sector's potential due to inefficiencies in the fiscal regime, notably low tax rates, generous tax exemptions and holidays, and various forms of tax avoidance and evasion in the sector. The sign of success of economic transformation in Zambia will be an increase in overall government revenue associated with a rebalancing of the sources of revenue resulting from expansion and dynamism of non-mining sectors. In this perspective, Zambia still has a long way to go on the economic transformation road.

Several policy and structural factors have inhibited the achievement of optimal revenue mobilization from the mining sector in Zambia. The key factor is the nature of Mining Development Agreements (MDAs) signed between the government and mining companies, whereby only a few mines effectively pay taxes due to the stabilization clauses embedded in the contracts that last up to 20 years. Adam et al., (2014a, b, p. 210) assert that "by international standards, the tax structure embedded in the

MDAs was overly liberal, generous and biased toward the taxation of rents that, at the time of negotiation, were historically low" (also see Adam & Simpasa, 2010). The fiscal regime enables mining companies to minimize their tax liabilities thanks to generous provisions on tax deductibility and extended loss carry-over privileges. The provision allowing companies to deduct 100% of capital expenditures implies that tax deductions remain high for extended periods, given that mines always need to invest not only in expansion but also in maintenance of their equipment. The pervasive use of special incentives to attract and retain private investors in the mining sector is, as Conrad (2014, p. 97) pointed out, "tantamount to an individualized tax system." Most importantly, the "locked in" incentives in the MDAs due to long-duration stability clauses imply that the Zambian economy does not fully benefit from mineral booms. As Fraser and Larmer (2010, p. 15) put it referring to the MDAs signed during the privatization of state mining enterprises, "any money that was made from mining was expatriated before Zambians could see the benefits of the 'boom'."

Moreover, ambiguities in the definitions of rules for the application of tax instruments create avenues for tax minimization, even by honest taxpayers, and evidently an avenue for corruption in tax assessment. For example, the levy of mineral royalty may be based on production or processed output, which certainly implies different values of the royalty base. The absence of clear guidelines can result in substantial losses of government revenue even without ill intentions on the part of the taxpayer or the tax assessor.

The last issue worth mentioning here is the legacy of indebtedness that has characterized the mining sector since independence. On the government side, ZCCM-IH inherited massive debt from its predecessor, including accrued pension benefits and other severance costs for laid off employees. This implies that a substantial portion of mining revenue goes to servicing the debts rather than financing development programs. On the private sector side, as the data presented in the next section show, a substantial fraction of foreign direct investment in mining is made of debt. This implies that the base for company income taxation is eroded by the deduction of interest payments. In cases where the companies operating in Zambia are branches of international corporations and borrow internally, then debt financing of investments in the mines becomes a conduit for corporate profit shifting. Ultimately, mining corporations benefit from mineral booms more than the mining workers, the government, and the national economy. The 2013 Africa Progress Report recounted a chilling finding of the first EITI report on Zambia that "between 2005 and 2009, half a million Zambians employed in the mining sector were carrying a higher tax burden than companies" (Africa Progress Panel, 2013, p. 63).

Due to these policy and structural factors, the country has not captured its optimal benefits from mining exploitation. Suboptimal mobilization of tax and non-tax revenue from mining implies that increases in international demand and price of minerals become "cashless booms" (Conrad, 2014, p. 222)[12] for the country, thus frustrating expectations of mining-led development.

Low performance in government revenue mobilization can also be due to the adverse effects of the mineral bounty on government policy. The expectation of revenue growth from the expansion of mineral production and increases in international demand and price of commodities may crowd out domestic revenue mobilization from other sources as politicians avoid making difficult policy decisions—like taxation of the economic and political elite—to gain and maintain political support. This argument has been advanced as one of the explanations for the suboptimal gains from mineral booms in Zambia since independence (Larmer, 2010).

Foreign Exchange Generation by the Mining Sector

The mining sector is a potential source of foreign exchange earnings through exports, external financing in the form of foreign direct investment (FDI) and external borrowing. On balance, the country's success on this front has been less than satisfactory. In other words, the country has performed below potential in attracting foreign capital and accumulating foreign exchange reserves, while at the same time, it has faced severe external debt distress, some of which is associated with leveraged investments in the mining sector as illustrated in this section.

[12] Also see Adam and Simpasa (2010, p. 86).

Leveraged Foreign Direct Investment in Mining

While we have not been able to obtain historical time series data on FDI specifically flowing into the mining sector, we can make inferences from the trend of total investment on the basis that the mining sector is the primary recipient of FDI in the country. In 2015, the sector received 67% of the stock of FDI in the country (Table 5.6). The ratio has declined since then, settling at 56% in 2020 (Bank of Zambia 2016, 2021).

Historical data show that there was negligible foreign direct investment in the country during the era of state control of the mining sector from the 1970s through the 1990s (Fig. 5.4). This era also witnessed low international copper prices, which disincentivized foreign direct investment. Despite the re-privatization of mines starting in the early 1990s, FDI remained low and only started to increase at the turn of this century. However, we cannot attribute this upward trend in FDI solely to the domestic policy environment as it coincides with an international primary commodity boom, characterized by a steep increase in international copper prices.

Table 5.6 Stock of FDI liabilities by sector in Zambia in 2015 and 2020, million US$

	FDI stock in 2015		*FDI stock in 2020*		*Change 2015–2020*
	US$ million	*Share of total*	*US$ million*	*Share of total*	
Mining and quarrying	11,132.3	67%	8,513.5	56%	−24%
Manufacturing	2189.2	13%	2,824.4	19%	29%
Wholesale and retail trade	537.2	3%	959.2	6%	79%
Agriculture	181.9	1%	879.3	6%	383%
Commercial banks	539	3%	735.8	5%	37%
Real estate	382.4	2%	622.5	4%	63%
Construction	99.6	1%	407.3	3%	309%
Electricity	263.1	2%	167	1%	−37%
Accommodation and food	1236.6	7%	99.4	1%	−92%
Other sectors	147.1	1%	−70	0%	−148%

Sources Bank of Zambia: *Foreign Private Investment & Investor Perceptions in Zambia*, editions 2016 and 2021

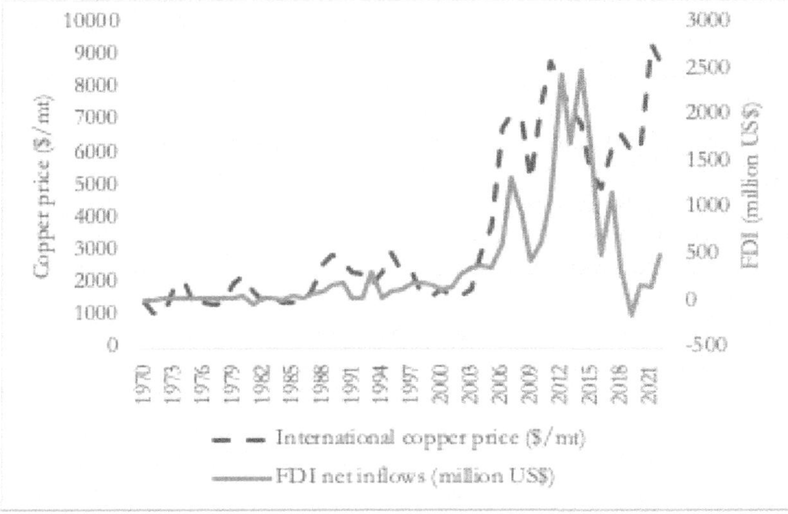

Fig. 5.4 FDI into Zambia and international copper prices, 1970–2022 (*Sources* Authors' construction using data from UNCTAD [FDI] and World Bank Pink Sheets [coper price])

Net foreign direct investment inflows declined dramatically from a peak of $2.5 billion in 2014, turning negative in 2019. The decline in FDI started in the context of a sharp reduction in international copper prices during 2011–2016. While copper prices have now recovered their pre-2011 level, FDI flows to Zambia are still at one-fifth of their 2014 level ($540 million in 2022).

External Debt

Zambia's external debt increased steadily until the end of the 1980s and stabilized until 2002. As the country was classified as a heavily indebted poor country, it qualified for debt forgiveness, which drastically reduced the debt stock from a peak of $7.5 billion in 2004 to a low of $2.2 billion in 2006. However, thereafter, external borrowing resumed, largely on commercial terms as the country was classified as a lower middle-income country. The debt stock reached a historical peak of \$30 billion in 2020.[13]

As external debt accumulation accelerated, its composition increasingly shifted away from concessional debt toward higher-interest loans, with an increasing resort to sovereign and non-Paris Club loans, especially from China. At the same time, the share of concessional debt dropped from a peak of 57.5% in 2005 to a low of 6.7% in 2022. The shift of debt composition toward non-concessional loans implied higher interest on new debt commitments. Hence, each new dollar borrowed implied a heavier debt service burden, draining more government revenue away from public investment and social service provision.

Additional concurrent developments contributed to the worsening of Zambia's debt burden since the mid-2000s. During this period, the government took on an increasing share of loans denominated in US dollars, at a time when the dollar was appreciating while the Zambian Kwacha was depreciating. In economic terms, this implies that servicing external debt increasingly required the country to spend more Kwachas for each dollar to be paid. Thus, as the debt service exploded in the 2010s, it continued to eat up an increasing share of government revenue, with the ratio peaking at 60% in 2019. The acceleration of the debt burden relative to exports and government revenue was a recipe for debt distress. But this was debt distress foretold over the past decades.

The analysis of developing countries' external indebtedness often tends to overlook the importance of private debt embedded in foreign direct investment. Data from the Bank of Zambia's surveys on foreign investment and investors indicate that external debt constitutes a major instrument of FDI in the mining sector (Fig. 5.5). Over 2013–2015, the share of debt exceeded 80% of FDI liability inflows. In 2018 and 2019 external borrowing helped offset large dividend outflows. In those two years, debt represented 3.5 times and 3.9 times the equity capital flows, respectively.

The private sector has been an important contributor to the acceleration of the country's external debt over the past two decades. The mining sector accounts for the largest share of private sector debt associated with foreign direct investment. In fact, private sector borrowing has exceeded general government debt, although the gap has gradually narrowed since

[13] The data quoted in this paragraph is from the World Bank's International Debt Statistics.

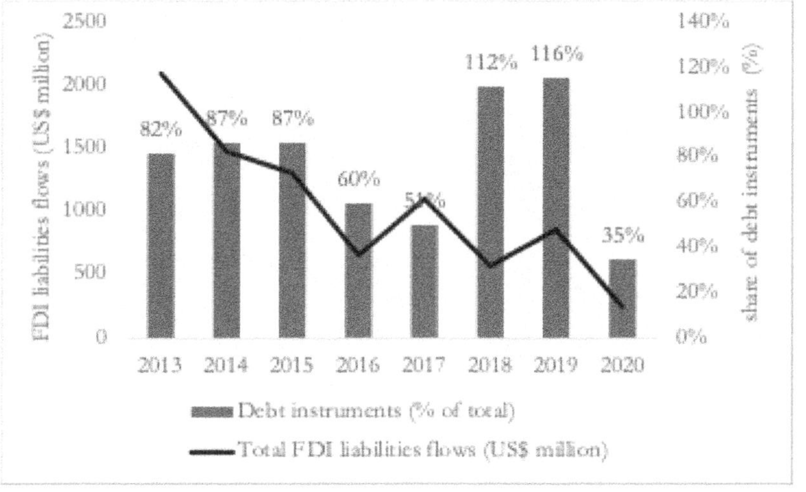

Fig. 5.5 Flows of FDI liabilities into the private sector, 2013–2020 (*Sources* Authors' construction using data from the Bank of Zambia in *Foreign Private Investment & Investor Perceptions in Zambia*, editions 2013–2021)

2017 as can be seen in Fig. 5.6. In 2015, the stock of private sector debt stood at $14.6 billion against $6.7 for government debt. In 2020, the respective amounts were $15.9 billion and $13.8 billion.

The reliance on external debt as an instrument of foreign direct investment poses two important problems. First, it raises the country's overall external debt burden and its vulnerability to shocks that can plunge it into debt distress. Second, debt financing by foreign corporations erodes the tax base through deductions of interest payments from taxable corporate income. This undermines efforts to raise government revenue from the mining sector which is dominated by foreign corporations. Low revenue mobilization further undermines the country's debt servicing capacity, further exacerbating the risks of debt distress. It is clear, therefore, that while Zambia's tenuous debt situation is a result of complex factors, the mode of external financing of the mining sector has also played a significant role in the country's debt problems. Controlling external debt accumulation will require substantial improvements in revenue generation from mining, which poses the central question about the design and efficiency of the fiscal regime governing the mining sector.

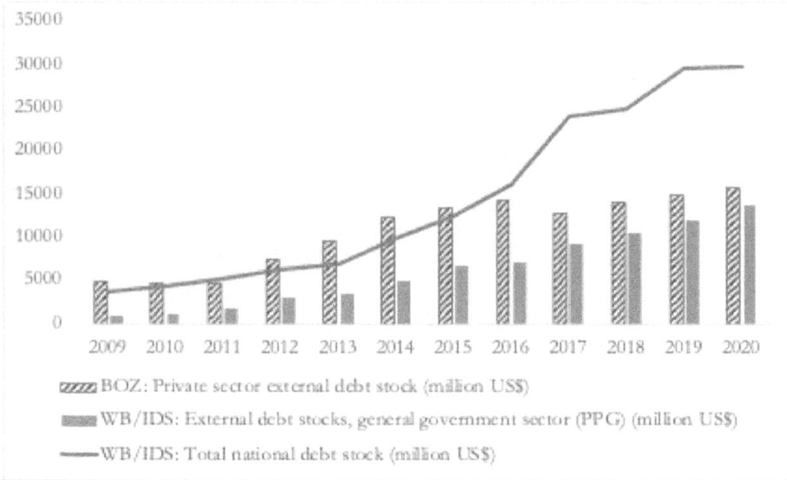

Fig. 5.6 Stock of external debt owed by the private sector and the government in Zambia (million US$) (*Source* Authors' construction using data from the World Bank's International Debt Service [WB/IDS] and the Bank of Zambia [BOZ])

Foreign Exchange Earnings: Has Zambia Cashed in on Mineral Booms?

The mining sector has been the largest source of foreign exchange across sectors through foreign direct investment and exports of minerals. According to data from the Bank of Zambia, the mining sector generated over 30% of the total supply of foreign exchange over 2013–2021 (Table 5.7). Foreign financial institutions come next with 16.3%. In contrast, the mining and quarrying sector accounts for only 2.8% of total demand for (use of) foreign exchange. The main users are public administration (14.7%), financial intermediaries (12.7%), and wholesale and retail trade (11%).

However, even though the mining and quarrying sector supplies the largest share of foreign exchange among sectors, the question remains as to whether it has performed up to its potential in terms of generating hard currency flowing into the country. Mineral booms are expected to be associated with increased foreign exchange accumulation. Indeed, the

Table 5.7 Supply (inflows) and demand (use) of foreign exchange by sector in Zambia, total over 2013–2021 (million US$)

	Supply (inflows)		*Demand (use)*	
	Amount	*Share (%)*	*Amount*	*Share (%)*
Mining and quarrying	23,807.2	30.8	1956.9	2.8
Foreign financial institutions	12,597.7	16.3	9017.1	12.7
Domestic financial intermediaries	6064.4	7.8	6321.7	8.9
Bank of Zambia	4078.2	5.3	2780.9	3.9
Households	3530.4	4.6	4172.1	5.9
Electricity, gas and water supply	3283.7	4.2	4474.1	6.3
Wholesale and retail trade	3145.8	4.1	7814.8	11.0
Transport, storage and communication	3051.2	3.9	4402.3	6.2
Manufacturing	2898.9	3.7	6248.6	8.8
Construction	2807.3	3.6	1660.4	2.3
Agriculture, hunting, and forestry	1980.6	2.6	1808.1	2.5
Health and social work	1496.5	1.9	545.2	0.8
Community and social service activities	1333.3	1.7	241.4	0.3
Public administration and defense; compulsory social security	791.8	1.0	10,491	14.7
Real estate, renting, and business activities	603.9	0.8	478.3	0.7
International organizations and bodies	575.0	0.7	40.6	0.1
Hotels and restaurants	317.8	0.4	122.3	0.2
Education	277.5	0.4	96.2	0.1
Forex Bureaus	103.9	0.1	3713.9	5.2
Other business activities	4629.1	6.0	4740.7	6.7
Total	77,374.3	100.0	71,126.9	100

Source Authors' construction using data from the Bank of Zambia

data indicate that Zambia has recorded substantial foreign exchange accumulation in the context of the sustained increase in copper prices over the past two decades (Fig. 5.7). The stock of foreign exchange reserves rose steadily from $247 million in 2003 at the start of the price boom to $2.4 billion in 2012 before the 2014–2016 commodity price crash. Foreign exchange reserves declined steadily from a peak of $2.5 billion in 2014 to a 10-year low of $1 billion in 2020.

Has Zambia effectively leveraged its potential in foreign exchange generation from the mining sector? Most importantly, has the country

Fig. 5.7 Foreign exchange accumulation in Zambia through copper price cycles (*Source* Authors' construction using data from the World Bank [Pink Sheets] IMF [International Financial Statistics])

reaped the benefits of mineral export booms in terms of foreign exchange earnings that effectively contribute to meeting the country's international financing needs? The amount of foreign exchange earnings (written as forex in the equation below) from commodity exports that effectively flow through the Central Bank can be estimated as:

$$Forex\ earnings = Exports - Company\ Forex\ use - Forex\ retention\ abroad \quad (5.1)$$

During commodity booms, the volume of exports increases, and this is evident in the data, especially during the commodity booms since the early 2000s. Companies use their foreign exchange earnings to cover the purchase of production inputs including machinery, raw material, services, and to service their external debt. As exhibited in the previous section, external borrowing has been a predominant instrument of foreign direct investment in the mining sector. This leads to high debt service liabilities which must be covered by export proceeds. The debt-dominated financing structure of mining houses therefore constitutes a constraint to foreign exchange accumulation in the country, limiting resources available to cover the import needs of the Zambian economy outside of the mining sector.

The amount of export proceeds retained abroad by mining companies depends on both their own external obligations as well as the fiscal regime and foreign exchange regulations. In some countries the government sets rules regarding repatriation of export proceeds as a means of optimizing the foreign exchange gains for the country. In the case of Ghana, for instance, the retention rates (minimum and maximum) are negotiated between the government and gold mining companies within Development Agreements (Chapter 3 in this book). In the case of Zambia, until the establishment of the Bank of Zambia's Export Proceeds Tracking Framework directives in December 2023 (which became effective in January 2024) (Bank of Zambia, 2023), mining companies and other exporting firms faced no regulatory obligations to repatriate foreign exchange earnings from their exports. Without a regulation on repatriation of export proceeds, it is impossible for the country to reach its potential in terms of foreign exchange earnings from mineral exploitation.

Examination of the trend of mineral exports and foreign exchange earnings from the mining and quarrying sector indeed shows a disconnect between the two. As Fig. 5.8 illustrates, the volume of exports of major minerals (copper, cobalt, and gold) and the supply of foreign exchange by the mineral sector have diverged and the gap has widened since 2016. As a result, the relative contribution of the mining and quarrying sector has declined steadily over the past decade, with the ratio of foreign exchange earnings to total exports dropping from 48% in 2014 to only 12% in 2021. The disconnect between mineral exports and foreign exchange inflows is partly attributed to the lax regulation that leaves a free hand to mining companies as to whether they repatriate their export proceeds and how much.

Kwacha, the "Commodity Currency"

At Zambia's independence in 1964, mining contributed 92% of total exports. Twenty-eight years later in 1992, copper, cobalt and gold were still accounting for 91% of total exports. The share of mining has declined since then, but the sector still carries a commanding share of the country's exports. In 2021, copper, cobalt, and gold accounted for 74.6% of total exports of goods and services. Due to this dependence on

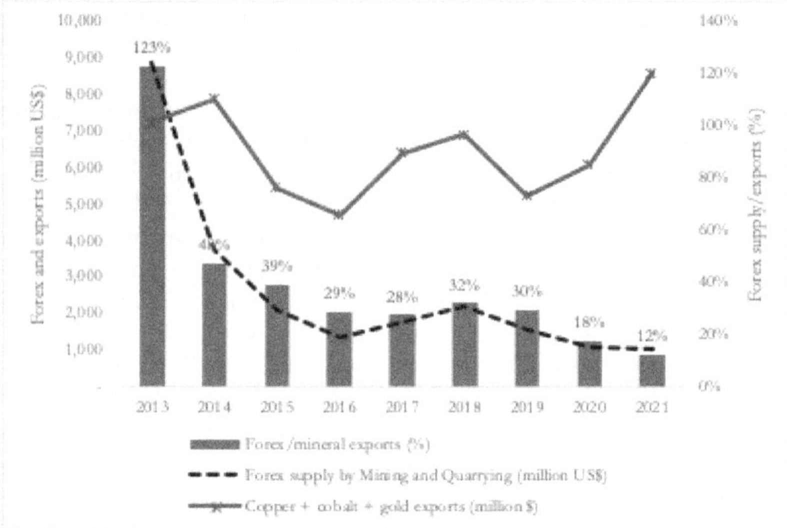

Fig. 5.8 Mineral exports and foreign exchange supply by the mining sector in Zambia (*Source* Authors' construction using data from the Bank of Zambia)

the mineral sector, the country is highly vulnerable to shocks to the prices and demand for mineral commodities. Indeed, the country's terms of trade are strongly influenced by movements of mineral prices, with immediate effects on the exchange rate of the Kwacha against the US dollar. In fact, as commodity exports go, so goes the exchange rate of the national currency, Kwacha; hence the epithet of "commodity currency" (Bova, 2012; Cashin et al., 2002, 2004; Ngandu, 2005). The linkages between commodity exports and the terms of trade and the implications for the exchange are the primary mechanisms for the Dutch disease effects of mineral resource exploitation. During commodity booms, improvements in the terms of trade lead to exchange rate appreciation, which undermines the export competitiveness of non-extractive sectors. During commodity export slumps, the terms of trade deteriorate, and the exchange rate depreciates. To the extent that there is sufficient production capacity and international demand for non-resource sector products, this would help the country to weather the storm through a rebound of non-extractive exports. However, as Zambia depends heavily on imports of equipment and raw material, a collapse of commodity

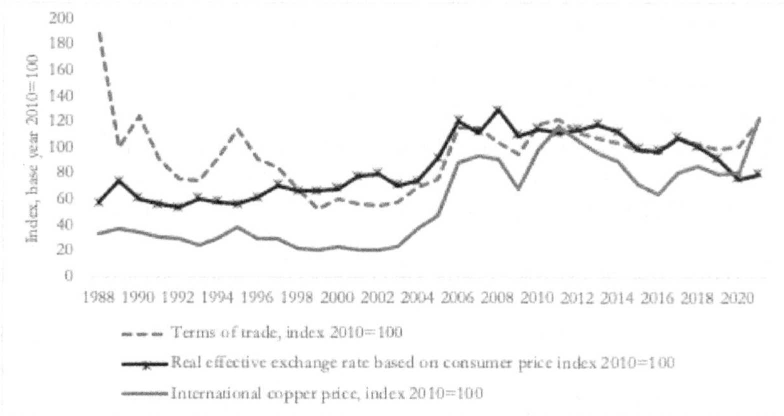

Fig. 5.9 Copper price, terms of trade, and the real exchange rate in Zambia, 1988–2021 (*Sources* Authors' construction using data from the World Bank [Pink Sheets] and the IMF [International Financial Statistics])

exports undermines its import capacity, suffocating economic activity in the non-resource sectors.

Indeed, the data show that movements in international copper prices have been closely related to movements in the real exchange rate of the Kwacha (Fig. 5.9). Specifically, increases in copper prices have been followed by appreciation of the real exchange rate, especially from the early 2000s. So, while mineral booms may yield increased foreign exchange earnings, this comes at a cost in terms of a loss in export competitiveness in non-mining sectors due to real exchange rate appreciation. In contrast, periods of declining mineral prices are accompanied by depreciation of the national currency, which raises the import bill and puts upward pressure on inflation, thereby eroding the living standards of the population.

Mining and Offshore Wealth Accumulation

Zambia on the Global Wealth Accumulation Bandwagon?

The past two decades have witnessed an unprecedented accumulation of private wealth globally in the context of growth acceleration, commodity booms, and financial integration. Africa has also experienced private wealth accumulation, albeit at a relatively lower rate. While estimates vary across sources due to disparities in measurement and scope, private wealth in Africa has reached impressive levels, ranging between $1.9 trillion and $2.4 trillion as of 2022 depending on the source used.[14] According to Capgemini's, 2023 *Global Wealth Report*, private wealth held by high-net-worth African individuals increased from $839 billion in 2008 to $1.9 trillion in 2022 (Capgemini, 2023). That is a 121% increase or a 5.8% annual compound growth rate over the period. These rates are slightly lower than those of private wealth of HNWIs at the global level over that period, which stood at 153% and 6.9%, respectively.

It is important to note, however, that wealth accumulation is heavily concentrated within a small fraction of the population benefiting from the increased affluence. This can be gleaned by comparing the continent's share of wealth vs. the number of HNWIs in the world. In 2022, Africa accounted for 2.2% of global wealth, while Africans classified as HNWIs represented only 0.9% of the global population of HNWIs. The data suggests that wealth accumulation in Africa has been accompanied by increasing inequality.

While Zambia has experienced relatively fast growth in private wealth over the past decade—rising by 22% from 2012 to 2022, it has performed relatively modestly in terms of the level of wealth compared to the average in continent and globally. Table 5.8 presents some highlights on private wealth and the number of high-net-worth individuals in top ranked African countries and includes Zambia for comparative purposes. Zambia also performs poorly relative to other mineral resource-rich countries. Figure 5.10 plots private wealth against mineral exports for mineral-dependent developing countries as classified by UNCTAD (2023). Clearly, Zambia is punching below its weight in terms of leveraging its mineral resources to generate wealth. As can be seen in the figure, Zambia is below the trend line, meaning that it is generating less wealth than is feasible given its mineral exports.

The other important issue besides underperforming in leveraging mineral resources is that private wealth accumulation only benefits a very small fraction of the Zambian population. The estimates presented here concern the wealth of the high-net-worth individuals, who own $1 million or more in liquid assets. There are only 900 of those individuals

[14] See Capgemini (2023), Credit Suisse (2022); Henley and Partners (2023); AfrAsia Bank (2021)

Table 5.8 Estimates of private wealth in Zambia and selected African countries in 2022

	Stock of private wealth ($bn)	*Number of HNWIs ($1m+)*	*Number of multi-millionaires ($10m+)*	*Growth of number of millionaires over 2012–2022*
South Africa	651	39,300	2080	−21%
Egypt	307	16,900	880	−25%
Nigeria	228	10,000	510	−30%
Morocco	125	5000	220	28%
Kenya	91	8500	340	30%
Ghana	59	2900	120	24%
Zambia	14	900	30	22%
Africa	2400	138,000	6200	
Zambia's share in Africa	*0.6%*	*0.6%*	*0.5%*	

Sources Wealth estimates are from wealth reports by AfrAsia Bank, Henley & Partners, and Credit Suisse

Notes HNWI = high-net-worth individuals, owning at least $1 million in liquid assets. HNWI numbers are rounded to the nearest 100. Multi-millionaire figures are rounded to the nearest 10. The numbers include only people living in each country (residents). Other African countries not included in the table that have larger stocks of private wealth than Zambia (in descending order of wealth amount) are Tanzania, Angola, Ethiopia, Mauritius, Côte d'Ivoire, Uganda, Namibia, Mozambique, and Botswana

in the country. This is 4.5 out of 100,000 Zambians (based on 2022 population). Thus, for ordinary Zambian citizens, wealth accumulation is an alien concept, as their main concern is whether they can afford decent housing, feed their family, send their children to school, and pay for healthcare. As shown in the data presented in the next section, poverty levels remain high, and vulnerability to shocks remains a serious issue as illustrated by the uptick in poverty since 2015 due to shocks to agricultural production and the Covid-19 pandemic. Therefore, Zambia's dual policy challenge is how to generate more wealth from mineral resources and—more importantly—how to ensure that the wealth benefits most of the Zambian population.

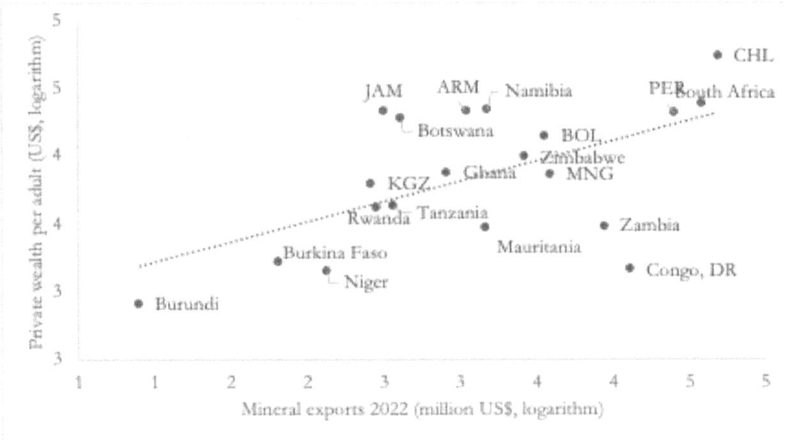

Fig. 5.10 Private wealth and mineral exports among mineral-dependent developing countries in 2022 (*Source* Authors' construction using data from Henley & Partners [wealth] and UNCTAD [mineral exports])

Offshore Licit and Illicit Wealth

A substantial fraction of private wealth is held abroad in various forms, including liquid and semi-liquid assets in financial systems as well as physical high-value assets such as real estate and precious metals. While the relative preference between domestic and foreign holding of private wealth varies by country, evidence suggests that African wealth holders tend to have a relatively high preference for holding their wealth abroad. In a sense, African wealthy individuals exhibit a "negative home bias," contrary to the conventional expectation that investors would prefer domestic assets which they deem less risky than foreign assets. A study by Collier et al. (2001) found that about 40% of Africa's private wealth was held abroad, compared to 39% for the Middle East and only 10% for Latin America. They estimated that the exodus of capital had caused GDP in Africa to be 16% lower than it would have been if the capital had been retained and invested in the continent. The implication is that holding of private wealth in offshore jurisdictions, regardless of whether the wealth is licit or not, causes significant economic losses for the source country.

Various estimates have been developed to assess the value of wealth held offshore. The main estimates are based on surveys focused on affluent people, which are published in various wealth reports including those by AfrAsia Bank, Henley & Partners, Capgemini, and Credit Suisse. These estimates do not engage with the question of legality of the wealth. The second category consists of holdings in financial institutions by non-bank entities as reported by the Bank of International Settlements. These assets are held in the form bank deposits and various non-liquid assets. Again, these data do not distinguish between licit and illicit wealth. The third category consists of estimates of wealth accumulated through capital flight and the more general phenomenon of illicit financial flows. The methodology consists of adding to annual outflows the estimated interest earnings on the stocks of wealth accumulated over time. It is difficult to disentangle between capital flight proceeds that are invested vs. consumed. The wealth accumulated through capital flight is by default deemed illicit because of illicit acquisition of the wealth at home (predicate crime), illicit transfer in violation of capital account regulations, and illicit holding of wealth abroad, hidden away from the tax and regulatory authorities abroad and at the source. Below, we present some estimates of the second and third categories of offshore wealth in the case of Zambia.

Figure 5.11 presents the trend of quarterly asset holdings by Zambian non-bank private agents in all banks and financial institutions reporting to the BIS from 2005 to the first quarter of 2023. As can be seen on the graph, bank holdings increased dramatically in 2015 and have remained high since. From December 2014 to March 2015, bank holdings by non-bank Zambian individuals and businesses jumped by 99% from \$2.5 billion to \$4.9 billion. The graph shows that the start of the copper boom corresponds with rapid accumulation of bank holdings in BIS-reporting banks, but the relationship is not sustained past 2018.

Next, we examine the accumulation of offshore wealth through capital flight. The trend of the stock of capital flight is presented in Fig. 5.12, along with the international price of copper. The stock of capital flight is estimated as the compounded value of past outflows capitalized at the 3-month US Treasury Bill rate. As of 2022, the stock of capital flight stood at \$86.9 billion. With a stock of external debt of \$28.7 billion that year, it means that the country was a clear "net creditor" to the rest of the world. A critical nuance, however, is that while the external debt is a public liability resting on the shoulders of the Zambian people, the wealth stashed abroad originating from capital flight is privately owned and therefore cannot be used to pay off the country's external debt. Therefore, efforts to achieve the country's financial stability must include

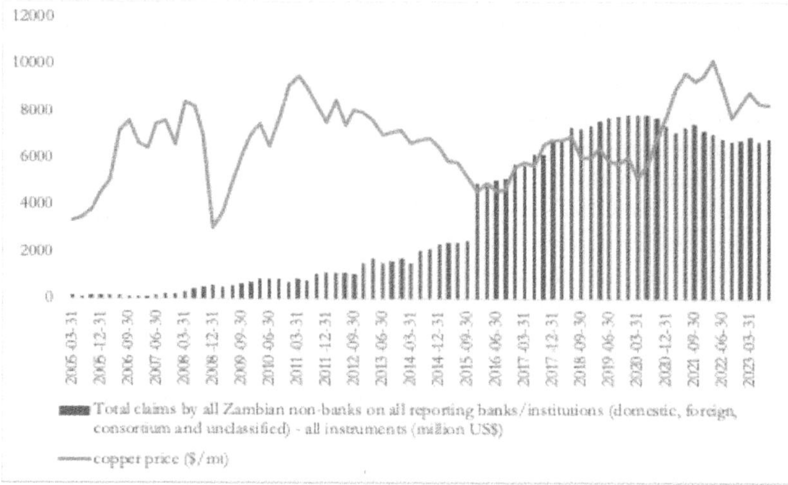

Fig. 5.11 Claims by non-bank Zambian agents on BIS-reporting banks and financial institutions, 2005–2023 (*Source* Authors' construction using data from the Bank of International Settlements [bank holdings] and the World Bank's Pink Sheets [copper price])

strategies to stem the hemorrhage through capital flight and repatriate the private wealth stashed abroad.

Capital flight accumulation increased from the early 1990s, and it shifted into higher gear from 2015, a period marked by the increase in copper prices. The key linkages between the accumulation of private offshore wealth and capital flight involve mineral export misinvoicing and the repatriation of profits from mining exploitation. Unlike licit wealth held abroad legally and transparently, which can generate taxable income and can be repatriated for investment at home, the wealth accumulated from capital flight is a net loss to Zambia. The government earns no tax revenue from such wealth as it is hidden or disguised to remove connections with the beneficial owners and predicate criminal activities that may have generated the funds initially. Illicit offshore wealth is unlikely to be repatriated and invested in Zambia for fear of prosecution of its illicit origins.

Strategies to stem capital flight and repatriate private wealth stashed abroad must be tailored to the type of wealth, especially whether it is

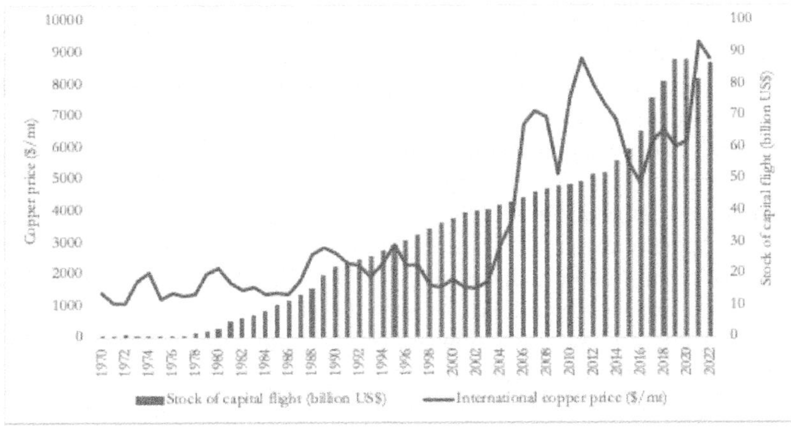

Fig. 5.12 Accumulation (stock) of capital flight from Zambia and copper price, 1970–2022 (*Source* Authors' construction using data from Ndikumana and Boyce [2025] [capital flight] and the World Bank's Pink Sheets [copper price])

licit or illicit. For licit wealth held legally abroad, the focus should be on establishing economic incentives that make repatriation appealing for asset holders in terms of returns to investment considering economic and political risks. In practice, policies aimed at inducing the repatriation of legitimate private offshore wealth should be part of the overall strategy for promoting domestic investment and private sector development.

Dealing with illicit private wealth held abroad is more complicated. The first issue is that such wealth is typically disguised to conceal the identity of the beneficial owners and the predicate crime that generated it. Second, even when the wealth is tracked and identified, there are important legal and administrative hurdles that hinder the repatriation of the funds. Some countries have attempted to grant time-bound amnesties to holders of offshore wealth, waiving prosecution against transgression of exchange controls, tax liabilities, and obligations to demonstrate the legitimacy of the origin of their wealth. South Africa adopted a series of tax amnesties in 1995, 2005, and 2006 as well as voluntary wealth disclosure programs aimed at enticing repatriation of offshore wealth and increasing tax compliance (Aboobaker et al., 2022). These measures yielded disappointing results on both goals. Only modest tax revenues were mobilized through these initiatives due to several structural and institutional constraints. The first constraint was the limited technical capacity of the South African Revenue Service to audit and investigate transgressions of tax laws and exchange controls. The other factor was the extensive use and abuse of transfer pricing by multinational corporations operating in key sectors notably mining.

Tax amnesties in South Africa also scored a failing grade on the objective of curbing capital flight. In fact, capital flight accelerated in the post-Apartheid period when tax amnesties were implemented in the context of economic liberalization (Aboobaker et al., 2022). The problem is that high-net-worth individuals who hold assets abroad wield significant economic and political power, which enables them to stifle efforts aimed at enforcing the rules on taxation and capital controls. These political economy factors make it hard to design and implement an effective policy to curb capital flight-fueled private wealth accumulation offshore and induce the repatriation of wealth held abroad. South Africa's experience with tax amnesties and economic liberalization as a means for stopping capital flight and enticing repatriation of private wealth held offshore carries important lessons for Zambia should the country consider adopting these strategies to tackle the problem of capital flight and to discourage the practice of stashing private wealth in foreign lands.

So, in the end, has mining made Zambia wealthier? Has mining exploitation generated commensurate wealth for the country? The answer depends on who you ask. For the 900 Zambian HNWIs (Henry & Partners, 2023) who live in a world of affluence, the answer is a definite yes. It is a yes also for the extractive multinational corporations operating in Zambia that stack up massive profits from mineral exploitation in their offshore accounts. But for ordinary Zambian citizens who are engaged in the mining sector, wealth accumulation remains an elusive concept. So is the case for most Zambians who are not employed in mining, whose dreams of reaping "spillover benefits" from mining remain just that—only a dream.

Has Mining Contributed to Poverty Alleviation in Zambia?

Mining has the potential to generate income for those who are employed in the sector and to improve the living conditions in the concerned communities and nationally through the funding of development programs. In fact, under the post-independence socialist regime, the government mandated state mining firms to operate a "cradle-to-grave policy," providing social services including free education for mine workers' children, in addition to subsidized food, housing, power, transportation, and water (Lee, 2009).

Mining also affects people's wellbeing indirectly through spillover effects at both local and regional levels. Mineral exploitation produces what can be called "local-level multiplier" effects that can be magnified at the regional and national levels (Adam et al., 2014a, b, p. 214). These effects are stronger if local demand for goods and services is high and concentrated on goods that are intensive in unskilled labor. Overall, the strength of the spillover effects depends on the intensity of forward and backward linkages between mines and the local economy.[15] These linkages between mining and the local economy do not happen by chance. They need to be enabled and enhanced by a deliberate industrial policy that aims to incentivize, even constrain (notably within the mining Development Agreements) mining companies to source their inputs and services from the domestic economy as much as possible. One of the important criticisms of the mining sector in Zambia is that mining companies establish linkages primarily with suppliers, manufacturers, and markets outside of the country (Fraser & Lungu, 2007). When mining remains an "island economy," the overall welfare gains are limited.

There is relatively limited empirical evidence on the micro-level linkages between mining exploitation and the wellbeing of the population in the mining zones and surrounding areas in Zambia. A study by Alexander Lippert (2014) attempted to fill this gap by testing three hypotheses: (1) An increase in copper production improves living standards and reduces unemployment in areas around the mines relative to the rest of the country; (2) The positive spillovers of increased mineral production extend to the rural hinterland of mining cities, neighboring districts, and the population along the copper transportation route; (3) The positive spillover effects diminish with distance from mines and become insignificant beyond a certain point.

The empirical evidence from the study by Lippert (2014) largely supports these hypotheses. Specifically, the study finds that following an increase in copper production, households in the mining areas record significant improvements in per capita expenditure, housing conditions,

[15] See Morris et al. (2012) for a conceptual discussion of policy and structural factors that influence the linkages between extractive sectors and the rest of the economy.

child health, and access to drinking water and electricity. The results indicate that the effects are broadly distributed, suggesting a reduction in poverty without an increase in inequality. Moreover, the positive effects extend to the localities away from the mines along the transport routes, but they diminish monotonically with distance from the mines and vanish after about 75 km. Finally, these positive effects accrue to both urban and rural areas around the mining centers. While these results are suggestive of positive gains from mineral exploitation at the micro level, they need to be further investigated to confirm whether and to what extent the Zambian population benefits from mining exploitation.

In addition to the complexity of the linkages between mining exploitation and poverty, assessing these linkages is complicated by imperfections in the measurement of poverty and social wellbeing. Nonetheless, despite the imperfections in the estimates, the data broadly indicates that poverty remains high in Zambia even by Sub-Saharan African standards, although it has trended downward since the 1990s.

According to data from the World Bank's Poverty & Inequality Indicators,[16] in 2015, 12.8 million Zambians lived in poverty. That means that in 24 years (since 1991), the number of poor people more than doubled in the country—up from 5.8 million. During this period, the percentage of Zambian poor people relative to Sub-Saharan Africa rose from 1.4% to 1.9%, implying that on average the number of poor people increased faster in Zambia than in other African countries.

A disaggregated analysis of poverty and social wellbeing by province sheds some light on the connection between mining and poverty. The question of interest is whether regions that host mineral resources are better off in terms of poverty reduction and improvement in measures of social development and welfare. The map in Fig. 5.13 shows the location of minerals with color coding reflecting the level of poverty. The map indicates that, indeed, regions that are most endowed in minerals, notably copper, have lower levels of poverty as is the case for the Copperbelt, Central, and North-Western regions. Considering other minerals such as gold and gemstones solidifies this insight.

The examination of the trend in poverty between 1996 and 2022 across regions shows that poverty rates are lower in mineral-rich regions such as Copperbelt, Central, and North-Western (Table 5.9). This

[16] The World Bank's data on Poverty and Inequality Indicators can be found online here: https://pip.worldbank.org/poverty-calculator.

Fig. 5.13 Location of minerals and poverty incidence in Zambia by province (2022) (*Source* Authors' design with assistance from Dr. Didier Wayoro. Poverty data are from ZAMSTAT)

suggests that the proximity to mining sites generates economic opportunities that give a comparative advantage to neighboring communities relative to those located in areas with no mining activity. Moreover, poverty declined much faster in mineral-rich low-poverty regions than in their counterparts that do not have minerals and where initial poverty rates were higher. In other words, there has been poverty divergence across regions over time which is somewhat associated with mining activity.

The data show, however, that poverty incidence at the national level rose from 54% in 2015 to 60% in 2022, a rate that had not been observed since 2010. Across regions, the increase in poverty over the 2015–2022 period is more pronounced in regions that had lower initial poverty rates which are also endowed in minerals, except Lusaka. The deterioration of

Table 5.9 Evolution of poverty incidence in Zambia from 1996 to 2022

	Poverty rate (%)			*Change in poverty rate (%)*		*Extreme poverty (%)*		*Change in extreme poverty (%)*
	1996	*2015*	*2022*	*1996 to 2015*	*2015 to 2022*	*2015*	*2022*	*2015 to 2022*
Lusaka	58	20	27.0	−53.4	33.7	11	16.5	50.0
Copperbelt	65	31	35.9	−44.8	16.6	18.2	23.4	28.6
Central	84	56	67.5	−19.6	20.1	39.8	55.4	39.2
Southern	83	58	63.5	−23.5	10.2	38.1	50.9	33.6
North-Western	90	66	61.6	−31.6	−7.2	48.4	50.6	4.5
Muchinga		69	82.6		19.2	54.4	73.1	34.4
Eastern	85	70	76.4	−10.1	9.1	55.9	62.7	12.2
Northern	87	80	78.0	−10.3	−2.1	67.6	65.3	−3.4
Luapula	87	81	77.3	−11.1	−4.7	67.7	69.8	3.1
Western	88	82	78.6	−10.7	−4.4	73	61.6	−15.6
Zambia	78	54	60.0	−23.1	10.3	40.8	48.0	17.6

Sources Authors' compilation using data from ZAMSTAT: https://zambia.opendataforafrica.org/olwrslb/poverty-statistics-1991-2015?regionId=ZM-06#; Key Poverty Highlights of the 2022 Living Conditions Monitoring Survey Results, 22 September 2023

living standards was due to the marked decline in GDP growth starting in 2015, declining FDI in the mining sector which reduced job creation in the sector, and the droughts of 2015 that adversely affected power supply and agricultural production. The upward trend of poverty is expected to be reversed gradually with the consolidation of recovery from the COVID-19 pandemic, a reversal of the decline in FDI and improvement in fiscal stability following the restructuring of external debt. Obviously, the timing and strength of this expected recovery remains unknown.

The data on other indicators of wellbeing and social development tell a similar story of disparities across regions in favor of those endowed with mineral resources. According to survey data from ZMSTAT in 2015, mining regions exhibit higher levels of education, better access to formal finance as indicated by ownership of an account in a bank or financial institution, household wealth, and lower infant mortality (Table 5.10). This suggests that, indeed, mining generates various avenues for improving social wellbeing over time. The flip side of the coin is that proximity

Table 5.10 Indicators of wellbeing in Zambia by province in 2015

Region	*Years of education*	*Owns a bank account (%)*	*Wealth index (min 1-max 5)*	*Infant mortality (per 1000 live births)*
Central	7.8	16	3.2	67.7
Copperbelt	8.7	27	3.8	60.9
Eastern	6	10	2.6	94.9
Luapula	7	10	2.6	95.6
Lusaka	8.8	33	4.1	64.3
Muchinga	6.9	9	2.4	90.6
Northern	6.9	8	2.4	85.1
North-Western	7.9	19	2.8	55.8
Southern	7.8	14	3.2	62.6
Western	6.7	9	2.3	77.9
Zambia	7.5	16	3	74.2

Sources Authors' compilation using data from ZAMSTAT and DHS Zambia 2018[17]

to mining exposes the household's welfare to adverse effects of shocks to production, demand, and prices of minerals given the low diversification of income sources. This is further justification for the need to leverage mineral resource endowment to promote economic diversification, notably by investing mining revenue into infrastructure that is needed to stimulate activities in non-mining sectors. Economic diversification will indeed be the best gauge of Zambia's performance in development-oriented management of its mineral resources.

Conclusion

Mining has always been an integral part of economic activity in Zambia, long before the Europeans arrived in the area and snatched it from the indigenous people. The colonial regime cemented the control of the sector by foreign corporations by engineering a resource management regime geared to serving the interests of European capitalists and the British Empire. The attempt by the Kenneth Kaunda regime to reverse the colonial legacy through nationalization of mines was unsuccessful, and the government of Frederick Chiluba restored private ownership of

[17] https://dhsprogram.com/data/available-datasets.cfm.

the mines in 1991, keeping only state minority shareholding. The analysis in this chapter concurs with the dominant evidence in the literature suggesting that the regulatory model and the fiscal regime governing the mining sector have yielded sub-optimal outcomes in terms of the benefits of mining exploitation accruing to the state and the Zambian people.

Zambia remains a strategically important player on the global stage as a mining producer, and its importance is further amplified by the global agenda to foster a transition to clean energy fueled in major part by "critical minerals." The critical importance of these minerals gives Zambia an opportunity to leverage its endowment to drive the national development agenda and transition to a higher growth path and reach higher levels of living standards. To achieve those goals, however, the country needs to undertake substantial reconfiguration of the management of the mining sector and its strategic position in the global economy along the mineral value chain. Below we highlight some of the changes that are required for ushering a new era of gainful exploitation of minerals in Zambia.

The ultimate measure of Zambia's success will be its capacity to leverage its mining endowment to drive a robust agenda of economic transformation. This entails success by relative attrition of the mining sector. The agenda requires a paradigm shift in the management of the sector, specifically to increase national stakes in mining, optimizing fiscal revenue and increasing foreign exchange earnings repatriated into the country, reinvesting revenue from mining in the expansion of the production base of the country, and fostering dynamic economy-wide spillover effects from mining exploitation. To the extent that such transformational changes take place, a gradual decline in the relative share of mining in the economy in favor of an increase in manufacturing would be the testimony of success in terms of graduation from primary commodity dependence.

To increase revenue generation and overall gains from mining, a business-as-usual approach will not work. Instead, there is a need for a paradigmatic shift in the management of the mining sector toward increased equity holding by the government and Zambian private investors in new and existing mines. The standard concession-based model whereby the government counts primarily on mineral royalty and corporate income tax has proven to generate an unbalanced distribution of the gains in favor of foreign corporations. In this respect, Zambia could take a cue from its neighbor Botswana, which has shifted to equity holding in the diamonds company DeBeers, while also promoting domestic processing of diamonds to move up the value chain, thus increasing government revenue, foreign exchange earnings, employment, and overall spillovers in the economy. The increase in government shareholding in mines can be paid for with future revenue shares, thus removing the barrier of liquidity as a constraint to the transition to a beneficial mode of management of the mining sector.

The country must do better in leveraging its mining resources in terms of foreign exchange earnings both from mineral exports and foreign direct investment. This is critically important for overcoming the current debt challenges and preventing future debt distress. Two things are clear from the analysis in this study: mineral export booms have not generated commensurate foreign exchange earnings flowing back into the country, and the high debt content of foreign direct investment has exacerbated the country's precarious net external position. There is, therefore, a need for systematic and transparent enforcement of the rules on the repatriation of foreign exchange earned from mineral exports, as well as provisions determining the mechanisms of repatriation of export earnings into the country.

Another important tool for leveraging Zambia's mineral endowment is the design of an effective saving and investment strategy, enabling the country to accumulate savings during commodity booms that will be used to finance productive investment and to cushion the effects of adverse shocks on the economy. The Zambian government should seriously consider setting up a sovereign wealth fund, learning from the experience of other resource-rich countries that have established such vehicles. It is never too late to get started.

References

Aboobaker, A., Naidoo, K., & Ndikumana, L. (2022). South Africa: Capital Flight, State Capture and Inequality. In L. Ndikumana & J. K. Boyce (Eds.), *On the Trail of Capital Flight from Africa: The Takers and the Enablers* (pp. 149–192). Oxford University Press.

Acemoglu, D., Johnson, S., & Robinson, J. A. (2001). The Colonial Origins of Comparative Development: An Empirical Investigation. *American Economic Review, 91*(5), 1369–1401.

Adam, C. S., A. Lippert and A. M. Simpasa (2014). Mining in Zambia: Revitalization and the challenges of inclusive prosperity. *In Christopher*, A., P. Collier, and M. Gondwe (Eds.). Zambia: Building Prosperity from Resource Wealth. Oxford: Oxford University Press, pp. 201-226.

Adam, C., & Simpasa, A. M. (2011). Copper mining in Zambia: From collapse to recovery. *Plundered Nations*, 304-350.

Adam, C. S., & Simpasa, A. M. (2010). The economics of the copper price boom in Zambia. In A. Fraser & M. Larmer (Eds.), *Zambia, Mining, and Neoliberalism: Boom and Bust on the Globalized Copperbelt* (pp. 59–90). Palgrave MacMillan.

Adam, C. S., & Simpasa, A. M. (2011). Copper mining in Zambia: From collapse to recovery. In P. Collier & A. J. Venables (Eds.), *Plundered Nations? Successes and Failures in Natural Resource Extraction* (pp. 304–350). Palgrave Macmillan.

Adam, C. S., Lippert, A., & Simpasa, A. M. (2014a). Mining in Zambia: Revitalization and the Challenges of Inclusive Prosperity. In A. Christopher, P. Collier, & M. Gondwe (Eds.), *Zambia: Building Prosperity from Resource Wealth* (pp. 201–226). Oxford University Press.

Adam, C. S., Collier, P., & Gondwe, M. (Eds.). (2014b). *Zambia: Building Prosperity from Resource Wealth.* Oxford University Press.

AfrAsia Bank. (2021). *Africa Wealth Report 2021.* AfrAsia Bank.

Africa Progress Panel. (2013). *Equity in Extractives: Stewarding Africa's Natural Resources for All. Africa Progress Report 2013.* Africa Progress Panel.

Andersson, P., & Kayizzi-Mugerwa, S. (1993). External Shocks and the Search for Diversification in Zambia. In M. Blomstrom & M. Lundahl (Eds.), *Economic Crisis in Africa: Perspectives on Policy Responses* (pp. 143–161). Routledge.

Aron, J., & Elbadawi, I. A. (1992). *Parallel Markets, the Foreign Exchange Auction and Exchange Rate Unification in Zambia* (Working Paper No. 909). The World Bank.

Baldwin, R. (1966). *Economic Development and Export Growth: A study of Northern Rhodesia, 1920–1960.* University of California Press.

Banda, W. (2020). *Selection of Zambia's Optimal Copper Mining Excess Profit Tax.* School of Mines, University of Zambia, Lusaka, Zambia.

Bank of Zambia. (2016). *Foreign Private Investment & Investor Perceptions in Zambia—2016. Accelerating Export Diversification and Industrialization for Inclusive Growth.* Lusaka: Bank of Zambia, Balance of Payments Statistical Committee.

Bank of Zambia. (2021). *2021 Private Sector Foreign Investment and Investor Perception Survey Report: Promoting Investment for Sustainable Growth and Job Creation.* Bank of Zambia, Balance of Payments Statistical Committee.

Bigsten, A., & Kayizzi-Mugerwa, S. (2000). *The Political Economy of Policy Failure in Zambia* (Working Papers in Economics No. 23). Department of Economics, Göteborg University.

Bova, E. (2012). Copper Boom and Bust in Zambia: The Commodity-Currency Link. *Journal of Development Studies, 48*(6), 768–782.

Capgemini. (2023). *World Wealth Report 2023*. Capgemini Research Institute.
Cashin, P. A., Céspedes, L. F., & Sahay, R. (2002). *Keynes, Cocoa, and Copper: In Search of Commodity Currencies* (Working Paper No. WP/02/223). International Monetary Fund.
Cashin, P. A., Céspedes, L. F., & Sahay, R. (2004). Commodity Currencies and the Real Exchange Rate. *Journal of Development Economics, 75*(1), 239–268.
Chansa, F., Mubanga, N., Mudenda, D., & Ndulo, M. (2021). Industrial Policy in Context: Comparative Experiences From Chile and Zambia. *Zambia Social Science Journal, 7*(1), 2.
Chitonge, H. (2021). *Industrial Policy and the Transformation of the Colonial Economy in Africa: The Zambian Experience*. Routledge.
Collier, P., Hoeffler, A., & Pattillo, C. (2001). Flight Capital as a Portfolio Choice. *The World Bank Economic Review, 15*(1), 55–80.
Conrad, R. F. (2014). Mineral Taxation in Zambia. In C. S. Adam, P. Collier, & M. Gondwe (Eds.), *Zambia: Building Prosperity from Resource Wealth* (pp. 82–109). Oxford University Press.
Craig, J. (2001). Putting privatization into practice: The case of Zambia Consolidated Copper Mines Limited. *The Journal of Modern African Studies, 39*(3), 389–410.
Craig, J. R. (1999). *State Enterprise and Privatization in Zambia 1968–1998*. PhD thesis, University of Leeds
Credit Suisse. (2022). *Global Wealth Databook 2022*. Credit Suisse.
Cunningham, S. (1981). *The Copper Industry in Zambia. Foreign Mining Companies in a Developing Country*. Praeger Publishing.
Daniel, P., Keen, M., & McPherson, C. (Eds.). (2010). *The Taxation of Petroleum and Minerals: Principles, Problems and Practice*. Routledge.
Fessehaie, J. (2012). What Determines the Breadth and Depth of Zambia's Backward Linkages to Copper Mining? The Role of Public Policy and Value Chain Dynamics. *Resources Policy, 37*(4), 443–451.
Fraser, A., and J. Lungu. 2007. *For Whom the Windfalls? Winners and Losers in the Privatization of Zambia's Copper Mines*. Mine Watch Zambia.
Fraser, A., & Larmer, M. (Eds.). (2010). *Zambia, Mining, and Neoliberalism: Boom and Bust on the Globalized Copperbelt*. Palgrave MacMillan.
Henley & Partners. (2023). *Africa Wealth Report 2023*. Henley & Partners.
International Council on Mining and Metals (ICMM). (2014). *Enhancing Mining's Contribution to the Zambian Economy and Society*. Chamber of Mines/ICMM.
Larmer, M. (2010). Historical Perspectives of Zambia's Mining Booms and Busts. In A. Fraser & M. Larmer (Eds.), *Zambia, Mining, and Neoliberalism: Boom and Bust on the Globalized Copperbelt* (pp. 31–58). Palgrave MacMillan.

Lee, C. K. (2009). Raw Encounters: Chinese Managers, African Workers and the Politics of Casualization in Africa's Chinese Enclaves. *The China Quarterly, 199*, 647–666.

Liebenthal, R., & Cheelo, C. (2020). The Boom–Bust Cycle of Global Copper Prices, Structural Change, and Industrial Development in Zambia. In J. Page & F. Tarp (Eds.), *Mining for Change: Natural Resources and Industry in Africa* (pp. 397–421). Oxford University Press.

Lippert, A. (2014). *Spill-Overs of a Resource Boom: Evidence From Zambian Copper Mines* (Working Paper No. 131). Oxford Centre for the Analysis of Resource Rich Economies, University of Oxford.

Lombe, W., & Mwakacheya, B. (2017). *Experience of Mining Fiscal Reform and Renegotiation of Mining Contracts: The Case of Zambia*. Third World Network-Africa.

Lundstøl, O., & Isaksen, J. (2018). *Zambia's Mining Windfall Tax* (WIDER Working Paper No. 2018/51). UNU-WIDER.

Manley, D. (2017). *Ninth Time Lucky: Is Zambia's Mining Tax the Best Approach to an Uncertain Future? NRGI Briefing October 2017*. National Centre for Development Studies.

Martin, A. (1972). *Minding Their Own Business: Zambia's Struggle Against Western Control*. Hutchinson of London.

McPherson, C. (2010). State Participation in the Natural Resource Sectors. In P. Daniel, M. Keen, & C. McPherson (Eds.), *The Taxation of Petroleum and Minerals: Principles, Problems and Practice* (pp. 263–288). Routledge.

Meller, P., & Simpasa, A. M. (2011). *Role of Copper in the Chilean & Zambian Economies: Main Economic and Policy Issues* (Working Paper No. 43). Global Development Network.

Morris, M., Kaplinsky, R., & Kaplan, D. (2012). 'One Thing Leads to Another'—Commodities, Linkages and Industrial Development. *Resources Policy, 37*(4), 408–416.

Mudenda, D., Bulawayo, M., & Ndulo, M. (2022). The Financialisation of Commodity Markets: The Case of Copper in Zambia. *Journal of Development Economics and Finance, 1*(2), 227–253.

Mudenda, G., & Bardouille, R. (1988). *Technological Development and Educational Policy: The Case of the Mining Industry in Zambia* (p. 71). UNESCO.

Musambachime, M. C. (2016). *Wealth from the Rocks: Mining and Smelting of Metals in Pre-Colonial Zambia*. Xlibris Corporation.

Musonda, F., & Christopher, A. (1999). Trade Liberalization in Zambia: 1970–1995. In T. Oyejide & J. Gunning (Eds.), *Regional Integration and Liberalization in Sub-Saharan Africa* (Vol. 2, pp. 451–546). Palgrave Macmillan.

Ndikumana, L. (2023). *Capital Flight From Natural Resource-Dependent African Countries: Updated Estimates and Analysis for the Cases of Cameroon,*

Ghana, and Zambia, 1970–2021 (PERI Working Paper No. 582). Political Economy Research Institute, University of Massachusetts Amherst.

Ndikumana, L. , & Boyce, J. K. (2025). *New Estimates of Capital Flight from African Countries, 1970–2022.* PERI Research Report (January).

Ndulo, M. (1986). Mining Legislation and Mineral Development in Zambia. *Cornell International Law Journal, 19*, 1.

Ndulo, M. (1977). The Requirement of Domestic Participation in New Mining Ventures in Zambia. *Comparative and International Law Journal of Southern Africa, 10*(3), 257–280.

Ndulo, M., & Sakala, M. (1987). *Stabilization Policy in Zambia: 1976–85* (World Employment Program Working Paper No. 13). International Labour Organization.

Ngandu, S. (2005). *Mineral Prices and the Exchange Rate: What Does the Literature Say?* Human Sciences Research Council.

Pickbourn, L., Nkurunziza, J. D., & Ndikumana, L. (2022). *Growing the Good and Shrinking the Bad: Output-Emissions Elasticities and Green Industrial Policy in Commodity-Dependent Developing Countries* (UNCTAD Research Paper No. 84). United Nations Conference on Trade and Development.

Radetzki, M. (2016). *State Mineral Enterprises: An Investigation Into Their Impact on International Mineral Markets.* Routledge.

Reeve, W. H. (1963). *The Geology and Mineral Resources of Northern Rhodesia* (Bulletin of the Geological Survey No. 3). Ministry of Mines.

Roberts, A. D. (1982). Notes Towards a Financial History of Copper Mining in Northern Rhodesia. *Canadian Journal of African Studies, 16*(2), 347–359.

Roberts, A. D. (1976). *A History of Zambia.* Heinemann.

Robinson, A. E. (1933). The Economic Problem: Part Three. In J. M. Davis (Ed.), *Modern Industry and the African* (pp. 131–226). MacMillan.

RST and Anglo American Corporation. (1970). *Mining Yearbook of Zambia* 1970. Copper Industry Service Bureau.

Saasa, O. S. (1987). *Zambia's Policies Towards Foreign Investment: The Case of the Mining and Non-Mining Sectors* (Research Report No. 79). Scandinavian Institute of African Studies.

Sherpa. (2011). *Specific instance regarding Glencore International AG and First Quantum Minerals Ltd. and their alleged violations of the OCED guidelines for multinational enterprises via the activities of Mopani Copper Mines Plc. in Zambia.*

Sikamo, J. A., Mwanza, A., & Mweemba, C. (2016). Copper Mining in Zambia—History and Future. *Journal of South Africa Institute of Mining and Metallurgy, 116*, 1–6.

Simpasa, A., Hailu, D., Levine, S., & Tibana, R. (2013). *Capturing Mineral Revenues in Zambia: Past Trends and Future Prospects* (UNDP Discussion Paper). United Nations Development Programme.

Simson, H. (1985). *Zambia: A Country Study*. Scandinavian Institute of African Studies.

Simutanyi, N. (2008). Copper Mining in Zambia: The Developmental Legacy of Privatization. *Institute for Security Studies Papers, 2008*(165), 16.

Tembo, A. (2019). After the Deluge: Appraising the 1970 Mufulira Mine Disaster in Zambia. *Historia, 64*(2), 109–131.

UNCTAD. (2023). *State of Commodity Dependence 2023*. United Nations.

Whitworth, A. (2015). Explaining Zambian Poverty: A History of (Nonagriculture) Economic Policy Since Independence. *Journal of International Development, 27*(7), 953–986.

World Bank. (2011). *What Would It Take for Zambia's Copper Mining Industry to Achieve Its Potential?* (Report No. 62378-ZM). Finance & Private Sector Development Unit, Africa Region.

World Trade Organization. (2009). *Trade Policy Review. Report of the Secretariat: Zambia*. June 22. Geneva: WTO.

ZEITI. (2023). *ZEITI Final Report 2022*. Zambia Extractive Industries Transparency Initiative (ZEITI).

CHAPTER 6

Zambian "Missing" Copper, Gemstones, and Gold: Dark Spots in International Commodity Trade

Dale Mudenda and Léonce Ndikumana

Introduction

Capital flight from natural resource-rich developing countries like Zambia prevents them from leveraging their resources to meet their development financing needs. Indeed, evidence shows that oil and mineral-rich African countries tend to experience more capital flight than their non-resource-dependent counterparts. As of 2022, eight out of the top ten African countries with the highest amount of capital flight were oil and mineral-rich countries (the exceptions are Ethiopia and Morocco) (Ndikumana & Boyce, 2025).[1] Zambia is in the eleventh position. Updated estimates put total capital flight from Zambia since 1970 at $79.6 billion as of 2022. An analysis of capital flight from Zambia, along with Cameroon and Ghana is presented in the second chapter of this book.

[1] The top 10 countries with the highest cumulative amount of capital flight as of 2022 are, in ascending order of volume of capital flight: Nigeria, South Africa, Morocco, Algeria, Angola, Ethiopia, Mozambique, Cameroon, the Republic of Congo, and Ghana (Ndikumana and Boyce, 2025).

L. Ndikumana, *Capital Flight from Cameroon, Ghana, and Zambia*, https://doi.org/10.1007/978-3-032-22770-6_6

The problem of illicit financial flows, of which capital flight is a subset,[2] has generated interest among policy making institutions notably the African Union, the United Nations Economic Commission for Africa, the United Nations Conference on Trade and Development (UNCTAD), the World Bank, as well as in academia and policy-oriented think tanks. Researchers have sought to understand the extent and mechanisms of illicit capital outflows, with the aim of informing the design and implementation of policies aimed at stemming the financial hemorrhage suffered by developing countries.

Trade misinvoicing, whereby the value of imported and exported goods is intentionally either underinvoiced or overinvoiced, has been identified as a major mechanism of illicit financial flows (UNCTAD, 2016, 2020; Bananomi et al., 2024). Firms obtain foreign exchange and move capital out of the country by underinvoicing exports while importers gain access to unrecorded foreign exchange by overinvoicing imports. Empirical studies on African countries have established that trade misinvoicing constitutes a substantial mechanism of the capital flight (Ndikumana & Boyce, 2010, 2022, 2025; Ndikumana et al., 2015). A few studies have examined the problem of trade misinvoicing in individual African countries, including Lemi (2019) for Ethiopia, Kwaramba et al. (2016) for Zimbabwe, and Mpenya et al. (2016) for Cameroon. A multi-country study by UNCTAD (2016) examined the extent of trade misinvoicing of various commodities including copper from Zambia and Chile, cocoa from Côte d'Ivoire, oil from Nigeria and gold, iron ore, silver, and platinum from South Africa. The volume edited by Ndikumana and Boyce (2022) contains in-depth analysis of export misinvoicing for the cases of Angola (oil), Côte d'Ivoire (cocoa), and South Africa (minerals).

This case study on Zambia builds on past studies on trade misinvoicing and extends the analysis by further refining the empirical methodology in important ways. First, the UNCTAD (2016) study examined the extent of copper misinvoicing in Zambia, but it focused on copper ores (SITC 682 or HS 74) and excluded copper concentrates recorded under SITC 2831 (or HS 26). This chapter includes both the HS 74 and HS 26

[2] Illicit financial flows is a broader phenomenon than capital flight. Beyond unrecorded flows, it also includes recorded flows that are illicit because they originate from illicit activities, are transferred illegally, or are hidden offshore outside of the view of the regulator. See Ndikumana et al. (2015) for a detailed discussion of the distinction between the two phenomena.

categories to get a comprehensive measure of copper exports. Secondly, while previous studies (UNCTAD, 2016; Ndikumana et al., 2015; Ndikumana & Boyce, 2010) applied a fixed CIF/FOB ratio of 10% in mirror trade data comparisons, as was commonly done in literature, here we use product-level and partner-specific CIF/FOB ratios estimates published in the OECD's International Trade by Commodity Statistics. The fact that these ratios are country, product, and time specific enables us to obtain a more accurate measure of trade misinvoicing.

Finally, while previous studies identified the major trading partners in trade misinvoicing, little work had been done to investigate what lies behind the observed large gaps in mirror trade statistics. This chapter examines triangular trade for countries where bilateral trade exhibits large gaps in exports and imports, to explore whether some of Zambia's recorded exports are subsequently sold to third parties. Evidence from such an analysis can provide useful input into the design of strategies to curb capital flight and combat corporate tax evasion.

This chapter proceeds as follows. The next section provides a brief overview of the relevant literature on trade misinvoicing, followed by a presentation of the methodology used to estimate commodity export misinvoicing. The subsequent three sections present the results for the cases of copper, gemstones, and gold, respectively. The last section concludes this chapter with a summary of the findings and some policy recommendations.

Trade Misinvoicing as a Channel of Capital Flight

The economic literature has investigated the issue of trade misinvoicing, mainly as a channel of capital flight. The focus has been on the estimation of the magnitude of trade misinvoicing and the analysis of its motives and determinants, with the aim of shedding light on strategies to deter the phenomenon as a means of curbing illicit capital flows (Classen & Naude, 1993; Tandon & Rao, 2017; UNCTAD, 2016; Yalta, 2010). The empirical evidence shows that developing countries lose substantial amounts of funds through trade misinvoicing. For example, Yalta (2010) investigated the extent of trade misinvoicing for Turkey vis-à-vis its major trading partners for the period 1970 to 2007 and found that exports were underinvoiced while imports from China were overinvoiced. Jha and Nguyen (2014) found an increasing trend of trade misinvoicing estimated at US$186 billion between 1988 and 2012 in India. Similar evidence of large trade misinvoicing was uncovered by Fisman and Wei (2009) between Egypt and the United States. The study by Mahmood and Azhar (2001) on Pakistan and its 14 key trading partners revealed that exporters overinvoiced exports by US$ 2.4 billion over 10 years.

Total trade misinvoicing for a sample of 30 African countries amounted to $725.9 billion over the 1970–2022 period (Ndikumana & Boyce, 2025). Net outflows via export underinvoicing, whereby exporters understate the true value of their exports to retain some of the proceeds offshore, amounted to $719 billion over this period. Net import overinvoicing amounted to $6.6 billion.

Studies on individual African countries have found large volumes of trade misinvoicing. For example, Rustomjee (1991) estimated that exports from South Africa were underinvoiced by an average of 21% over the period 1970–1988. Ndikumana and Boyce (2022) analyzed the magnitudes of capital flight, adjusted for trade misinvoicing for Angola, Côte d'Ivoire, and South Africa from 1970 to 2018. They estimated the net trade misinvoicing outflows at US$133.5 billion for South Africa over 1998–2018 and $14.9 billion for Côte d'Ivoire. Lemi (2019) estimated that between 2008 and 2016 Ethiopia lost U$6–36 billion through trade misinvoicing with advanced economies, and US$15–78 billion with emerging countries.

In the case of Zambia, existing studies show that trade misinvoicing is a major conduit of capital flight. Ndikumana and Boyce (2025) estimated that from 1970 to 2022, Zambia lost $16.9 billion through trade misinvoicing, with $38.3 billion through import overinvoicing partially offset by $21.4 billion in export overinvoicing. UNCTAD (2016) found substantial discrepancies in copper export statistics, whereby exports declared by Zambia exceed the value of imports declared by its trading partner. As the top declared destination of Zambian copper is Switzerland, these discrepancies may be partly attributed to the merchanting by Glencore, a Swiss trading firm, which also owned shares in Mopani Copper Mine until it sold them to the Zambian government in early 2021.

The literature has identified several motivations for trade misinvoicing, including evasion of customs duties and circumventing capital controls (Patnaik et al., 2012; Buehn & Ichler, 2011; Boyce & Ndikumana, 2022). The argument is that high import duties, taxes, and restrictions on capital account transactions induce firms to underinvoice their merchandise exports as a way of evading these costs. Overinvoicing of imports and underinvoicing of exports also enables firms to access foreign exchange through illegal means, especially in contexts of shortage of foreign exchange and restricted access to hard currency.

Firms may also be tempted to overinvoice exports in situations where exports are incentivized through export promotion schemes such as duty drawbacks enabling firms to maximize profits (Epaphra, 2015; Henry, 2016; Lemi, 2019; Spanjers & Solomon, 2017). However, for export overinvoicing to make economic sense for the firm, the gains from export promotion incentives would have to exceed the costs of acquiring the extra hard currency beyond the true value of exports (which must be surrendered to the central bank).

Another reason for export misinvoicing is to avoid the cost associated with administrative barriers, weak regulation and poor enforcement of rules, and unstable economic policy and political environment that could trigger state expropriation of private assets. Hence, in a context plagued by bureaucratic bottlenecks, including lengthy paperwork and delays in administrative authorizations, traders tend to resort to corruption and underinvoicing to expedite clearance while disguising export underinvoicing (Buehn & Ichler, 2011; Patnaik et al., 2012).

Transit trade has also been cited as an explanation of observed gaps in mirror trade statistics. If a transit country is incorrectly recorded as a destination country, this generates discrepancies due to asymmetric recording between the source and the ultimate destination of the exports. However, one important question is why exports would be recorded as destined to a country that is only a transit station or trading hub. This is in violation of international conventions and norms governing the recording of international trade transactions to which all countries officially adhere (see UN DESA, 2011).

Estimation of Export Misinvoicing

Export misinvoicing is estimated in this chapter using a methodology initially developed by Bhagwati (1964) and subsequently refined and applied in subsequent studies (Chang et al., 1997; Ndikumana & Boyce, 2010, 2022). The method is based on the principle of double entry in cross-border trade whereby the exporter's statistics are mirrored in the importer's books. Specifically, the method compares the value of exports reported by the exporting country to the value of the imports reported by its partner, accounting for the cost of insurance and freight.

An alternative method uses a "price filter" comparing the prices reported by the importer and exporter to the benchmark market prices or a "normal price range" of the relevant products, to identify "abnormally underpriced" exports. This is a valuable complement to the method based on mirror trade statistics using the value of imports and exports. A major challenge with the price filter method, however, is that it requires transaction level data using standard classifications, which are difficult to access and use due to privacy concerns. Moreover, the "normal price range" does not capture the often-substantial product heterogeneity associated with the degree of processing as in the case of gold. Detailed descriptions of the methodology and applications can be found in Bonanomi et al. (2024). Ahene-Codjoe et al. (2022) applied the method to the case of commodity exports from Ghana.

While trade misinvoicing can be estimated for exports and imports, this chapter only examines misinvoicing of exports of minerals, focusing on copper, gold, and gemstones. The computation algorithm adopted in this chapter considers that exports from a country must match the imports of its trading partner once adjusted for the cost of insurance and freight *(cif)*. Considering Zambia as exporting country (z) of a mineral product *(k)* (alternatively copper, gold, gemstones) and an importing partner *(j)* at time *t*, export misinvoicing of the mineral product (noted as *DX*) is calculated as follows:

$$DX_{zt}^{k} = M_{jt}^{k} - (1 + cif)X_{zt}^{k} \tag{6.1}$$

where *M* is the value of imports declared by the partner, *X* is the value of exports declared by Zambia, and *cif* is the ratio of *cif* to *fob* value of exports representing the cost of insurance and freight. A positive value of *DX* represents export underinvoicing or unrecorded capital outflows from Zambia through exports, while a negative value reflects export overinvoicing resulting in unrecorded capital inflows into the country.

The estimation of bilateral misinvoicing is based on the principle that every transaction is recorded twice: once from the perspective of the reporter (Zambia) who declares the export, and second from the perspective of its importing partner *j*. However, one weakness of the estimation based on the comparison of mirror trade statistics is the possibility of generating large export misinvoicing, largely "false positives," in instances where the reported destination in Zambia's books is a trading hub (such as Switzerland) rather than the final point of sale (Lepissier,

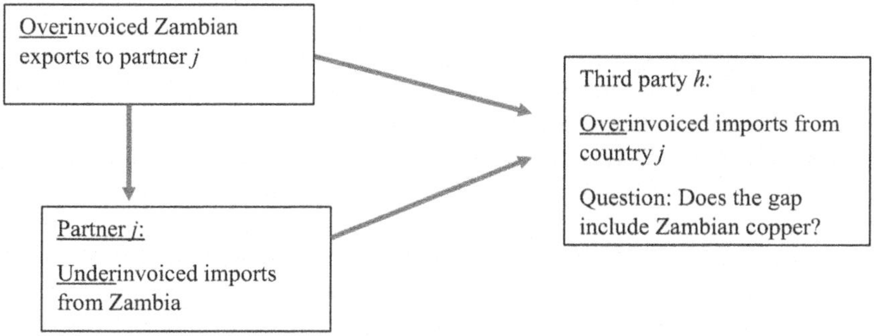

Fig. 6.1 Triangular trade from Zambia's perspective: case of export overinvoicing (*Source* Authors' construction)

2021). Commodities are often re-exported to a third country without being recorded in the hub-hosting country. We explore this scenario using a triangular trade analysis to investigate whether mineral commodities sold to partner country *j* with large trade gaps with Zambia, such as Switzerland, may have been sold to third-party countries as schematically presented in Fig. 6.1.

The statistical reconciliation process entails implementing Eq. 6.1 for trading partner *j*, and its own key trading partners (*h*) that may have a direct or no direct trade links with Zambia. The objective is to examine whether trade between countries *h* and *j* as well as with their respective partners may explain the discrepancies in mirror trade statistics between Zambia and partner *j*. Specifically, the goal is to check whether a portion of the commodities seemingly registered as heading to partner j ends up in third-party country *h*.

Data Sources

We use two datasets to estimate export misinvoicing: The OECD International Trade by Commodity Statistics database where we obtain estimates of the cost of insurance and freight *(cif)* for bilateral trade at the product and partner level; the United Nations Commodity Trade (Comtrade) database where we source data on exports and imports classified following the United Nations nomenclature for trade classification—the harmonized system (HS) and standard international trade classification (SITC). For copper exports we extracted data at four-digit level codes HS 2603 containing copper ores and concentrates and HS7401 to HS 7419 containing articles made of copper for the period 1995 to 2021. We considered non-monetary gold reported under HS codes 7108, 7109, and 7012, and gemstones recorded under HS codes 7103 and 2616.

One challenge associated with the analysis of mirror trade data is the presence of unmatched or "orphaned transactions," whereby Zambia reports exports to a partner, while the latter's books show no imports from Zambia, or vice versa. To minimize the bias arising from such mismatches in reporting, we eliminate observations with unmatched flows from the computation of export misinvoicing. In an accompanying exercise, we attempt to explore the fate of unmatched flows through triangular trade analysis. The statistical reconciliation process entails implementing Eq. 6.1 for Zambia's trading partners that exhibit large discrepancies in mirror trade and their key trading partners that may have a direct or indirect trade linkage with Zambia as depicted in Fig. 6.1.

The "Missing Zambian Copper"

Copper Export Misinvoicing

Table 6.1 reports Zambia's copper exports to the top 10 destinations from 1995 to 2021 ranked by the cumulative value of exports over the study period. The data show that Zambia's copper exports are concentrated in a few countries, with the top three export destinations—Switzerland, China, and Singapore, accounting for 94% of the total exports in 2021.

The data show a shift in the destination of Zambia's copper exports from countries like India, Saudi Arabia, and Thailand in the 1990s to new markets in China, Singapore, and Switzerland from the early 2000s. The privatization of copper mines in the late 1990s and early 2000s attracted new investors from Western and Asian Countries.

The data in Table 6.2 presents the cumulative value of exports to the major partners including years with unmatched observations or orphaned trade flows. Zambia reports more copper exports to some countries than their respective reported imports from Zambia. Most of the copper is reported to be exported to Switzerland, while the latter reports virtually no copper imports from Zambia. The situation is also observed for copper recorded in Zambia as shipped to Singapore, South Africa, and the United Kingdom, albeit at a much smaller scale.

Table 6.1 Top ten copper destinations Zambia's copper exports in selected years from 1995 to 2021 (million, nominal US$)

Countries	*1995*		*2010*		*2014*		*2021*	
	Amount	%	*Amount*	%	*Amount*	%	*Amount*	%
Switzerland	0.00	0.0	2980.8	59.3	4260.4	58.7	4549.1	53.6
China	0.2	0.0	1293.8	25.8	1728.4	23.8	1948.2	23.0
Singapore	59.9	6.7	0.0	0.0	265.5	3.7	1489.8	17.6
South Africa	6.1	0.7	226.2	4.5	195.0	2.7	48.6	0.6
United Kingdom	3.2	0.4	105.3	2.1	64.8	0.9	0.0	0.0
United Arab Emirates	0.0	0.0	175.6	3.5	133.2	1.8	0.1	0.0
Thailand	128.7	14.4	5.0	0.1	0.0	0.0	0.0	0.0
Saudi Arabia	112.6	12.6	23.9	0.5	0.0	0.0	0.0	0.0
Egypt, Arab Rep	0.0	0.0	49.2	1.0	0.0	0.0	0.0	0.0
India	84.3	9.4	0.0	0.0	25.2	0.3	0.7	0.0
Total top 10 partners	395.0	44	4859.80	96.8	6672.5	91.90	8036.5	94.80
World	892.9	100	5022.9	100	7252.1	100	8481.8	100

Source Authors' compilation using data from Comtrade

Table 6.2 Trade of Zambian copper, as reported, including observations with unmatched reporting, 1995–2021 (million, constant 2021 US$)

	Amounts (million constant 2021US$)			*Share (percent) in:*	
Partner	*Partners' imports*	*Zambia's exports*	*Difference (cif-adjusted)*	*Partners' imports*	*Zambia's exports*
China	41,203.2	21,329.5	18,332.8	41.7	19.2
Egypt	4153.2	1327.6	2713.6	4.2	1.2
India	5638.5	1037.5	4528.5	5.7	0.9
Saudi Arabia	6423.0	1476.1	4825.2	6.5	1.3
Singapore	561.1	5706.7	−5544.7	0.6	5.1
South Africa	3318.4	4696.2	−1725.2	3.4	4.2
Switzerland	0.0	58,508.0	−62,350.9	0.0	52.6
Thailand	3300.9	1692.7	1478.0	3.3	1.5
United Arab Emirates	8675.9	1764.1	6762.7	8.8	1.6
United Kingdom	190.5	4916.6	−5094.7	0.2	4.4
Total 10 partners	73,464.9	102,455.0	−36,726.6	74.4	92.1
World	98,798.5	111,282.4	−19,978.0	100.0	100.0

Source Authors' computations

Some countries report receiving more copper from Zambia than the latter has exported there, especially in the case of trade with China. Such gaps are also observed in trade with the United Arab Emirates, Thailand, Egypt, Saudi Arabia, and India.

The results presented in Table 6.3 show both underinvoicing and apparent overinvoicing of copper exports. Copper exports to China are underinvoiced to the tune of $18.4 billion (constant 2021 US$) over 1995–2021. The underinvoicing of copper exports to a major trading partner like China is a genuine problem for in Zambia, as it is a channel of capital flight and a loss of customs revenue.

There is also underinvoicing of copper exported to the United Arab Emirates ($6.9 billion), India ($4.1 billion), and Saudi Arabia ($3.2 billion). The discrepancies are marginal in the case of exports to Thailand and Egypt.

The gaps in bilateral trade with some partners deserve some attention as they suggest apparent export overinvoicing whereby they report smaller amounts of copper imports than the value of exports reported by Zambia

Table 6.3 Estimated export misinvoicing of copper from Zambia, considering only matched reporting over 1995–2021 (million, constant 2021 US$)

Partner	*Partner's imports*	*Zambia's exports*	*Export misinvoicing*
China	41,097.6	21,329.5	18,361.7
Egypt	2187.9	1300.0	775.5
India	5218.5	1037.5	4108.8
Saudi Arabia	4564.4	1270.9	3186.6
Singapore	435.8	5705.9	−5,639.8
South Africa	3318.4	4696.2	−1725.0
Switzerland	0.0	3064.1	−3254.1
Thailand	2089.9	1692.7	263.6
United Arab Emirates	8675.9	1628.2	6910.9
United Kingdom	185.9	3031.6	−3075.6
Total 10 partners	67,763.1	44,756.7	19,912.6
World	98,798.5	111,282.4	−19,755.9

Source Authors' computations

to these countries. This is the case for Switzerland. Accounting for c.i.f., Zambia's exports to Switzerland exceed the latter's recorded imports by $3.2 billion over 1995–2021. Such discrepancies cannot be justified by standard motives of export misinvoicing. So, what is behind those large gaps in mirror copper trade statistics between Zambia and Switzerland? A plausible reason is the fact that Switzerland is a major trading hub-hosting companies involved in "merchanting" of primary commodities. A Swiss company may buy copper from Zambia and store it in bonded warehouses on the London Metal Exchange, possibly for a relatively long time, before reselling it to the ultimate destination without the copper ever officially entering Switzerland (Lépissier, 2021). Upon reselling the copper, it is not recorded as a re-export from the United Kingdom (LME). Such arrangements create gaps when one attempts to track copper export flows from the source to the destination using mirror trade statistics.

Furthermore, mining firms engage in activities that enable them to earn higher returns on copper exports than reported in benchmark LME official reports. First, while the value of exports is recorded at the border crossing based on the LME price, exporters can speculate on prices by storing the copper in bonded warehouses for some time, offloading it on the market once the price increases. The discrepancies in mirror trade statistics also arise when sellers hedge the sale by buying futures or options that allow them to lock in a certain price while the physical deal is closed at the spot price of the time of delivery (Östensson, 2018). The lag between the time of export and the time of reporting at the destination can blur the trade flows, making it difficult to reconcile the quantities, prices, and values of the traded goods at the source and at the destination.

Mineral traders can also engage in practices aimed at maximizing their profits that could result in export discrepancies. Mining managers interviewed by the authors stated that the reconciliation of mirror trade data requires knowing three important elements. The first element is the exact quantity sold by the mining company to the importing country. Second is the timing of the sale relative to the dates of imports from Zambia; and finally, the price at which the copper is ultimately sold to the export market by the exporter. This is because exporters such as Glencore could store copper in warehouses and export it later. The opacity of export flows is further compounded by intra-company trade that allows exporters to under-declare the values of copper exported to related entities.

Another issue with mirror trade statistics is that copper mines tend to smelt different copper grades, obtained from different mines and even from other countries, to produce more refined and higher quality copper used in pharmaceuticals and other specialized industries. This kind of copper is sold at higher prices than recorded in national statistics, which are based on LME prices, resulting in statistical discrepancies. In the case of Zambia, mining firms import copper ores from the Democratic Republic of Congo (DRC) for smelting, which they then export together with copper from their own mines. This copper may be recorded by the importing country as originating from either Zambia or the DRC. Thus, the transparency of trade statistics may be compromised as the copper originating from the DRC can erroneously be recorded as originating from Zambia.

Triangular Copper Trade Analysis

The results presented above showed that although Zambia reports exporting over 54% of its copper to Switzerland, the later reports no imports of copper from Zambia. Yet, Switzerland declares high values of copper exports to third countries in Comtrade. This suggests that Swiss companies may be rerouting Zambian copper to third-party countries that may exhibit symmetric gaps in trade statistics with Zambia or those without strong trade links with Zambia that trade with Switzerland.

All major destination markets for copper from Switzerland are, therefore, potential sources of the gaps in mirror copper trade statistics between Zambia and Switzerland.

Table 6.4 presents the results of the analysis of copper trade between Switzerland and its major trading partners. The main destination of copper exported by Switzerland is Germany. Over 1995–2021, Germany accounted for 43.6% of Switzerland's exports and 40% of total imports reported by its partners. The other partners are Austria, France, Italy, and the United States, which together account for 64% of total imports and 75.6% of Switzerland's exports over the same period.

The analysis of the mirror trade data shows that Germany declared a larger amount of copper imports than what Switzerland declared as exports. Adjusting for the cost of insurance and freight yields a gap of $702 million. For the other countries, it's the other way around: they declare less imports from Switzerland than the latter declares as exports to them. The cumulative excess imports for the four partners (Austria, France, Italy, and the United States) amount to $816 million.

The first question raised by these results is whether those gaps could account for the observed discrepancies in Zambia-Switzerland copper trade statistics. It is possible that the gap with Germany could indeed include some of the copper recorded by Zambia as exported to Switzerland that is not recorded by the latter as imports. A possible scenario is

Table 6.4 Switzerland's copper exports to its main partners, including matched reporting only from 1995 to 2021 (million, constant 2021 US$)

	Total (million, constant 2021 US$)			*Shares of total (%)*	
	Partner's imports	*Switzerland's exports*	*Export misinvoicing*	*Partner's imports*	*Switzerland's exports*
Austria	1313.3	1544.6	−254.3	6.1	8.5
France	1347.0	1459.9	−125.0	6.2	8.0
Germany	8701.6	7944.3	702.0	40.1	43.6
Italy	1728.1	1846.0	−141.2	8.0	10.1
United States	793.1	994.2	−295.5	3.7	5.5
Total top partners	13,883.1	13,789.0	−114.0	64.0	75.6
World	21,687.2	18,232.8	3378.1	100.0	100.0

Source Authors' computations

that the German importer knows for sure that they bought the copper from a Swiss entity, but the Swiss entity does not record it as its copper export given its awareness that it originated from Zambia. In that scenario, Zambia's copper exports would have been routed through Switzerland, but ending up in Germany, where the Zambian origin is not recorded. It is difficult to assess the likelihood and the share of copper associated with such scenarios from the aggregate statistics.

How about the gaps with the other four countries? These gaps could explain the Switzerland-Zambia gap if importers in these countries are able to identify the cargo as containing Zambian copper and hence recording it as being imported from Zambia (rather than Switzerland), while Swiss traders record it as their own export. In this scenario, Switzerland would have served as a transit or merchanting station for Zambian copper that is sold to the ultimate destination as Swiss copper.

It is difficult to know how much of the Zambia-Switzerland trade gap reflects any of these observed discrepancies between Switzerland and its main trading partners. It is particularly important to note that there are statistical gaps in copper trade between Switzerland and other copper exporters as well. So, it is not possible to know, from aggregate statistics, the share that is accounted for by Zambia's "missing copper." The Zambia-Switzerland copper trade gaps remain an unsolved puzzle.

Trading in Gemstones: Glaring Gaps in Export Statistics

Exports of Gemstones

Zambia is endowed with substantial reserves of gemstones, notably emeralds, amethyst, tourmalines, and recently discovered sugilite. The mining of gemstones began during the colonial era by private investors in the Kafubu area of the Copperbelt. However, in 1971, as part of the nationalization program, the government took over the sector under the Mining Development Corporation (Sliwa & Nguluwe, 1984). The discovery of higher quality gems by indigenous people fueled illegal artisanal and small-scale mining. To curb illegal mining, the government established a restricted mining zone in Lufwanyama and forcibly removed the population from there. A new state-owned agency, the Reserved Minerals Corporation, was given monopoly over mining and prospection rights (Sliwa & Nguluwe, 1984). By 1980, Kagem Mining Ltd. (owned by

Reserved Minerals at 55% and Hagura at 45%, an Indian-Israeli corporation) was authorized to conduct exploration and mining in the Kafubu area. A privatization agreement was signed between the mining company Hagura and the Government of Zambia in May 2001 (Mashikinyi, 2020). In 2022, the government had 25% of the shares in Kagem mine, which is the largest emeralds mine in the world. In addition to Kagem, there are a few other large privately owned gemstone mines such as Gemcanton, Grizzly, Chatete, and Kariba Minerals, which is owned by ZCCM-IH.

The gemstones subsector has historically remained at the periphery of the country's development strategy. Large formal firms exist alongside a large number of informal small-scale miners (some registered and others unregistered), and foreign buyers, which creates a fertile ground for export smuggling and misinvoicing, hence capital flight. The gemstone sector is not significantly contributing to the Zambian economy because substantial portions of gemstone revenue are not accounted for due to smuggling (Hilson, 2020). In 2010, the government issued about 500 ten-year gemstone mining licenses, of which 345 were for emerald.

Most of the artisanal miners are Zambian, often backed by foreign traders (MCTI, 2020). This is because the Mines and Minerals Development Act No. 11 of 2015 restricted artisanal mining rights to citizens or cooperatives that are wholly owned by citizens (Banda & Chanda, 2021). Zambian-owned artisanal small mining entities tend to be backed by private sponsors who give them mining equipment, loans, and inputs, and purchase their output for exports.

In 2020, the Ministry of Commerce, Trade and Industry formulated an export diversification strategy focused on gold and gemstones. The strategy identified important problems in the gemstone sector, including illegal trading, crime in mining areas, smuggling, environmental degradation and fragmentation of farming land. The strategy targets building capacity and amalgamation of ASM to minimize fragmentation and promote value addition in gold and gemstones. The strategy also encourages the use of appropriate, affordable, and safe technology through the dissemination of relevant information, provision of extension services, and technology demonstrations. Furthermore, the government commits to working with miners associations to facilitate access to funding. The strategy projected that the contribution of gold and gemstones to GDP would rise to 1% by 2025 compared to less than 0.1% in 2022.

Large-scale gemstone producers sell their production either through auctions in Zambia and abroad or directly to hand-picked established clients, such as Ashok Jewelers of India. For example, Kagem undertakes quarterly auction sales mainly in Singapore and India, and at times within Lusaka. The government-owned Kariba Minerals used to auction its amethyst in India, but it later resorted to using established networks after regulatory changes in India. Most artisanal small miners sell in the informal markets to local and foreign traders that finance their operations. These arrangements provide a fertile ground for smuggling and capital flight given that unregistered miners cannot sell their minerals through formal markets.

Zambia is among the world's top producers and exporters of quality emeralds and other gemstones alongside Colombia, Brazil, Ethiopia,[3] and Zimbabwe (Geology.com; Mashikinyi, 2020). The country's gemstone exports increased from US$38.7 million in 2010 to US$101.4 million in 2021. Table 6.5 presents exports to and imports from the top 10 partners, including unmatched reporting. The top 3 partners account for 72% of all gemstone imports from Zambia: India (38%), Singapore (16%), and the United States (18%). The largest discrepancies are observed in trade with the United States and India, which are also the largest buyers of Zambian gemstones. While the United States recorded $492.9 million worth of imports of gemstones from Zambia, the latter registered only $25 million of gemstone exports to the United States. The corresponding numbers for India are $1 billion (imports) and $590 million (exports).

The reverse outcome is observed in the case of trade with South Africa and the United Kingdom, which recorded less imports than Zambia's reported exports of gemstones. However, the absolute amounts are much smaller than the gaps recorded in trade with India and the United States.

Misinvoicing of Gemstone Exports

The observed discrepancies in mirror trade statistics point to export misinvoicing. This section presents estimates of gemstone export misinvoicing using the methodology described earlier in this chapter. The results presented in Table 6.6 show substantial underinvoicing of gemstone exports destined to India ($407.7 million) and the United States ($415.9 million) over 1995–2021. Underinvoicing is also observed, albeit to a lesser extent, for gemstones exported to Thailand ($66.9 million) and

[3] A large amount of high-quality opal was discovered in Wegal Tena, Wolo Province in Ethiopia (Rondeau et al., 2010).

Table 6.5 Trade of Zambia's gemstones, including unmatched reporting: Cumulative value over 1995–2021 (million, constant 2021 US$)

	Partner's imports		*Zambia's exports*		*Difference*	
	Value ('000$)	*Percent*	*Value ('000$)*	*Percent*	*Raw*	cif-*adjusted*
India	1040.6	38.1	590.4	42.5	450.2	407.4
Singapore	442.9	16.2	333.2	24.0	109.6	92.0
Hong Kong, SAR	124.3	4.6	122.1	8.8	2.1	1.4
Switzerland	48.6	1.8	49.2	3.5	−0.6	−3.0
South Africa	30.7	1.1	58.6	4.2	−27.9	−28.2
United Kingdom	29.3	1.1	45.7	3.3	−16.3	−17.3
United States	492.9	18.0	25.0	1.8	467.9	467.7
Thailand	124.7	4.6	24.7	1.8	100.0	100.0
Israel	35.5	1.3	25.6	1.8	9.9	8.6
United Arab Emirates	96.3	3.5	48.1	3.5	48.1	48.1
Top 10 partners	2465.7	90.3	1322.7	95.3	1143.0	1076.9
World	2730.8	100.0	1387.9	100.0	1343.0	1273.0

Source Authors' computations

the United Arab Emirates ($44.4 million). We note, however, that some exports to Singapore, South Africa, and the United Kingdom cannot be traced in these partners' imports statistics. Zambia lost a cumulative amount of $829 billion through misinvoicing of gemstones exported to the group of 10 top partners considered in the table from 1995 to 2021. Considering all partners (the world), the cumulative loss amounts to $1.2 billion.

The trading partners where significant discrepancies in gemstone trade statistics are recorded share the characteristic of hosting auction centers (India and Singapore) or serving as major trading hubs for precious metals (South Africa and the United Kingdom). This raises the question of whether the merchanting hosted in these countries may induce, enable, or facilitate mis-recording of the quantity and value of gemstones exported from Zambia. In the case of South Africa and the United Kingdom, the results may reflect the fact that some gemstones reported in Zambia's books as exported to these countries are warehoused there, not reported

Table 6.6 Estimated misinvoicing of gemstone exports from Zambia over 1995–2021, considering only matched reporting (millions, constant 2021 US$)

	Partner's imports	*Zambia's exports*	*Export misinvoicing*
India	1040.6	590.4	407.7
Singapore	222.1	261.9	−54.5
Hong Kong, SAR	124.3	122.1	−6.5
Switzerland	24.6	25.2	−2.5
South Africa	30.6	58.6	−33.4
United Kingdom	23.7	45.7	−25.3
United States	442.8	25.0	415.9
Thailand	93.3	24.7	66.9
Israel	35.4	18.1	16.2
United Arab Emirates	93.4	45.0	44.4
Total for top partners	2130.8	1216.7	828.9
World	2730.8	1387.9	1244.1

Source Authors' computations

as imports, and later sold to other countries. A similar phenomenon is observed for Zambian copper exports to Switzerland discussed in the previous section.

One important factor that facilitates and induces misinvoicing of gemstone exports is the fact that the sector remains largely informal and fragmented. Furthermore, the trading system allows producers to auction their output abroad to buyers from various countries. The gemstones cross the border without a reference price for tax purposes. This makes it difficult to trace the quantity and value of the gemstones that are exported from Zambia as well as the real benefits to the economy in terms of government revenue and foreign exchange earnings.

On the "Gold Trail"

Gold: A Sector With a Substantial Unexploited Potential

Although gold mining has existed before the colonial period, the sector has remained peripheral to Zambia's development strategy, which focused on copper. For most of the post-independence period, gold mining has been dominated by informal artisanal small-scale gold mining (ASGM). These producers lack access to affordable investment capital, face poor infrastructure, and poor geological knowledge of the sector. Moreover, the gold sector has been associated with environmental degradation due to unregulated exploitation. The influx of foreign gold traders has generated little or no tangible contribution to wealth creation and poverty reduction in the local communities.

Recently, there has been a spate of gold re-discoveries, with an estimated 300 findings in Luano, Vubwi, Lundazi, Mwinilunga, Mpika, Rufunsa, and Petauke districts. The areas are mainly dominated by ASGM with only one large formal gold mine, the Kanshishi gold mine in Northwestern Province. However, many other mines such as Mopani Copper Mine produce and export smaller quantities of gold as a by-product of copper mining. Most of the gold produced by small-scale miners is sold in informal markets to foreigners, mainly Chinese, Russians, and Indians that patronize the gold panning sites (Hilson, 2020). This unregulated trading environment is conducive for capital flight through gold smuggling and export underinvoicing.

Recently the government embraced the ASGM and recognized its potential to contribute to social economic development. To curb illicit gold exports and improve revenue generation from the sector, the government developed a basic framework for guiding ASGM formalization. Recognizing that the existing licensing schemes were not suitable for the rapidly growing ASGM, the government updated the Mines and Minerals Development Act of 2015 by adding a "gold panning certificate" as a requirement for ASGM, which can only be issued to citizens or cooperatives comprising of citizens only. Certificate holders are required to pay mineral loyalty and other taxes, maintain production and financial reports, and comply with the environmental management requirements. Policymakers perceive the certificate to be "user-friendly and useful in legalizing anarchic pockets of gold rush activity" (Hilson, 2020). The certificate was promoted as not only affordable but also as a tool to enhance trust and security of tenure for ASGM.

In 2020, the government developed a national export diversification strategy for gold and gemstones. The strategy classifies gold as a strategic mineral of interest (Ministry of Commerce Trade and Industry (MCTI) and Ministry of Minerals and Mines Development [MMMD], 2020), and it mandated ZCCM-IH to explore and develop the gold subsector to ensure maximum benefits for the state and the Zambian people. ZCCM-IH is expected to buy gold from the ASGM and other gold mining entities, with the aim of eliminating middlemen and facilitating the sale of gold through formal markets to enhance revenue collection and formalize the sector.

Moreover, since 2020, gold has been adopted as a strategic reserve by the Bank of Zambia. Thus, the Bank of Zambia buys gold directly from formal suppliers, specifically Kansanshi gold mine. The gold from ASGM continues to be mainly traded in the informal markets. Figure 6.2 illustrates the organization of gold production and sales and the players involved. As Zambia does not have refinery capacity, once the gold is purchased by the Bank of Zambia, it is shipped to the Rand Refinery Limited (RRL) in South Africa for refining, remaining a property of the Bank of Zambia.

According to our interviews with Bank of Zambia officials, the Bank's gold is shipped out for refinery by the mining houses which also export their own gold. The gold shipped to the refinery in South Africa by the Bank of Zambia is not recorded in South Africa's trade statistics as it remains a property of the Bank of Zambia. The refined gold can be retained in South Africa for safe keeping or could be exported to other countries by or on behalf of the Bank of Zambia.

Figure 6.3 shows the trend in Zambia's gold exports as reported in the Balance of Payments and in Comtrade. Two important observations emerge from the data. The first is a remarkable increase in reported gold exports starting from 2008. According to BoP data, gold exports

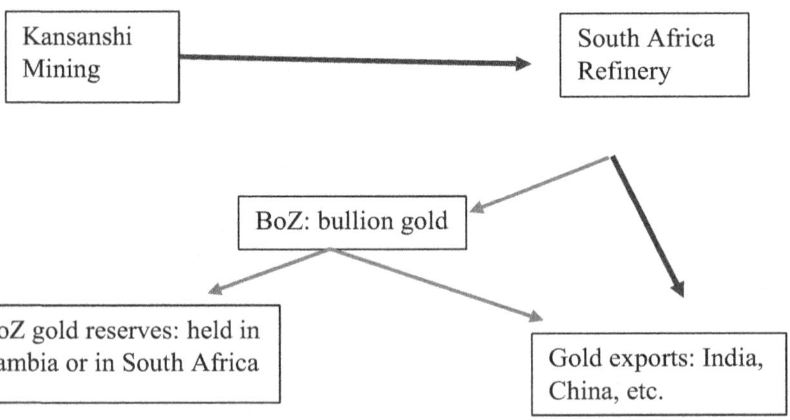

Fig. 6.2 The flow of gold produced in Zambia (*Source* Authors' construction)

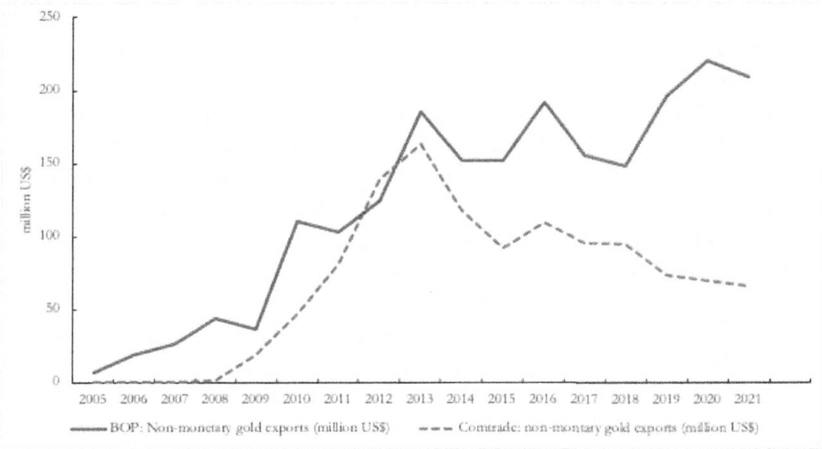

Fig. 6.3 Trend of official gold exports from Zambia: BOP and Comtrade (million, nominal US$) (*Source* Authors' construction using data from the Bank of Zambia and Comtrade)

increased from US$44 million in 2008 to US$185.6 million in 2013, reaching US$220.5 million in 2020. The second observation is a growing discrepancy between the value of gold exports reported in the balance of payments compared to Comtrade, starting in 2013. In that year, the BoP reported $22 million more than Comtrade; the gap reached $139 million in 2021. We could not find an explanation for the gap.

Gold Export Misinvoicing

Data from Comtrade show large discrepancies between the values of gold exports declared by Zambia and the amounts of gold imports recorded by the two partners (Table 6.7). While Zambia's statistics show that South Africa is the destination of all its gold (97.5%), the UAE reports as having imported nearly all gold from Zambia (92.5%). Zambia declared $1.3 billion of gold exports, but South Africa recorded only $227,000 of gold imports from Zambia. One wonders then where the $1 billion worth of Zambian gold exports went. Trade with the UAE shows the opposite scenario, with $1.8 billion of gold imports recorded in the UAE while Zambia only shows $19.8 million of gold exports to that destination. These discrepancies in mirror gold trade statistics point to export misinvoicing as a conduit for capital flight, which is documented in Table 6.7.

The results show that most of Zambia's gold exports are not matched with the destination indicated at the origin. Comparison of partner data taking account of the cost of insurance and freight reveals significant underinvoicing of gold exports destined to the UAE, to the tune of $1.6 billion (Table 8, panel a). This suggests that Zambia is losing substantial amount of tax revenue and foreign exchange through the manipulation of gold exports to the UAE. The discrepancies have exploded since 2018. Panel (b) of Table 6.8 presents the results over 2019–2021. During the 3-year period, the UAE recorded $1.5 billion of gold imports, while Zambia reported $196 million of gold imports, implying gold export misinvoicing of $1.5 billion. Relative to the rest of the world, estimated gold export misinvoicing stands at $1.5 billion for the 3 years.

Table 6.7 Zambia's Gold trade as reported including unmatched reporting: Cumulative amounts over 2001–2021 (million, constant 2021 US$)

	Partner's imports		*Zambia's exports*	
	Amount	*Percent*	*Amount*	*Percent*
South Africa	0.2	0.0	1352.8	97.5
United Arab Emirates	1827.7	92.7	19.8	1.4
World	1972.5	100.0	1388.2	100.0

Source Authors' computations

Table 6.8 Zambia's gold trade as reported including matched reporting only: cumulative amounts over 2001–2021 (million, constant 2021 US$)

Panel a: 2001–2021	Partner's imports	Zambia's exports	Export misinvoicing
South Africa	0.2	113.5	−118.0
United Arab Emirates	1642.2	7.8	1634.0
World	1972.5	1353.1	544.8
Panel b: 2019–2021	Partner's imports	Zambia's exports	Export misinvoicing
South Africa	0	0	0
United Arab Emirates	1548.2	0.2	1548.0
World	1690.1	215.7	1464.3

Source Authors' computations

Gold Trade and the UAE Hub

As Zambia does not have gold refineries, it relies on the Rand Refinery Limited in South Africa where Zambia-based mining houses send their gold for refining. The refined gold is then sold to third parties by the mining houses. Since Zambian gold is not recorded by South Africa as an import, and it is not recorded as an export or a re-export going out South Africa, this creates major accounting problems, obscuring the gold value chain.

A question emerging from these statistics is: what is the destination of the gold registered by Zambia as exported to South Africa which is not recorded as import by South Africa? As the UAE is the main buyer of Zambian gold, the question is: is Zambian gold coming out of Rand Refinery Limited thereafter exported to the UAE, where it is reported as Zambian gold? How would the UAE importers know that it is Zambian gold that they are buying from South Africa? Answering these questions would require detailed investigation down to the transaction level.

As a first attempt to explore the role of the UAE as a possible destination of Zambian gold routed through South Africa, we examine gold trade between South Africa and the UAE. Table 6.9 presents the cumulative value of gold trade between South Africa and the UAE from 2001 to 2021. The figures in the first row include all years including unmatched trade flows, while those in the second row exclude observations with unmatched flows. The results show that the UAE reports more gold imports from South Africa ($11.5 billion) than the latter's reported exports to the former ($35.6 million). This suggests that South Africa possibly serves as a transit for gold originating from other countries, including Zambia, and destined to the UAE. The statistical discrepancies raise the following questions : what is the true market value assigned to Zambian gold routed through South Africa that ends up in the UAE? What fraction of the final gold value accrues to Zambia? What benefits does Zambia draw from gold trade going through South Africa in terms of fiscal revenue and repatriation of foreign exchange earnings? These are fundamental questions that have critical implications for Zambia's economic development that deserve to be investigated, which requires improved transparency in the handling and reporting of statistics on gold trade throughout the entire value chain.

Table 6.9 Gold trade between South Africa and the United Arab Emirates over 2001–2021 (million, constant 2021 US$)

	UAE's imports	*SA's exports*	*cif-adjusted difference*
All years, including unmatched flows	11,559.1	35.6	11,522.3
Only years with matched flows	729.6	35.6	692.8

Source Authors' computations

Conclusion

This chapter analyzed trade statistics to investigate the extent of minerals export misinvoicing as a channel of capital flight, focusing on copper, gemstones and gold. In the case of copper, the analysis reveals major discrepancies between Zambian recorded exports and imports as recorded by its trading partners. Specifically, while Zambia records Switzerland as the primary destination of its copper exports, Switzerland reports virtually no copper imports from Zambia. Further analysis reveals that the observed large gaps cannot be explained by discrepancies in copper trade between Switzerland and its main trading partners. The reverse situation of export underinvoicing is observed with some partners, led by China, which is the second destination of Zambia's copper exports. However, the gaps do not offset each other: on balance, over $19.9 billion (constant 2021 $) of Zambia's copper exports cannot be traced in partners' import statistics. This chapter discusses some possible explanations for the observed gaps. Ultimately, the discrepancies in Zambia-Switzerland copper trade remains a mystery.

While Zambia is endowed with substantial reserves in gemstones (emeralds, amethyst, tourmalines, and sugilite), the subsector has remained at the periphery of the national strategy for mining sector development. The gemstone subsector remains dominated by informal mining and is highly exposed to export smuggling. The analysis of mirror trade statistics reveals substantial discrepancies in trade with the United States and India, which are also the largest buyers of Zambian gemstones. Our estimations show a cumulative loss of $1.2 billion due to gemstone export underinvoicing over the period 1995–2021.

Gold trade statistics exhibit substantial discrepancies between gold exports recorded in Zambia and gold imports recorded by its trading partners. While Zambia's records show South Africa as the primary destination of its gold ($1.3 billion over 2021–2021), the UAE is the top importer of Zambian gold ($1.8 billion) according to partner data in Comtrade. One possible piece of the puzzle may be South Africa's role as a regional gold refinery hub. Indeed, while Zambia records South Africa as the top destination of its gold exports, South Africa's statistics show virtually no gold imports from Zambia. Further detailed analysis suggests that the gold going through South Africa may end up in the United Arab Emirates, which is an important importer of gold from South Africa. These recording asymmetries make it impossible to track gold trade to assess the accuracy of the reporting of gold exports, government revenue collection, and repatriation of export earnings, which are critical tools for leveraging mineral resources to finance economic development process and combat capital flight occurring through trade misinvoicing.

The analysis of export misinvoicing of minerals reveals structural deficiencies in the reporting of transactions along the value chain. These deficiencies suggest that the country is not collecting an adequate value of its mineral endowments especially in terms of government revenue and foreign exchange earnings. The evidence calls for deep reforms in the mining sector to improve regulatory efficiency, transparency, and accountability on the part of all involved parties and in all transactions from investment, production, government revenue collection, exporting, and foreign exchange repatriation.

Bibliography

Ahene-Codjoe, A. A., Alu, A. A., & Mehrotra, R. (2022). Abnormal Pricing in International Commodity Trading: Evidence From Ghana. *International Economics, 172,* 331–348.

Albertin, M. G., Yontcheva, B., Devlin, D., & Devine, H. (2021). *Tax Avoidance in Sub-Saharan Africa's Mining Sector*. International Monetary Fund.

Banda, W., & Chanda, E. K. (2021). A Proposed Cooperatives Strategy for Artisanal and Small-Scale Gold Mining Sector in Zambia. *Resources Policy, 70,* Article 101909.

Bhagwati, J., Krueger, A., & Wibulswasdi, C. (1974). Capital Flight From LDC's: A Statistical Analysis. In J. Bhagwati (Ed.), *Illegal Transactions in International Trade* (pp. 148–154). North Holland.

Bhagwati, J. N. (1964). On the Under-Invoicing of Imports. In J. Bhagwati (Ed.), *Illegal Transactions in International Trade* (pp. 138–147). North Holland.

Boyce, J. K., & Ndikumana, L. (2001). Is Africa a Net Creditor? New Estimates of Capital Flight From Severely Indebted Sub-Saharan African Countries, 1970–1996. *Journal of Development Studies, 38*(2), 27–56.

Boyce, J. K., & Ndikumana, L. (2010). Measurement of Capital Flight: Methodology and Results for Sub-Saharan African Countries. *African Development Review, 22*(4), 471–481.

Boyce, J. K., & Ndikumana, L. (2015). Strategies for Addressing Capital Flight. In S. I. Ajayi & L. Ndikumana (Eds.), *Capital Flight from Africa: Causes, Effects and Policy Issues* (pp. 393–417). Oxford University Press.

Boyce and Ndikumana (Eds.) (2022). On the Trail of Capital Flight from Africa. The Takers and the Enablers. Oxford: Oxford University Press

Buehn, A., & Eichler, S. (2011). Trade Mis-invoicing: The Dark Side of World Trade. *The World Economy, 34*(8), 1263–1287.

Carbonnier, G., Brugger, F., Bürgi Bonanomi, E., Dzanku, F. M., & Insisienmay, S. (2024). *Missing Dollars: Illicit Financial Flows from Commodity Trade*. Brill. (International Development Policy Series no. 17. Geneva Graduate Institute of International and Development Studies).

Chang, K. P. H., & Cumby, R. E. (1991). Capital Flight in Sub-Saharan African Countries. In I. Husain & J. Underwood (Eds.), *African External Finance in the 1990s* (pp. 162–187). World Bank.

Chang, P. K., Claessens, S., & Cumby, R. E. (1997). Conceptual and methodological issues in the measurement of capital flight. International Journal of Finance & Economics, 2(2), 101-119.

Claessens, S. and D. Naude, D. (1993). Recent Estimates of Capital Flight. World Bank Policy Research working Paper NO. 1186. Washington, DC: The World Bank.

Collier, P., Hoeffler, A., & Pattillo, C. (2001). *Flight Capital as a Portfolio Choice*. World Bank, Development Research Group and International Monetary Fund.

de Boyrie, M. E., Nelson, J. A., & Pak, S. J. (2007). Capital Movement Through Trade Mis-invoicing: The Case of Africa. *Journal of Financial Crime, 14*(4), 474–489.

Fisman, R., & Wei, S. J. (2009). The Smuggling of Art, and the Art of Smuggling: Uncovering the Illicit Trade in Cultural Property and Antiques. *American Economic Journal: Applied Economics, 1*(3), 82–96.

Epaphra, M. (2015). Tax rates and tax evasion: Evidence from missing imports in Tanzania. MPRA Paper No. 62328 (February).

Geda, A., & Yimer, A. (2016). Capital Flight and Its Determinants: The Case of Ethiopia. *African Development Review, 28*(S1), 39–49.

Henry, J. S. 2016. The Price of Offshore - Data by Region. The Global Haven Industry: http://globalhavenindustry.com/price-of-offshore-menu

Hilson, G. (2020). The 'Zambia Model': A blueprint for formalizing artisanal and small-scale mining in sub-Saharan Africa?. Resources Policy, 68, 101765.

IMF and IDA (2000). *Decision Point Document for the Enhanced Heavily Indebted Poor Countries (HIPC) Initiative*. World Bank: IMF and International Development Association (IDA).

Jha, R., & Nguyen, T. (2014). *Trade Misinvoicing and Macroeconomic Outcomes in India* (Working Paper No. 31). Centre for Applied Macroeconomic Analysis.

Kambani, S. M. (2003). Small-Scale Mining and Cleaner Production Issues in Zambia. *Journal of Cleaner Production, 11*, 141–146.

Kwaramba, M., Mahonye, N., & Mandishara, L. (2016). Capital Flight and Trade Mis-invoicing in Zimbabwe. *African Development Review, 28*, 50–64.

Leins, S., Kesselring, R., & Schulz, Y. (2019). Value Works: Effects of Financialization Along the Copper Value Chain. SNIS Working Papers.

Lemi, A. (2019). Catch Me if You Can: Trade Mis-invoicing and Capital Flight in Ethiopia. *Ethiopian Journal of Economics, 28*(1), 1–48.

Lépissier, A. (2021). A methodological toolkit to understand complex policy problems: applications to climate change and illicit finance. Doctoral dissertation, University of California, Santa Barbara.

Ljungberg, D., & Friedel, C. (2014). *Does Natural Resource Abundance Cause Capital Flight?* Stockholm School of Economics (unpublished).

Mahmood, Z. and M. Azhar (2001). On overinvoicing of exports in Pakistan. The Pakistan Development Review, 40(3), 173-185.

Mashikinyi, M. (2020). *Investigating the Technical, Financial and Regulatory Challenges in the Zambian Gemstone Mining Sector: A Case Study of Gemcanton Investment Holdings Limited*. MA Thesis, University of Zambia.

MCTI & MMMD, (2020). *Zambia: Export Diversification Strategy for Gold and Gemstones*.Lusaka, Zambia: Zambia's Ministry of Commerce, Trade and Industry (MCTI) & Ministry of Mines and Minerals Development (MMMD).

Mpenya, A. H. T., Metseyem, C., & Epo, B. N. (2016). Natural Resources and Capital Flight in Cameroon. *African Development Review, 28*(S1), 88–99.

Mudenda, D., Bulawayo, M., & Ndulo, C. (2020). The Financialization of Commodity Markets: The Case of Copper in Zambia. *Journal of Development Economics and Finance, 1*(2), 227–253.

Ndikumana, L., & Boyce, J. K. (2025). *New Estimates of Capital Flight from African Countries, 1970–2022*. PERI Research Report (January).

Ndikumana, L., & Boyce, J. K. (2022). Capital Flight from Angola, Côte d'Ivoire, and South Africa: An Overview. In L. Ndikumana & J. K. Boyce (Eds.), *On the Trail of Capital Flight from Africa: The Takers and the Enablers* (pp. 10–36). Oxford University Press.

Ndikumana, L., Boyce, J. K., & Ndiaye, A. S. (2015). Capital Flight from Africa: Measurement and Drivers. In S. I. Ajayi & L. Ndikumana (Eds.), *Capital*

Flight from Africa: Causes, Effects and Policy Issues (pp. 15–54). Oxford University Press.
Ndikumana, L., & Boyce, J. K. (2010). Measurement of Capital Flight: Methodology and Results for Sub-Saharan African Countries". *African Development Review, 22*(4), 471–481.
Ndikumana, L., & Sarr, M. (2019). Capital Flight, Foreign Direct Investment and Natural Resources in Africa. *Resources Policy, 63,* Article 101427.
Ndulo, M. (1986). Mining Legislation and Mineral Development in Zambia. *Cornell International Law Journal, 19*(1), 1–34.
Östensson, O. (2018). Misinvoicing in mineral trade: what do we really know? Mineral Economics, 31(1), 77-86.
Patnaik, I., Shah, A., & Gupta, A. S. (2012). Determinants of Trade Misinvoicing. *Open Economies Review, 23*(5), 891–910.
Prescott, G. W., Baird, M., Geenen, S., Nkuba, B., Phelps, J., & Webb, E. L. (2022). Formalizing Artisanal and Small-Scale Gold Mining: A Grand Challenge of the Minamata Convention. *One Earth, 5*(3), 242–251.
Qureshi, T. M., & Mahmood, Z. (2015). *The Size of Trade Mis-invoicing in Pakistan* (MPRA Paper No. 65801).
Reeve, W. H. (1963). *The Geology and Mineral Resources of Northern Rhodesia* (Bulletin of the Geological Survey No. 3). Ministry of Labour and Mines, Northern Rhodesia.
Rondeau, B., Fritsch, E., Mazzero, F., Gauthier, J. P., Cenki-Tok, B., Bekele, E., & Gaillou, E. (2010). Play-of-Color Opal From Wegel Tena, Wollo Province, Ethiopia. *Gems and Gemology, 46*(2), 90–105.
Rustomjee, Z. (1991). Capital flight under Apartheid. Transformation: Critical Perspectives on Southern Africa, 19, 89-103.
Sikamo, J., Mwanza, A., & Mweemba, C. (2016). Copper Mining in Zambia: A History and Future. *Journal of the Southern African Institute of Mining and Metallurgy, 116*(6), 491–496.
Siwale, A., & Siwale, T. (2017). Has the Promise of Formalizing Artisanal and Small-Scale Mining (ASM) Failed? The Case of Zambia. *The Extractive Industries and Society, 4*(1), 191–201.
Sliwa, A. S., & Nguluwe, C. A. (1984). Geological Setting of Zambian Emerald Deposits. *Precambrian Research, 25*(1–3), 213–228.
Spanjers, J. and Solomon (2017). Illicit financial flows to and from developing countries: 2005-2014. Washington, DC: Global Financial Integrity. http://www.gfintegrity.org/wp-content/uploads/2017/05/GFI-IFF-Report-2017_final.pdf
Tandon, S. and R. K. Rao (2017). Trade Misinvoicing: What Can We Measure. National Institute of Public Finance and Policy, NIPFP Working Paper 200 (July).

UN DESA. (2011). International merchandise trade statistics: Concepts and definitions 2010. *Statistical Papers*, Vol. 52. United Nations, Department of Economic and Social Affairs (DESA).

UNCTAD. (2016). *Trade Mis-invoicing In Primary Commodities in Developing Countries: The Cases of Chile, Côte d'Ivoire, Nigeria, South Africa and Zambia*. UNCTAD.

UNCTAD. (2020). *Tackling illicit Financial Flows for Sustainable Development in Africa*. UNCTAD.

UNDP. (2011). *Illicit Financial Flows from the Least Developed Countries: 1990–2008*. UNDP.

Whitney, J. W. (1976). *Analysis of Copper Production, Processing, and Trade Patterns, 1950–1972*. Pennsylvania State University Press.

Yalta, A. Y. (2010). Effect of Capital Flight on Investment: Evidence From Emerging Markets. *Markets Finance & Trade, 46*(6), 40–54.

Zambia Development Agency and Zambia Statistical Agency. (2022). *2021 Survey on Private Sector Foreign Investment in Zambia, Annual report*. Bank of Zambia.

Zambia Development Agency and Zambia Statistical Agency. (2023). *2022 Survey on Private Sector Foreign Investment in Zambia, Annual Report*. Bank of Zambia.

ZCCM Investments Holdings Plc (various editions). *Annual Report and Financial Statements*. ZCCM-IH.

CHAPTER 7

Oil and the Cameroonian Economy: Dual Dependence and the Many Faces of the "Curse"

Léonce Ndikumana, Hans Tino Mpenya Ayamena, and Juste Lokossou

Introduction

Cameroon is one of the most endowed African countries with a wide range of overground and underground natural resources. In the words of Keutiben et al., (2022, p. 635), "nature has vastly well-endowed Cameroon." Nicknamed "Africa in miniature" (https://discover-cameroon.com/en/about-cameroon/), Cameroon is among the top 10 African richest countries in natural resources (World Bank, 2018) Indeed, what makes Cameroon special is not its endowment in absolute value of any single natural resource. It is rather the impressive combination of its strategic geographical position (coastal and tropical), the rich biodiversity with abundant agricultural potential, and vast oil and mineral reserves. This makes an impressive development potential. However, all that potential has remained just that. The story of Cameroon is, by and large, a story of unfulfilled development potential.

At independence, Cameroon boasted promising prospects for rapid growth and development. An illustrative comparator often used in the literature is with Malaysia, which has similar structural features, but has

L. Ndikumana, *Capital Flight from Cameroon, Ghana, and Zambia*,
https://doi.org/10.1007/978-3-032-22770-6_7

achieved massively better outcomes. At independence, Cameroon's per capita GDP of $936 was close to Malaysia's $1267; a 1.35 ratio in favor of the latter. Today, Malaysia's per capita income is nearly eight times that of Cameroon ($11,429 compared to $1467). This illustrates a story of unfulfilled development potential. Indeed, as Gauthier and Zeufack (2012, p. 155) lament, "With its abundant natural resource base, varied climate, and diverse population, Cameroon has the potential to be one of the richest countries in sub-Saharan Africa. However, like many resource-rich countries, it has suffered from the natural resource curse."

Instead of boasting impressive development outcomes, Cameroon is among African resource-rich countries with the unenviable reputation of suffering heavily from financial hemorrhage through capital flight. In a sense, capital flight has become a chronic manifestation of the "resource curse" that plagues many African countries that are endowed with natural resources in a context of poor institutions and weak regulatory frameworks (Ndikumana & Boyce, 2022; Ndikumana & Sarr, 2019). By 2022, Cameroon had lost a cumulative amount of $98 billion through capital flight since 1970, the eighth highest in Africa (Ndikumana & Boyce, 2025; Chapter 2 in this book).

This chapter aims to shed light on both the potential of the oil sector and the challenges that Cameroon has faced in converting that potential into real development outcomes. The objective is to provide some insights into why Cameroon has fallen through the trap of the corrosive linkages between natural resource endowment and capital flight, one of the reasons for its inability to fulfill its development potential. While Cameroon is a small oil producer from a global perspective and even by African standards, oil still represents an important sector of the economy, with high expectations regarding its contribution to economic development. The oil sector contributed 14.5% of GDP in the mid-1980s, but its share has declined significantly since then, down to only 5.4% in 2022. The generation of government revenue and foreign exchange earnings from oil has remained below potential. Moreover, the country has been trapped into natural resource dependence, with economic transformation remaining elusive; but not illusive, as there is a real basis for successful transformation. The main causes of this failed transformation include the inability to take advantage of oil revenue to expand non-oil sectors, to ramp up public investment in economic and social infrastructure, and to build forward and backward linkages within the economy. The leakages of the proceeds of oil revenue through an opaque management system

(Gauthier & Zeufack, 2011, 2012; Keutiben et al., 2022) as well as capital flight (Mpenya et al., 2016) have contributed to a resource-dependence trap. As a result, Cameroon has struggled to achieve and sustain strong economic growth, to eradicate poverty, and to reach other social development goals that other comparable resource-rich emerging countries such as Malaysia have achieved. The issue is not lack of resources; it is rather the inability to set up the right institutional and regulatory frameworks to leverage those resources.

The next section provides a historical overview of oil sector activities since the colonial era. As in other African resource-rich countries, such as Zambia with minerals (Chapter 5 in this volume) and Ghana with gold (Chapter 3), at the genesis of the exploration of oil, Cameroon suffered the "original sin" of external dominance, which it has struggled to overcome till today. The oil sector was dominated by foreign companies at the exploration stage; and this continued during the production stage later. The subsequent section describes the fiscal regime that governs the oil sector with an emphasis on the ownership structure of the upstream and downstream oil segments. It examines the incentives set up by the legal framework to attract private investment, highlighting innovations brought about by the 1999 Petroleum Code. Next, we examine the contribution of the oil sector to exports and foreign exchange earnings. The section also highlights the failure to diversify the export basket, further entrenching resource dependence. It also investigates the issue of export misinvoicing and provides estimates both at the aggregate level as well as relative to the main trading partners. The subsequent section presents evidence on the overall contribution of the oil sector to the Cameroonian economy and society. It is a tale of underperformance and an illustration of the many faces of the "curse." The section highlights how the failure to sustain high growth, initiate genuine economic transformation, and generate robust government revenue have contributed to the poor overall economic performance illustrated by persistent poverty and low social development indicators. The section also illustrates regional disparities along social economic outcomes. The last section concludes with a summary of the evidence and some policy recommendations.

Genesis of Oil Exploitation in Cameroon

The Colonial Beginnings

Cameroon's endowment in oil is related to its strategic geographic location, like its neighbors, Nigeria and Gabon. Geologists hypothesized that Cameroon, nested between the oil-rich regions of Nigeria to the north and Gabon to the south, likely contained significant oil reserves (Pokam Kamdem, 2022).

Oil exploration in Cameroon began under the German colonial rule, with the first documented indication discovery of hydrocarbon reserves in 1904 by the Westafrikanische Pflanzungsgesellschaft Victoria (WAPV), a German plantation company. Two wells were then drilled by the Internationale Bohrgesellschaft d'Erkelenz, reaching depths of 305 and 800 meters, respectively. However, these efforts failed to discover commercially viable oil reserves due to the lack of advanced geological knowledge leading to imprecise choices of drilling locations.

Oil exploration efforts continued when France and England took over Cameroon following Germany's defeat in World War I.[1] In 1923, Société Nationale du Cameroun (SNC), originally a timber company, was granted exploration rights. SNC's activities were supported by the Syndicat d'Etudes et de Recherches Pétrolifères de Logo-baba, which conducted geological surveys in the Douala basin, a territory then under French tutelage. Despite promising geological indicators, the exploration did not yield significant results during that period.

After World War II, the Bureau de Recherches de Pétrole (BRP), a French government entity, intensified exploration activities using detailed geological mapping and studies. The Société de Recherche et d'Exploitation des Pétroles du Cameroun (SEREPCA) was established in 1951, inheriting BRP's research permits. Between 1951 and 1959, SEREPCA drilled over 35,000 meters across various sites and discovered several small and medium-sized gas and oil reserves. These findings sustained the hope of eventually discovering substantial hydrocarbon reserves in Cameroon.

The transition from onshore to offshore exploration marked a significant shift in the exploration strategy. In 1961, SEREPCA expanded its exploration to the coastal and offshore areas, obtaining permits in the

[1] After World War I, Cameroon was placed under the tutelage of both France and England. The country was then divided into two, with East Cameroon under French rule and West Cameroon under British rule.

regions of Sanaga Cameroun and Rio del Rey.[2] This period also saw the entry of major international oil companies. Mobil Exploration Equatorial Africa (MEEA) acquired permits in 1965, followed by Shell Camerounaise de Recherches et d'Explorations (Shell CAMREX) in 1969, while Gulf Oil Company of Cameroon (CAMGOC), Amerada Petroleum Corporation Cameroon acquired permits in 1970, and Total Pakistan S.A. in 1972. Today, Cameroon's major oil reserves that are under exploitation are in the offshore Rio del Rey Basin (accounting for approximately 89% of known commercial reserves) and the Douala/Kribi-Campo Basin (hosting 11% of the reserves).

The Government vs. the Private Sector in the Oil Sector

Under the French tutelage, the government's role evolved from regulatory oversight to active participation in oil production in the context of a mixed economy (Pokam Kamdem, 2022). The Bureau de Recherches de Pétrole (BRP) played a significant role in preparing for the establishment of the Société de Recherche et d'Exploitation des Pétroles du Cameroun (SEREPCA).

The role of the French Commissioner in Cameroon, Théodore Paul Marchand, was central in reshaping the role of the state in the oil sector. In 1929, Commissioner Marchand revoked the permit of the Syndicat d'Etudes et de Recherches Pétrolifères de Logo-baba, accusing it of inactivity and instead favoring the Compagnie Française de Pétroles (CFP). This move underscored the French colonial administration's strategy to prioritize companies with state participation over purely private ventures. The Syndicat, the consortium involved in early oil exploration efforts, resisted this decision, arguing that the colonial administration's actions were biased toward fostering a state-dominated oil sector.

In the post-independence period, the Cameroonian government continued to fine tune its relationship with private oil companies. The initial monopoly held by SEREPCA was gradually eroded as new private

[2] On October 1, 1961, the two parts of Cameroon were reunified. This enabled the expansion of exploration to the western part of Cameroon, which shares a very long border with Nigeria, stretching from the north of the two countries to the coast. The Rio del Rel is located precisely in this part of Cameroon, which at that time was under British rule.

players, often subsidiaries of the "Seven Sisters"[3] oil giants, entered the market in the early 1960s. Cameroon participated in the Société Equatoriale de Raffinage (SER), holding a 5% stake in the Port-Gentil refinery from 1965 to 1973 (Pokam Kamdem, 2022).

During the 1970s, through entities like the Société Nationale d'Investissements (SNI) and the Caisse de Stabilisation des Prix des Hydrocarbures (CSPH), the state acquired majority stakes in national oil ventures. This included a 65% stake in the Société Nationale de Raffinage (SONARA) established in 1973 and a 51% stake in the Société Camerounaise des Dépôts Pétroliers (SCDP) created in 1979. The establishment of the Société Nationale des Hydrocarbures (SNH) on March 12, 1980, with 100% of government's shares, marked a significant shift in the governance of the oil sector, as the government sought to assert greater control over the sector (Perrot, 1988). SNH's mandate was twofold: (i) promoting the development of hydrocarbons in Cameroon; (ii) managing the state's interests in the oil sector including its shares in international oil companies and its quotas in crude oil production (see SNH's website). By January 1980, the government of Cameroon had negotiated a participation agreement with the French companies Elf SEREPCA and Pecten, securing the state a 20% stake in the capital of these companies. This arrangement extended to other companies that obtained exploration and production permits later. The Cameroonian oil management regime differed from that of its neighboring oil producers in its combination of shareholdings and production-sharing agreements, ensuring that the national company SNH received at least 60% of oil production (Pokam Kamdem, 2022). These provisions, coupled with royalties and taxes, aimed to enhance state control over the oil sector and maximize the benefits from oil exploitation for the government and the national economy (DSCN & DIAL, 1993; Perrot, 1988).

[3] Exxon, Mobil, Chevron, Gulf, Texaco, Shell, BP. These are multinationals who dominated the world oil industry between the years 1930 and 1970.

The Fiscal Regime of the Oil Sector

Ownership Structure and Industrial Organization

The Cameroonian oil sector is organized into two subsectors: upstream and downstream. The state has been significantly involved in organizing and managing the sector through four state-owned companies: Société Nationale des Hydrocarbures (SNH, National Hydrocarbons Corporation), Societe Nationale de Raffinage (SONARA, National Refining Company), Caisse de Stabilisation des Prix des Hydrocarbures (CSPH, Hydrocarbons Prices Stabilization Fund), and Société Camerounaise de Dépôts Pétroliers (SCDP, Cameroonian Petroleum Depot Company). These companies work alongside other public and private operators in the industry.

The Upstream Oil Sector

The upstream sector comprises of activities related to the granting of oil concessions, exploration, and crude oil production. The state is represented by SNH, a public industrial and commercial entity that has financial autonomy and is governed by the General Statute of Public Enterprises of Cameroon under the OHADA[4] law. The first set of SNH's responsibilities includes promoting, developing, and monitoring oil and gas activities nationwide. In this regard, SNH collaborates with international oil companies to ensure compliance with regulations and participates as an operator and runs the Mvia oil field since 2009.

The second set of SNH's responsibilities involves marketing the state's share of crude oil production on the international market through contracts. SNH also manages its own shares as an investor. It also sets the Cameroonian crude oil prices relative to Brent oil prices, considering quality differences, transport costs, and market demand conditions.

SNH's revenues from oil sales are transferred to the public Treasury after deduction of production costs. SNH operates under the direct supervision of the General Secretariat of the Presidency and collaborates with several ministries, including Mines, Energy, Finance, Commerce, Economy, and Environment. In 2005 Cameroon joined the Extractive

[4] "Organisation pour l'Harmonisation en Afrique du Droit des Affaires" (OHADA), translated in English as "Organization for the Harmonization of Corporate Law in Africa."

Industries Transparency Initiative (EITI) in a bid to improve efficiency in the management of the oil sector. Since then, SNH regularly publishes data on its key activities and undergoes external financial audits.

It is worth noting that SNH is a major corporation that is also involved in various activities besides exploitation, transport, refining, storage, and control of the quality of oil. Its other activities include insurance (Chanas Assurances S.A., with 45.26% of shares), ship repairs (Cameroon Shipyards and Industrial Engineering Ltd, 6.75%), and the hotel industry (Cameroon Hotels Corporation, 6.21%) (SNH, 2020).

Private companies, particularly multinationals, play a fundamental role in the upstream sector, primarily in exploration and extraction. The two major companies in the upstream sector are Perenco and Addax Petroleum.

Perenco: Perenco is Europe's leading independent oil and gas company and it has been active in Cameroon since 1993. The company operates both offshore and onshore, focusing on exploration and production. Since acquiring Total's shares in 2010, Parenco became the leading operator in Cameroon, with a presence in the Rio del Rey and Douala basins (Moudi and Ebome). It manages four production-sharing contracts, three of which are in production (Bolongo, Dissoni, Moabi), and one in the exploration phase (Bomana in the Rio Del Rey basin). It operates two Floating Storage and Offloading units (FSOs), Lobe and Kole. Perenco is also involved in gas projects in collaboration with SNH and the Norwegian company Golar LNG.

Addax Petroleum: Addax Petroleum has been engaged in Cameroon since 2002 and it is considered the second largest oil company in the country. It initially secured a license to explore oil offshore in the Rio del Rey basin and established its first oil production platform when it acquired Royal Dutch Shell's shares in Pecten Cameroon SA in 2011. Addax operates through two entities, Addax Petroleum Cameroon Company (APCC) and Addax Petroleum Cameroon Limited (APCL), both of which work closely with SNH and Perenco.

The Downstream Oil Sector

The downstream oil sector deals with crude oil derivatives and is predominantly operated by state-owned companies, namely SONARA, CSPH, and SCDP, alongside multinational and national companies engaged in import and distribution of oil products.

SONARA: Established by presidential decree on March 24, 1973, and inaugurated in 1981, SONARA is 96% state-owned, with the remaining 4% held by private oil companies. Initially designed to process light crude, SONARA has been upgrading its facilities since 2005 to refine heavy crude produced in Cameroon. However, following a fire in its factories on May 31, 2019, SONARA stopped its operations, and since then it is only involved in importing refined products. Before its shutdown in 2019, SONARA supplied 80% of the petroleum products consumed in the country, with the remaining 20% covered by imports by national and multinational companies through calls for competitive tenders issued by the CSPH.

CSPH: Created by Decree No. 74/458 on May 10, 1974 following the first oil crisis, CSPH's primary mission is to regulate the prices of hydrocarbons nationwide by absorbing price increases within its financial means. Initially, CSPH operated as a small institution managed by a supervisory committee under the authority of the Director of Prices of the Ministry of Trade. On August 26, 1998, under Decree No. 98/165, CSPH was reorganized into a modern, autonomous structure to enhance its operational efficiency and independence to better fulfill its mission of price regulation (CSPH-HPSF, 2021).

SCDP: Founded on July 1, 1979, SCDP is primarily responsible for the storage and distribution of petroleum products across the country, with a mandate to ensure the availability of petroleum products nationwide. It maintains strategic stocks, ensures compliance with administrative procedures, and collects the special tax on petroleum products (TSPP) on behalf of the state. SCDP operates a network of thirteen modern storage facilities across the country where it stores oil imported by multinational and national companies.

National and Multinational Oil Companies

Before 2000, the downstream oil sector was dominated by multinationals (Total, Elf, Texaco, Exxon Mobil). The liberalization of the sector during the 2000s allowed the entry of national companies and completely changed its landscape. Today about thirty companies (national and multinational) operate in the oil sector. The most important multinationals are Total Energies, which holds 18% of the capital of the SCDP, Corlay Cameroon (17%), and Ola Energy Cameroon (10%). The most important national companies are Tradex Cameroon (4% of SCDP capital), Neptune Oil Cameroon, Bocom Petroleum, Petrolex, Green Oil, and Blessing.

Total Cameroon: A subsidiary of the French oil group Total, Total Cameroon began its activities in Cameroon in 1947 and was involved in both the upstream and downstream segments of the oil sector. It controlled about 75% of the Cameroonian oil production from 1977 until 2010. Along with other companies, it played a significant role in the initial geological surveys and exploratory drilling in the 1940s. Other international participants included Shell, Mobil (now part of ExxonMobil), Elf Aquitaine (which later merged with Total), and Chevron (an American multinational).

Total Cameroon holds 19.7% stake in SONARA and 18% stake in SCDP. In 2010, Total sold its 75.8% stake in its upstream affiliate, Total E&P Cameroun, to Perenco. However, this sale did not include Total's downstream activities, where the company remains the leading distributor of oil products in Cameroon, accounting for commanding shares of key products notably kerosene (56%), super (22%), gasoil (18.6%), and fuel (18%) (2022 values) (SCDP, 2022).

Regulation of the Oil Sector

Given the importance of the oil sector in the Cameroonian economy, various laws have been enacted to regulate the activities in the sector. Table 7.1 presents the key regulatory acts chronologically with their respective mandates.

The regulation of the oil sector evolved in two major phases. The first period from the early 1960s to 1998 is characterized by the establishment of foundational laws and regulations, which primarily focused on attracting foreign investment and establishing basic operational guidelines for exploration and production activities. The second period starting in 1999 is marked by the enactment of the Petroleum Code of 1999, a comprehensive legal document prescribing the regulation of the upstream oil sector, and laws that liberalized the downstream oil sector. This period also saw greater participation in the oil sector by domestic actors, including the state, reflecting a shift toward a higher national stake in oil exploitation.

Table 7.1 Key regulatory acts governing the oil sector in Cameroon

Law number	*Date*	*Description*
		Upstream oil sector
64-LF-3	April 6, 1964	Governing mineral substances, complemented by Law No. 78/14 of December 29, 1978, and its application decree No. 64-DF-163 of May 26, 1964
64 LF-4	April 6, 1964	Establishing the basis, rates, and collection methods for fixed rights, royalties, and mining taxes; complemented and amended by Law No. 68-LF-13 of November 18, 1968
82–20	November 26, 1982	Specifying obligations for oil companies, amended by Law No. 89–15 of July 28, 1989
89/006	July 28, 1989	Authorizing the President of Cameroon to amend certain legislative provisions applicable to exploration and production activities of oil companies, and certain provisions of establishment agreements concluded between the government of Cameroon and oil companies
90/018	August 10, 1990	Authorizing the Government of Cameroon to conclude establishment agreements with oil companies holding exploration permits in sedimentary basins other than Rio del Rey
91/108	December 12, 1991	Establishing specific incentive measures to promote research and production activities in the Douala basin
95/13	August 8, 1995	Establishing specific measures for the promotion of hydrocarbon production activities from marginal fields within the national mining domain
98/003	April 14, 1998	Establishing specific fiscal measures for hydrocarbon research in the national mining domain
99/013	December 22, 1999	Introducing the Petroleum Code, complemented by its application decree (No. 2000/935/PM) of June 30, 2000, establishing the conditions for conducting oil sector activities. This law repealed all previous conflicting provisions from Law No. 64-LF-3 of April 6, 1964 to Law No. 98/003 of April 14, 1998
2019/008	April 25, 2019	Updating the Petroleum Code and abrogating all previous conflicting provisions, particularly those under Law No. 99/013 of December 22, 1999
Downstream oil sector		
95/135/ PM	March 03, 1995	Decree amending certain provisions of Decree 77/528 of 23 December 1997 regulating the storage and distribution of petroleum products

(continued)

Table 7.1 (continued)

Law number	*Date*	*Description*
2000/935/ PM	November, 13 2000	Order laying down the conditions for the pursuit of activities in the downstream petroleum sector and subsequent amendments
06–2001	October, 19 2001	Law on the organization of refining, import, export, transit, re-export, storage, mass transport, distribution, and marketing of hydrocarbons and hydrocarbon-derived products
022/ MINMEE	September, 28 2001	Decree specifying certain conditions for carrying out activities in the downstream petroleum sector

Source Authors' compilation from various official sources

Incentives Provided by the Petroleum Code of 1999

The Petroleum Code of December 22, 1999 introduced several fiscal and non-fiscal incentives aimed at encouraging foreign direct investment (FDI) into the upstream sector, including the following:

- Exemption from all taxes or duties after corporate taxes on profits and dividends.
- Exemption from all direct taxes on oil operations benefiting the state and local authorities. This also applies to the supply of goods and services, including studies directly related to oil operations (Articles 99, 105, and 106).
- The ability of foreign investors to repatriate the proceeds of their shares of hydrocarbons without paying exit duties and taxes (Article 109).
- Investor friendly foreign exchange regulations, including allowing expatriate workers and multinationals to transfer their profits abroad (Article 110).

Partly because of these incentives, FDI inflows into Cameroon's oil sector steadily increased between 1999 and 2005, led by Perenco, Addax Petroleum, and Total. By 2005, Cameroon had secured investment contracts with over 25 international companies, including those from the United States and China, drawn by the attractive tax regime and profit-sharing agreements. However, while FDI inflows remained steady and consistently above $600 million from 2014 onward, they have been lower compared to neighboring oil-rich countries such as Gabon and the Republic of Congo. Cameroon's ability to attract levels of foreign direct investment similar to its regional peers has been hampered by inadequate infrastructure and a complex legal system (Whiteaker, 2020).

The incentives provided by the Petroleum Code also led to increased oil production. By 2005, oil production had risen by 15% compared to pre-1999 levels, with Perenco and Total accounting for the bulk of the increase. The introduction of profit-sharing agreements and tax exemptions on services and equipment encouraged companies to modernize their operations, improving oil extraction efficiency. These regulations also provided flexibility in export operations with the removal of exit duties, a move that further encouraged investment in exploration and production, thus increasing government revenue (Presidency of the Republic of Cameroon, 2019).

Fostering Transparency—The EITI

Cameroon joined the Extractive Industries Transparency Initiative (EITI) in 2007 with the goal of promoting transparency and efficiency in the management of the oil sector. In the 2024 EITI report, however, Cameroon received a relatively low score (53 points) on implementing the 2019 EITI Standard (EITI 2024). The report pointed out significant issues with stakeholder engagement and planning processes. It noted that the ad hoc approach to work planning and the lack of substantive consultations with broader constituencies were critical areas needing improvement.

Furthermore, observers have expressed concerns about the inadequacy of the regulatory framework in promoting effective technology transfer (Foka, 2024). Despite the Petroleum Code's emphasis on local content and technology transfer, the implementation of these provisions has been inadequate. The regulations have not effectively fostered the transfer of appropriate technology to local entities, which is hindered by an inadequate legal environment and limited infrastructure.

Dominance of Multinational Corporations

The Cameroonian upstream oil sector is heavily dominated by multinational corporations, particularly in the exploration phase. For example,

British companies Gas du Cameroon and Afex hold 75% and 25%, respectively, of the Matanda block within the Douala/Kribi-Campo basin. Similarly, Perenco Rio del Rey, a Franco-British company, has full control over the Bomana block in the Rio Del Rey basin. In the Logone Birni basin, Yan Chang Logone Development Holding Co. Ltd, a Chinese company, also holds 100% of the Zina-Makary block. These figures underscore the complete reliance on foreign expertise and capital in the exploration of Cameroon's oil resources.

Multinational corporations also hold dominant positions in the production phase. For instance, Perenco Cameroon has a 75% stake in the Sanaga Sud field, which supplies natural gas to the Kribi power plant. In addition, Perenco holds a 75% stake in the Moabi field, a 40% stake in the Moudi field and 37.5% in the Dissoni Nord field. Addax Petroleum has a 70% stake in the Iroko field and 40% in the Mokoko Abana field. Perenco Rio del Rey holds 100% of the Bomana block, while Yan Chang Logone Development Holding Co. Ltd controls 100% of the Zina-Makary block.

The only Cameroonian entity involved in exploration and production is the state-owned SNH, which in most cases holds minority stakes in joint ventures with multinational corporations. For instance, SNH holds a 25% share in the Yoyo field alongside Noble Energy and a 50% share in the Moudi field with Perenco. However, no private local company is a significant operator or stakeholder, illustrating the challenges faced by domestic enterprises in competing within the capital-intensive and technologically demanding oil industry.

Production of Oil and Related Products

Crude Oil Production

Crude oil production in Cameroon has followed a downward trend from 8.7 million tons in 1969 to 5.8 million tons at the turn of the century (Fig. 7.1). It was estimated at 3.1 million tons in 2023, less than half the quantity registered in 1969. Episodes of recovery have been short-lived, such as over 1994–1999 and after the global financial crisis (2011–2015).

The trend of crude oil production does not appear to be correlated with oil prices. While oil prices were generally rising from 1975 to 1984, oil production was declining, except for a short-lived rise from 5.1 million tons in 1979 to 6.2 million tons in 1982. From 30,200 FCFA per metric ton in 1988, the price of crude oil started a long climb punctuated by

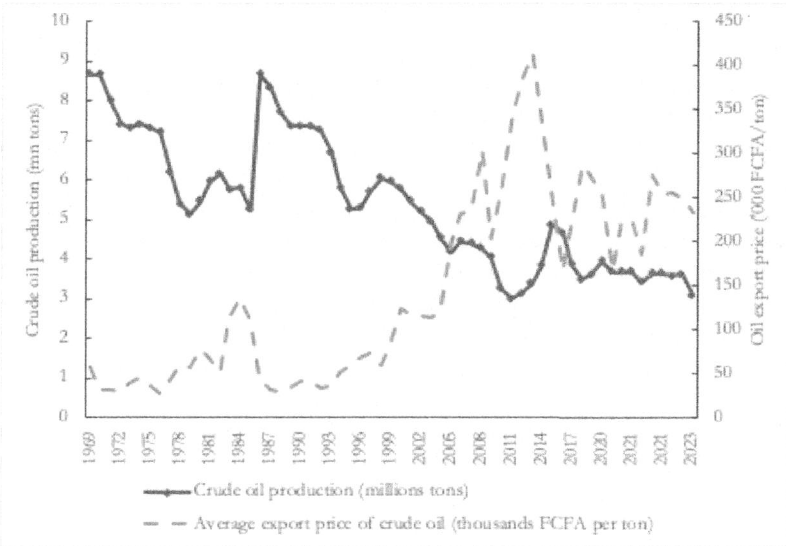

Fig. 7.1 Crude oil production in Cameroon and oil export price, 1969–2020 (*Source* Authors' construction using data from SNH and BEAC)

the global financial crisis in 2008. It peaked at 413,000 FCFA per ton in 2013 before collapsing in 2014. During that period, oil production steadily declined from 7.7 to 3.1 million tons. Since 2015, oil prices have exhibited wide fluctuations, which are not reflected in proportional variation in crude oil production. Overall, the data indicate no systematic connection between oil production and prices, suggesting that non-price factors drive crude oil production in Cameroon.

Crude Oil Production by Operator

To shed more light on the evolution of crude oil production, we examine the contribution by individual operators (Table 7.2). Total E&P maintained consistent production levels around 21 million barrels annually from 2005 to 2008, followed by a gradual decline in subsequent years. Pecten's production was stable at approximately 6 million barrels annually until 2011, after which it declined. The stability of production until the last decade may be attributed to strong established infrastructure and consistent operational strategies, with Total E&P's market dominance and Pecten's operational efficiency playing significant roles (SNH's website). The decline in oil production has been attributed to aging oil fields and reduced investments in new oil explorations.

After acquiring Total's shares, Perenco increased its production from around 3 million barrels in the mid-2000s to over 26 million barrels by 2015. This surge was driven by aggressive investment in redevelopment and optimization of existing fields, strategic operational expansion in the Rio del Rey and Douala basins, and the introduction of new technologies and efficient production techniques (Africa Energy Chamber, 2024; Energy Capital & Power, 2023; Parenco, 2023).

Addax began reporting production in 2011, with output increasing to peak at over 11 million barrels in 2014, before stabilizing at around 8–9 million barrels in the following years. Addax's performance in production was driven by investment in exploration and development projects, supported by a favorable regulatory environment and incentives aimed

Table 7.2 Crude oil production in Cameroon by operator (million barrels)

Year	*Total E&P*	*Pecten*	*Perenco*	*Addax*	*Others**	*All operators*
2005	20.2	7	2.9			30.1
2006	21.5	6.6	3.9			32.0
2007	21.6	6.2	3.5			31.3
2008	21.6	6	3.2			30.8
2009	17.4	6.3	3			26.7
2010	14.4	6.3	2.6			23.3
2011		5.6	16			21.6
2012			16.7	5.7		22.4
2013			18.2	6.1		24.3
2014			19.4	7.9	0.2	27.5
2015			26.1	8.7	0.1	34.9
2016			22.5	11.1	0.1	33.7
2017			17.5	10.2	0.4	28.1
2018			16.3	8.9		25.2
2019			17.2	8.8		26.0
2020			18.8	7.7		26.5
2021			18.4	7.2	0.02	25.6
2022			18.1	6.8	0.02	24.9

Source SNH database
*Others are RODEO, SNH, Gaz du Cameroun

at attracting foreign investment, with substantial backing from China Petrochemical Corporation (Cording & Nie, 2024).

The peak in crude oil production in 2015 can be attributed to high output from Perenco and Addax. However, this was followed by a decline due to natural depletion of oil reserves, operational challenges, and unfavorable global oil prices that adversely affected investment and production levels. Production was also negatively impacted during this period by governance and regulatory issues, including challenges in enforcing contracts and managing revenues (EITI, 2023). Other operators, notably RODEO, SNH, and Gaz du Cameroun contribute a negligible quantity of crude oil.

The contracts between private oil companies and the State are mostly production-sharing arrangements. Table 7.3 presents the State's production shares from 2005 to 2022. On average, the State's share has varied between 58% and 66.5% over that period.

Table 7.3 State's share of oil production in private companies (in percentage)

Year	*Total E&P*	*Pecten*	*RODEO*	*Perenco*	*Addax*	*GAZ du Cameroun*	*All operators*
2005	67.0	69.5		31.4			64.2
2006	67.1	69.5		41.8			64.5
2007	66.9	69.5		48.7			65.4
2008	67.3	69.5		49.9			65.9
2009	67.9	68.7		50.0			66.1
2010	68.1	69.0		52.0			66.5
2011		69.2		65.5			66.5
2012			26.9	64.9	69.3		66.0
2013			0.0	60.8	69.5		62.9
2014			18.2	58.9	62.1		59.4
2015			11.9	62.7	59.9		61.7
2016			14.6	62.4	54.1		59.5
2017				61.6	55.2	12.5	58.3
2018				60.3	64.0	13.3	61.6
2019				60.4	65.0	13.6	61.9
2020				56.9	66.2	3.5	59.6
2021				54.9	66.7	3.9	58.2
2022				56.3	66.6	6.2	59.1

Source SNH database

Oil Refinery and Supply of Oil Products to the Domestic Market

The government's strategy for oil sector development has traditionally aimed to minimize the country's dependence on imported oil by developing oil refineries to supply the domestic market. To that effect, SONARA was created in 1973 and inaugurated in 1981. It was designed to process light crude oil with a capacity of 2,100,000 tons per annum. The decision to establish a structure that can only process light crude oil turned out to be a major strategic mistake given that Cameroon's reserves contain primarily heavy crude oil. This implies high production costs for SONARA, undermining the company's competitiveness relative to imported oil.

The decision to set up SONARA's refinery to process light crude was reportedly motivated by the desire to guarantee the sustainability of the company in the long term given the limited amounts of national oil reserves. It was uncertain that the oil reserves of the Rio Del Rey basin, which was the only exploited site in the country at the time of creation of SONARA, could guarantee adequate supply of crude oil to the refinery in the long term. In addition, heavy crude oil is highly prized on the international market and therefore more expensive compared to light crude oil which is available from several neighboring countries (Nigeria, Gabon, Congo). Indeed, Nigeria was one of the main sources of light crude oil supply for SONARA.

However, the discovery of new oil fields in the Rio Del Rey basin, the entry into production of the Douala/Kribi-Campo basin in 1997, and the evolution of the technology used to process heavy crude oil led SONARA to review its strategy. Since 2005, SONARA upgraded and modernized its facilities to increase capacity to process heavy crude oil, in addition to light crude oil. This was expected to enable the company to export refined products in addition to supplying the local market.

On May 31, 2019, however, the fate of SONARA was shattered by a fire in its factory, causing all production units to shut down on June 1, 2019. While waiting for the rehabilitation of its production units, SONARA is engaged in the import of refined products.

Oil Exports and Foreign Exchange Earnings

Has Cameroon Succeeded in Leveraging Oil Price Booms?

Cameroon's oil exports have been influenced by world oil markets, which have exhibited significant fluctuations over time due to the vagaries of international commodity prices and exogenous shocks to oil production and demand. In the late 1960s and 1970s, crude oil prices were relatively low, but they started to increase significantly toward the end of the 1970s (Fig. 7.2). During this period oil exports increased, although not always proportional to price changes. Crude oil prices continued to be volatile through the 1980s, leading to volatility in Cameroon's oil exports.

The 1990s were characterized by moderate stability of global oil prices and Cameroon's oil exports. The introduction of new production technologies and improved global oil demand contributed to a more stable oil market. The economic crisis in the early 1990s and structural adjustment programs in Cameroon also played a role in these fluctuations.

The early 2000s marked a significant boom in oil prices, driven by rising global demand, geopolitical tensions that negatively affected oil supply, and economic growth in emerging markets. However, the global financial crisis of 2008 led to a sharp decline in oil prices and exports.

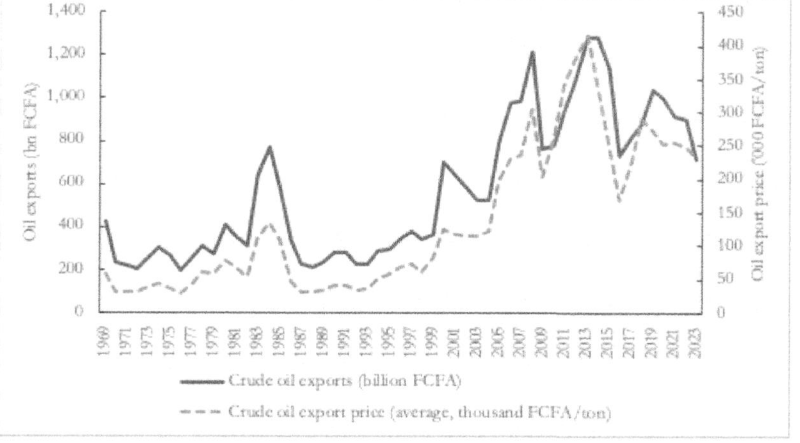

Fig. 7.2 Crude oil exports from Cameroon, 1969–2023 (*Source* Authors' construction using data from BEAC)

From 2010 onward, crude oil prices recovered but continued to fluctuate due to global economic conditions, technological advancements in oil extraction, and a shifting geopolitical landscape. Oil prices peaked in 2012 but declined thereafter till 2020. Oil exports followed a broadly similar trend. The period reflects the impact of global market oversupply, the emergence of alternative energy sources, and the COVID-19 pandemic, which significantly reduced global oil demand.

Foreign Exchange Earnings

The ability of the oil sector to generate foreign exchange earnings depends on many factors, including the trend in the volume of oil exports and the amount of export proceeds that are effectively channeled back into the country's reserves in the banking system. As can be seen in Fig. 7.3, the long-term trend of oil exports and foreign exchange reserves exhibits two major phases. Until 1994, both were low and relatively stable, except for a jump in 1984. From 1995 onward, both experienced an acceleration driven in major part by rising oil prices during the commodity booms that preceded the 2008 global financial crisis. Thereafter, the pace of oil exports decelerated and became more volatile, while foreign exchange reserves continued to accumulate rapidly when oil prices recovered from the 2014 slump.

To what extent has the oil sector contributed to foreign exchange accumulation? As indicated above, this depends on both the performance in terms of total exports, but also and very importantly on the extent to which the hard currency earned from exports is repatriated into the country. While the former depends on developments in demand and supply side of the oil markets, the latter depends on the fiscal regime that governs the oil sector.

The relative contribution of the oil sector to foreign exchange revenue generation has slowly but steadily declined over time, as illustrated in the falling share of oil in total exports (Fig. 7.4). In 1969, crude oil represented 53.7% of total exports. Today the ratio is just above 20%.

The country's chances to significantly diversify its exports have been hampered by its inability to develop the oil value chain through domestic refinery of crude oil. Refining oil domestically reduces the import bill and the dependence on the international oil markets for domestic consumption of oil products. At the same time, to the extent that refining capacity can be increased appropriately, it would also expand the export base.

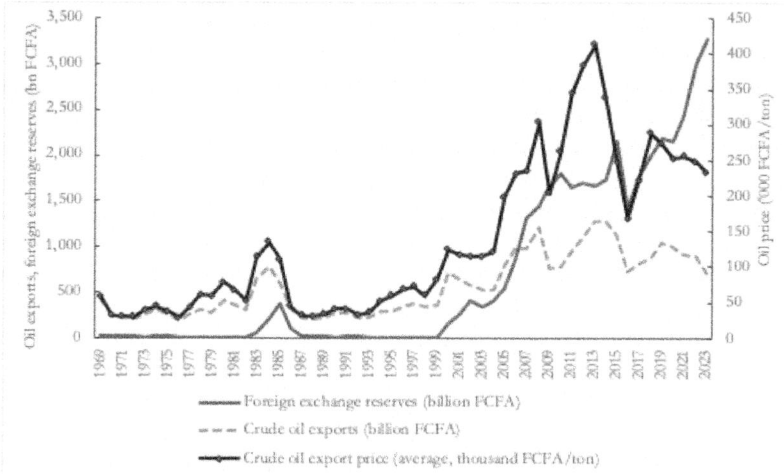

Fig. 7.3 Petroleum exports and foreign exchange reserves in Cameroon, 1969–2023 (*Source* Authors' construction using data from BEAC)

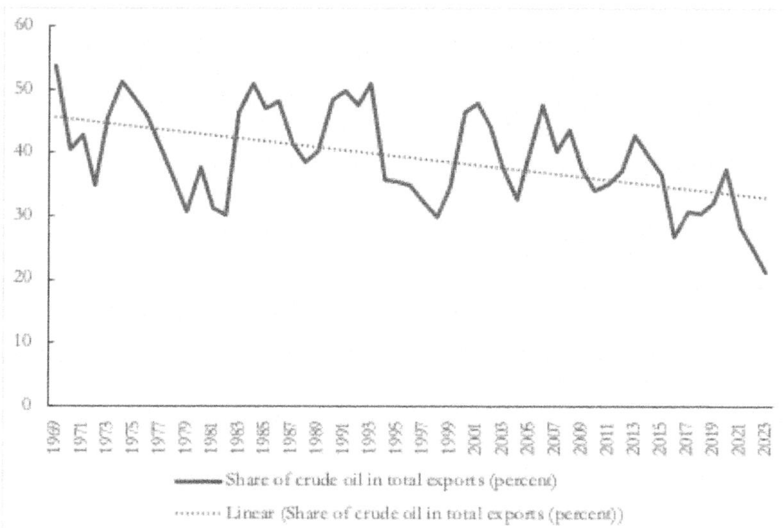

Fig. 7.4 Share of crude oil in Cameroon's total exports (percent) (*Source* Authors' construction using data from BEAC)

The refinery of oil was entrusted to SONARA, whose mandate was primarily to serve the needs for domestic fuel consumption. One structural challenge confronted by SONARA was the currency mismatch between its input expenditures and its sales revenues. The company's factory was set up to process light crude oil, which had to be imported, and hence paid for in hard currency, along with the other imported inputs and services. As the company's mandate was to serve primarily the domestic market, its sales were in the national currency (FCFA), implying that the company puts significant pressure on the country's foreign exchange reserves. Nonetheless, a major advantage is that by supplying the local market with oil products, the company also contributes to reducing the foreign exchange needs related to oil products. Therefore, the net effects on the foreign exchange reserves are an empirical question that can only be answered through careful examination of the data on the company's balance sheets, specifically by comparing its demand for foreign exchange to cover imports of inputs to the reduction in the use of foreign exchange implied by its supply of finished oil products to the domestic market.

Counting the Barrels: Oil Export Misinvoicing

The extractives sector has been historically exposed to export misinvoicing whereby exporters under-declare the value of their exports by manipulating export quantities or prices or both to earn extra hard currency that will not be surrendered to the authority, or by intentionally misreporting the type of products exported to benefit from reduced export levies.

Following the established approach for estimating export misinvoicing, we compare the value of oil exports as reported by Cameroon in the United Nations' Comtrade database to the value of oil imports as reported by its trading partners in the database. We consider oil products according to the international harmonized classification system, recorded under codes HS2709 to HS2715. The category HS2709 "Petroleum oils and oils obtained from bituminous minerals; crude" represents most of the oil exports, as the country exports mostly unprocessed oil. This category represents over 82% of Cameroon's reported total oil exports and 89% of its partners' reported oil imports from the country.

Oil export misinvoicing (XMISINV) relative to a trading route or partner j in year t is estimated as follows:

$$XMISINV_{jt} = M_{jt} - (1 + cif_{jt}/100) * X_{CMR,t} \tag{7.1}$$

The terms M_{jt}, $X_{CMR,t}$, and cif_{jt} represent, respectively, partner j's oil imports from Cameroon, Cameroon's oil exports to partner j, and the cost of insurance and freight factor for oil transport between Cameroon and partner j, which is reported in OECD ITIC database as a percentage of the CIF value of the partner's imports. This algorithm is repeated by HS category and the results are summed up by year to obtain total oil export misinvoicing. We consider only years where both Cameroon and its trading partner report a value for exports and imports, respectively. In a year where only one partner reports, export misinvoicing is set to zero. This approach, therefore, most likely underestimates the extent of export misinvoicing in cases where the failure to report was done deliberately to acquire unreported foreign exchange or to avoid export levies.

Table 7.4 presents total exports by Cameroon and imports by its partners considering all observations as well as considering only years where there is matched reporting. The results show substantial discrepancies between the value of oil exports declared by Cameroon and the values of imports declared by its partners for the category HS2709. Specifically, partners declare a substantially higher value than Cameroon. Partners' imports exceed Cameroon's c.i.f.-adjusted exports by a total of \$14.7 billion for HS2709 category over 2000–2021. In the case of category HS2710,[5] the difference is in the opposite direction, with Cameroon's exports exceeding its partner's imports by \$1.9 billion. Overall, mirror trade data show a net surplus of about \$13 billion of imports by partners over Cameroons exports for all HS categories combined. The study by Mpenya et al. (2016) estimated oil export misinvoicing amounting to \$7 billion over the 1995–2012 period, much more than for timber exports (\$1.7 billion). The results in that study are consistent with those in this chapter given that the latter covers a longer period.

The discrepancy of \$13 billion is typically interpreted as indicating oil export misinvoicing as a channel of capital flight. However, in the

[5] HS2710: Petroleum oils and oils from bituminous minerals, not crude; preparations n.e.c, containing by weight 70% or more of petroleum oils or oils from bituminous minerals; these being the basic constituents of the preparations; waste oils.

Table 7.4 Estimates of misinvoicing of oil exports from Cameroon over 2000–2021 (constant 2021 US$, million)

	All years		*Years with matched reporting only*		
HS Code	*Cameroon exports*	*Partners' imports*	*Cameroon exports*	*Partners' imports*	*Export misinvoicing*
2709	31,874.9	47,967.5	31,874.9	47,967.5	14,684.2
2710	5158.2	3610.0	5158.2	3610.0	−1935.4
2711	1512.3	1961.0	1,512.3	1961.0	318.5
2712	0.2	0.1	0.1	0.1	−0.1
2713	120.0	2.7	86.0	2.7	−92.8
2714	0.6	0.6	0.6	0.6	−0.1
2715	0.9	0.4	0.7	0.4	−0.3
Total	38,667.1	53,542.4	38,632.8	53,542.4	12,974.1

Source Authors' computations

case of Cameroon where the export of oil is primarily managed by the state company SNH, the standard incentives for misinvoicing do not apply. The discrepancies may partly reflect inadequacies in statistical reporting of oil exports. This issue deserves further investigation, especially focusing on the compilation of export statistics and their reporting to the UN Comtrade database. Transparency in the reporting of bilateral trade statistics is essential for preventing capital flight through trade misinvoicing.

To further investigate the discrepancies in oil trade statistics, we undertake an estimation by trading partner focusing on the top 8 partners that represent 66% of Cameroon's total oil exports and 71% of all its partners' oil imports. The respective values of oil trade and each partner's shares are presented in Table 7.5. The two leading trading partners are Spain which accounts for 21.7% of all partners' imports and 20% of Cameroon's oil exports, and Italy with shares of 14.3% and 12.9%, respectively.

The estimates of export misinvoicing by trading route are presented in Table 7.6. Export misinvoicing is estimated using, alternatively, the average cif factor across all HS categories (column 3) and the average cif for only HS2709 and HS 2710 (column 4) which represent over 90% of total oil exports. There is an overall discrepancy of $5.3 billion (col. 4) and $5.7 billion (column 5) between Cameroon's reported oil exports and its top 8 partners' reported imports. Specifically, the results indicate

Table 7.5 Top trading partners for Cameroon's oil, considering all years, over 2000–2021 (constant 2021 US$, million)

Trading partner (importer from Cameroon)	*Cameroon exports (million US$)*	*Partner's imports (million US$)*	*Partner's share (percent exports)*	*Partner's share (percent imports)*
China	3221.8	4713.9	8.3	8.8
France	2052.0	2151.3	5.3	4.0
India	2371.0	3771.5	6.1	7.0
Italy	5007.0	7674.2	12.9	14.3
Netherlands	927.2	899.4	2.4	1.7
Portugal	2573.3	2884.9	6.7	5.4
Spain	7800.6	11,620.4	20.2	21.7
United States	1471.3	4405.5	3.8	8.2
Top 8 partners	25,424.3	38,121.2	65.8	71.2
Total (all partners)	38,632.8	53,542.4	100.0	100.0
Percentage of total	65.8	71.2		

Source Authors' computation

that Cameroon systematically reports a smaller value of oil exports than its partners' reported oil imports from the country. The discrepancies are largest in the case of trade with the United States ($2.2 billion) and Spain ($1.1 billion).

The discrepancies in oil trade data suggest potential structural issues in the recording of oil exports that deserve to be investigated. Investigations of the sources of discrepancies in mirror trade statistics for oil exports would begin by exploring the case of leading trading partners. As oil exports are managed by SNH, it is unlikely that these discrepancies reflect the usual problems of export misinvoicing motivated by access to unrecorded foreign exchange and avoidance of export levies. They nonetheless call for attention with a view to identify strategies for ensuring consistent reporting of bilateral trade statistics as a means of preventing capital flight through export misinvoicing.

Table 7.6 Estimates of misinvoicing of Cameroon's oil exports vis-a-vis major partners, considering only years with matched reporting, over 2000–2021 (constant 2021 US$, million)

	Cameroon exports (1)	*Partners' imports (2)*	*Export misinvoicing (3)*	*Export misinvoicing (4)*
China	3221.8	3485.0	292.9	465.7
France	2039.9	2151.3	−5.6	38.5
India	2208.2	2927.3	664.9	777.0
Italy	5007.0	5865.5	597.1	604.1
Netherlands	833.0	733.6	513.0	528.3
Portugal	2572.8	2531.8	−128.8	−123.2
Spain	7800.6	9532.9	1119.5	1134.0
United States	1471.3	3374.0	2240.2	2283.6
Top 8 partners	25,154.6	30,601.4	5293.2	5708.0
Total (all partners)	38,667.1	53,542.4	12,974.1	10,423.0
Percentage of total	65.1	57.2	35.9	53.3

Source Authors' computations
Notes Export misinvoicing option (3): using the overall average cif/fob ratio across all HS categories; option (4): using only the average for HS2709&2710 (other categories account for very little exports while they have higher cif/fob ratios)

How Much Does the Oil Sector Contribute to the Cameroonian Economy?

A Story of Underperformance and the Many Faces of the "Curse"

Cameroon is a small oil producer from a global perspective. It is small even by African standards, ranking tenth among the continent's leading oil producers. Yet oil still represents an important sector of the Cameroonian economy, with high expectations regarding its contribution to economic development. The oil sector contributed 14.5% of GDP in 1986, but its share has declined significantly, estimated at only 5.4% in 2022.

More importantly, oil draws attention in Cameroon equally for what it contributes to the economy as for what it does not. The story of oil in Cameroon has been a story of unfulfilled expectations; a story of a sector that punches below its weight. Gauthier and Zeufack put it bluntly as follows: "With its abundant natural resource base, varied climate, and diverse population, Cameroon has the potential to be one of the richest countries in sub-Saharan Africa. However, like many resource-rich countries, it has suffered from the natural resources curse" (Gauthier & Zeufack, 2012, p. 155). There is little controversy in the literature that the oil sector in Cameroon has underperformed relative to its potential. Is it a story of "resource curse"? The nuances seem to be about the nature and mechanisms of the "curse," not about its existence.

The standard story of the natural resource curse is that the discovery and exploitation of a natural resource such as oil and minerals generate macroeconomic risks associated with the dominance of the primary commodity in exports, notably overvaluation of the national currency, vulnerability to terms of trade deterioration, unfavorable macroeconomic imbalances, and uneven growth due to limited backward and forward linkages in the overall economy. That is the classic "Dutch disease" (Benjamin et al., 1989). These effects, however, can be mitigated by appropriate macroeconomic, sectoral, and institutional policies that enable the country to harness, rather than suffer from resource dependence. In other words, good policies and efficient institutions are the antidote to the resource curse.[6,7] More specifically the key is whether a country establishes "producer friendly" institutions where "rent-seeking and production are complementary," or "grabber friendly" institutions, where "rent-seeking and production activities are competing" (Mehlum et al., 2006, pp. 2–3).

In the case of Cameroon, empirical and political economy studies have argued that the story of the oil sector is not a classic resource curse, but rather an "institutional curse" or a "governance curse." This argument is extended to other resources beyond oil, notably minerals and timber (Nting, 2019). In other words, Cameroon's inability to harness the potential of its oil sector has to do with the nature of institutions and governance structure that were established to manage the sector. Specifically at issue are decisions regarding (1) investment in the sector and the distribution of the benefits between the state and private enterprises, (2) the collection and management of government oil revenue,

[6] See Dietsche (2006) for a critical perspective on the argument that institutions are a "cure" to the "curse."

[7] Relatedly, there is evidence that the role of the quality of institutions in mitigating government revenue instability is stronger in natural resource-dependent African countries compared to their resource-scarce peers (Nikiema & Zore, 2024).

(3) the utilization of the oil revenue and its allocation between investment and government consumption, (4) an industrial policy to enhance the spillovers in the economy and economic transformation, and (5) the redistribution of the proceeds from oil to the population in the form of public services and social safety nets. An assessment of whether and to what extent Cameroon has suffered a "curse" of any type due to its oil endowment needs to consider the contribution of these mechanisms to the overall unsatisfactory performance.

From a long-term perspective, Cameroon has clearly underperformed relative to its potential, judging by its performance relative to other countries with comparable structural features. Figure 7.5 presents the trend of per capita GDP from 1960 Cameroon in comparison with Sub-Saharan African average and Malaysia. Malaysia and Cameroon share key structural features: small land size and population, geography (tropical), former colonies gaining independence only 3 years apart (1957 for Malaysia and 1960 for Cameroon), high endowment in primary commodities, and agriculture-based economies at independence.[8] But the similarities end there. In terms of economic performance since independence, the two countries belong to two different universes. In 2023 Malaysia's GDP per capita ($11,691) was eight times higher than Cameroon's ($1461).[9] In 1960, the ratio was just 1.4.

Some may argue that this is the typical African story; but in fact, it is not. Cameroon has underperformed even per African standards. Its GDP per capita has lied below SSA's average since independence, except for 1981–1992. Indeed, Cameroon experienced a "growth spurt" in the mid-1970s, with GDP per capita rising rapidly from $1124 in 1977, coinciding with the start of oil production, to $1,833 in 1986. The country, however, was unable to sustain the growth spurt, partly due to a decline in world prices of primary commodities including oil and minerals. GDP per capita was down to $1,060 in 1993, on the eve of the 1994 FCFA devaluation. It resumed steady but slow growth since then, remaining below the SSA average. The slow pace obviously widened the income gap relative to Malaysia which enjoyed robust and sustained growth through its post-independence period. Today Malaysia is an upper middle-income country

[8] See Gauthier and Zeufack (2012).

[9] World Development Indicators, 2023 values.

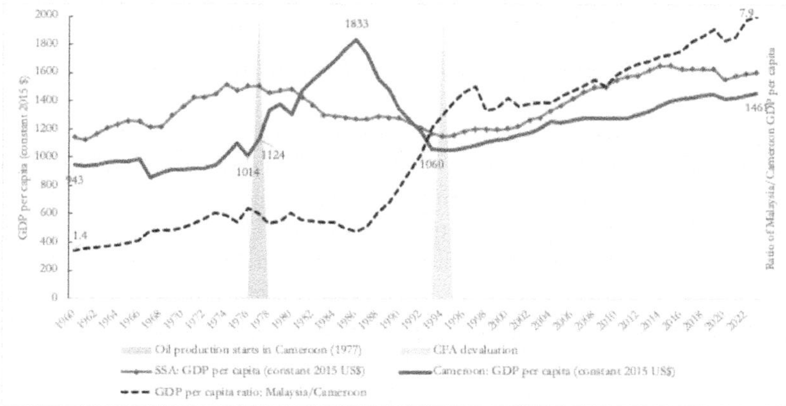

Fig. 7.5 Short lived "growth spurt" in Cameroon: Failure to sustain the gains from oil (*Source* Authors' construction using data from World Development Indicators)

(GNI per capita at $11,140) while Cameroon is still at the bottom of the lower middle-income group (GNI per capita at $1439).[10]

Cameroon's failure to harness its endowment in oil and other resources to generate strong growth explains the limited performance in all dimensions of economic and social development. What has happened to Cameroon's oil sector? Why did Malaysia succeed while Cameroon failed to leverage its natural resource potential? The answers to this complex question are also complex. They include a combination of bad policies and bad institutions that made it difficult for Cameroon to optimize revenue generation, and to mitigate the exogenous shocks that affect the resource sector and the economy in general. In the remainder of this section, we address some of these factors focusing on failed diversification and ineffective mobilization and management of government revenue from the oil sector. The section closes by presenting some stylized facts about poverty and social development and a discussion of possible linkages with the oil sector.

[10] According to World Bank classification lower middle-income economies are those with a GNI per capita between $1146 and $4515; upper middle-income economies are those with a GNI per capita between $4516 and $14,005 (https://datahelpdesk.worldbank.org/knowledgebase/articles/906519).

Elusive Economic Transformation

Resource-rich countries that have succeeded in reaching high levels of income and social development are those that managed to "graduate" from natural resource dependence. This typically occurs through steady transformation of the economy from a primary-sector-based economy into a manufacturing-based economy, driven by increased productivity supported by high investment and technological innovation. In the case of Cameroon, there has been little transformation of the structure of its economy since independence. The country has failed to industrialize as manifested by stagnant manufacturing production over time. Today, manufacturing value added represents less than 13% of GDP and its share has stagnated since the early 1990s. The economy is currently dominated by the services sector (50%), with a substantial share of the primary sector (24%). The share of the oil sector has declined significantly, from 14.5% in 1986 to only 5.4% in 2020.

The empirical economics literature has raised concerns about "premature deindustrialization"[11] in developing and emerging countries, whereby the industrial sector (and manufacturing especially) shrinks, not in favor of services necessarily as in advanced economies, but in favor of extractive sectors instead, arguably to take advantage of high commodity prices (Andreoni & Tregenna, 2021; Grabowski, 2015; Imbs, 2013; Tregenna, 2016).[12] In such cases, deindustrialization is characterized by entrenched dependence on primary commodities. In the case of Cameroon, industrialization in fact never took off to start with. Therefore, the term "deindustrialization" does not apply to Cameroon.

The failure of industrialization in Cameroon is manifested in the predominance of primary commodities in exports. As can be seen in Table 7.7, Cameroon's exports are dominated by mineral fuels, lubricants, and related materials that account for 50.8% of total exports today (average over 2020–2023), an increase from 33.6% in the 1990s. In contrast, the share of manufactured products in total exports is two percentage points lower today (6.8%) than in the 1970s (8.6%). By comparison, Malaysia has been riding a rapid manufacturing-driven economic transformation path. The share of manufactured goods in total

[11] Attention to the phenomenon of premature industrialization has increased, led by influential work by Dani Rodrik (Rodrik 2016).

[12] Also see Page et al. (2016).

exports rose from 13% in the 1970s to a commanding 77% in the 1990s and is at 69% today.

Another indicator of economic transformation is the sophistication of a country's export basket, which is a driver of global competitiveness. That can be gauged by the technology content of a country's exports. For Malaysia, "high-skill and technology-intensive manufactures" represented more than half of exports in the 1990s (54%) and the share is at 47% today. Cameroon's exports contain less than 2% of such sophisticated products. This means that Cameroon is still operating at a very low level of the global technology value chain, implying that it is also at the losing end regarding terms of trade.

Economic transformation requires leveraging natural resource revenue to scale up saving and investment, which helps to raise the production capacity and productivity. Economies that have successfully transformed into a manufacturing dominated structure are characterized by high saving and investment rates. This is evident in the case of Malaysia (Table 7.7). Not only its domestic saving rate has been high, but it also has exceeded domestic investment. In the 1990s, a 40% saving rate fueled a 33% investment rate, which helped sustain the high growth rate (averaging 7.2% in the decade). In contrast, Cameroon has posted lower saving and investment rates, with investment outpacing saving, leading to chronic resource gaps. This is one of the factors of the low average growth rates and the failure to fuel structural transformation of the economy.

A major driver of successful economic transformation and industrialization is a combination of good economic policies and high-quality institutions. Here again there is a sharp contrast between Cameroon and Malaysia. Malaysia's economic performance has been driven and sustained by high government efficiency in the delivery of services, regulation, and enforcement of the rule of law. Such an institutional environment promotes entrepreneurship, innovation, and investment. In contrast, Cameroon is at the opposite end of the spectrum in terms of quality of institutions. Perception of corruption is twice as high, with a current index of 27 compared to 50 on the scale of 0–100 (higher means less corruption). Indicators of effectiveness of the government are half of those of Malaysia. Clearly, weak institutions are a major constraint to economic transformation in Cameroon.

Table 7.7 Economic performance and institutional quality in Cameroon compared to Malaysia from 1970 to 2023

Indicator (averages)	*Cameroon*			*Malaysia*		
	1970s	*1990s*	*2020–2023*	*1970s*	*1990s*	*2020–2023*
GDP, growth, saving and investment						
GDP per capita (constant 2015 US$)	1067	1132	1443	2418	5474	11,691
GDP growth (percent)	7.3	0.2	3.6	8.2	7.2	5.2
Gross capital formation (percent of GDP)	21.4	16.8	17.8	23.7	36.3	22.7
Gross domestic savings (percent of GDP)	18.3	20.9	15.0	28.0	40.6	29.2
Export composition (percent of total)						
Mineral fuels, lubricants, and related materials	2.8	33.6	50.8	11.0	7.2	14.4
Manufactured goods	8.6	6.6	6.8	13.2	77.1	69.4
High-skill and technology-intensive manufactures		1.0	1.9		54.2	47.2
Governance and institutional quality						
Corruption perception score (0–100)		26	27 (2023)		49	50 (2023)
Control of corruption (0–5)		1.2	1.4		2.9	2.7
Government effectiveness (0–5)		1.5	1.6		3.1	3.5
Memorandum: Change in GDP per capita from 1970 to 2023: Cameroon: 59%; Malaysia: 538%						

Source Export composition from UNCTAD; GDP, growth, saving, investment, governance from World Development Indicators; Corruption perception index from Transparency International

The "Tragedy of Sediments"

The failure to achieve structural economic transformation in Cameroon reflects the phenomenon of "tragedy of sediments" that plagues oil-rich developing countries. The tragedy of sediments describes the paradox whereby a country remains trapped in a cycle of dependence on a finite resource such as oil. Rather than transitioning toward diversification and innovation, the country continues to layer new extractive efforts on top of previous ones—hence the term "sediments"—to sustain current levels of growth and revenue. That is the story of Cameroon. Several models predicted the depletion of Cameroon's oil reserves by the early 2000s, prompting the government to launch an intensified exploration campaign to expand and extend the life of its oil reserves (Djiofack, 2011). While this push to discover new oil reserves may delay the depletion, it deepens the reliance on a resource that is finite. Each new discovery, rather than solving the underlying issue, merely postpones the inevitable decline, trapping the economy further in layers of "sedimented dependence."

A country's chance of avoiding the full realization of the tragedy of sediments depends not on the sheer availability of oil but on the ability to foster independence from oil through innovation and economic diversification. Although the government of Cameroon has succeeded in establishing a fiscal regime that asserts its control over oil revenues, it has yet to channel these funds into sectors that can sustain long-term economic diversification (International Monetary Fund, 2022; World Bank, 2022). Economic transformation will require investments in industries beyond oil, such as manufacturing, renewable energy, and agro-industry, which could shield the economy from the volatility of oil markets.

The tragedy of sediments also ties into the broader theoretical concept of path dependence[13] by emphasizing how early decisions to prioritize oil extraction can lock the economy into a trajectory that is difficult to escape. Even as the government of Cameroon, through the SNH, controls some portion of the oil revenue, the lack of diversification reflects a failure to break free from the path that was set decades ago. Control over oil revenue has fostered political patronage and corruption, further entrenching the status quo and undermining efforts to reform the system (Rosellini, 2006). The cumulative effects of this behavior mirror the

[13] See North (1991; 1993).

layering of sediments, building a system that becomes harder to break up over time.

The tragedy of sediments offers an insightful perspective on the Cameroonian oil sector, besides existing frameworks such as the resource curse and *extractivism*, by highlighting the paradox of control and dependence. While the Cameroonian government has successfully taken control of the management of its oil sector, this very control has created a form of dependence that has proven difficult to escape. Unlike resource-rich countries that have successfully diversified their economies (Chile, Malaysia, Norway, Qatar, United Arab Emirates), Cameroon remains trapped into dependence on oil extraction until it can operate a regime shift toward a future beyond oil. While this theory acknowledges the agency of the Cameroonian government, it stresses that state control over oil resources does not necessarily guarantee long-run economic success. Rather, successful leveraging of oil exploitation requires a shift from extraction to diversification and innovation, enabling the country to truly overcome the tragedy of sediments.

Government Revenue Generation from the Oil Sector

The oil sector is expected to generate government revenue through various fiscal instruments such as corporate income tax and non-fiscal instruments such as oil rents and other levies. Government revenue collection has tracked oil production, increasing since the early 1990s till the 2008 global financial crisis (Fig. 7.6). However, revenue has fluctuated due to the volatility of international oil prices and fluctuations in oil production, exports, and imports. At its peak in 1991, oil revenue represented 65.7% of total government revenue. It declined hereafter, dipping below 30% in some years, but it recovered steadily from 2002, reaching another peak at 62.2% in 2007. Since then, oil revenue has broadly trended down, reaching an all-time low of 15.3% of total government revenue in 2015.

Has the oil sector generated government revenue in proportion to its potential? To shed light on this question, we compare Cameroon with other oil exporters, looking at oil rents generated in relation to the potential as indicated by the volume of oil exports. The data indicate that Cameroon has underperformed relative to the volume of exports and relative to other African oil exporters. As can be seen in Fig. 7.7, Cameroon is below the trend line, meaning that the oil sector has generated less

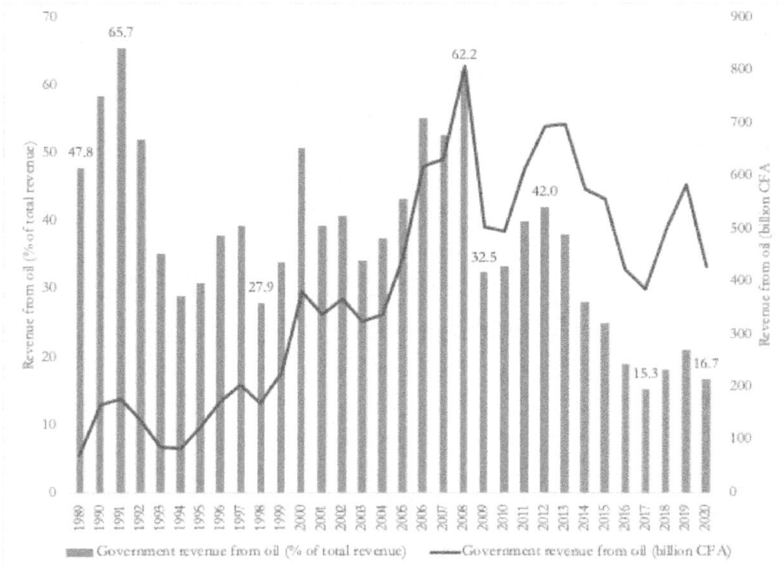

Fig. 7.6 Government revenue from oil in Cameroon, 1989–2020 (*Source* Authors' construction using data from BEAC)

rents than potentially feasible given the volume of oil exports. This raises questions as to whether the rates of rents are too low and whether the rents are not collected efficiently.

The ability of the oil sector to contribute to growth and economic transformation depends not only on the level of government revenue that is mobilized, but also and very importantly on how the revenue is managed. The first question is about how much revenue is spent and what fraction is saved for future investment. There is no commonly agreed rule about the optimal split between the two allocations. On the one hand, a developing country like Cameroon needs to maximize investment of the oil revenue to expand productive capacity to stimulate growth and economic transformation. On the other hand, some of the revenue must be saved to finance investment in the future, and to help cushion the economy against exogenous shocks. The second decision is about allocation of the oil revenue between productive activities and non-productive

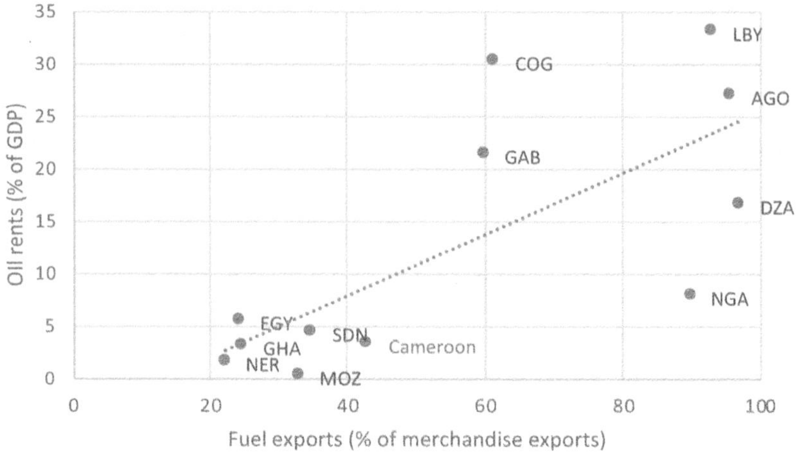

Fig. 7.7 Oil rents and fuel exports: Cameroon compared to other African oil exporting countries (average 2010–2021) (*Source* Authors' construction using data from the World Bank's World Development Indictors)

consumption. The third decision concerns the establishment of mechanisms of transparency in the management of the oil revenue to enhance efficiency and accountability. The fourth is the decision about mechanisms of distribution of the oil revenue between the state and the local communities hosting the oil reserves. All these decisions ultimately affect the overall efficiency of the use of oil revenue in terms of economic transformation, the benefits to communities, social cohesion, and political stability.

The most important factor that drives the efficiency of the use and allocation of government oil revenue is the quality of institutions and the regulatory framework governing the management of oil revenue. In this regard, the weakness of the institutional framework as illustrated earlier (Table 7.7) constitutes a major constraint to efficient oil revenue management in Cameroon. High-quality institutions were a major reason for efficient management of oil revenue and the impressive economic performance in the case of Malaysia. As Gauthier and Zeufack put it, "Transparency in oil revenue management has allowed the oil sector to become a central piece of Malaysia's economic policy and development. … In stark contrast, because of the lack of transparency in Cameroon, the oil sector has remained an enclave and has not been engaged systematically in the medium- to long-term development planning for the country" (Gauthier & Zeufack, 2012, p. 160).

Transparency problems have characterized oil revenue management in Cameroon since the beginning of oil exploitation in the 1970s. At that time, oil revenue management was under the control of the Presidency, which compromised independence and accountability. It was reported that oil revenue was held in some "secret accounts" (DeLancey, 2019), thus shielding it from public scrutiny (Gauthier & Zeufack, 2012; Keutiben et al., 2022). Over time, reforms have been undertaken to increase transparency and efficiency in oil revenue management. This started with the creation of the Société Nationale des Hydrocarbures (SNH) in 1980 (Decree of 12/03/1980) with the dual mandate of promoting the development of hydrocarbons in Cameroon and managing the state's interests in the oil sector including its shares in international oil companies and crude oil production (SNH's website). The SNH serves both as a regulator of the oil sector and a joint-venture associate in all oil activities undertaken by private oil producing companies. This dual role as a regulator and an operator can be a source of complexity and even opacity in the management of oil revenue (Gauthier & Zeufack, 2012, p. 161).

Further reforms were undertaken in the context of reforms sponsored by the Bretton Woods Institutions, notably the standby agreements with the IMF in 1991 and the HIPC initiative in late 1990s-early 2000s. Another boost came with the country's entry into the EITI in 2007, which was expected to improve the reporting of tax and non-tax payments by oil companies.

One important instrument for increasing transparency in the management of oil revenue is fiscal transparency, notably through disclosure of information on the level and financing of government spending in the budget process. In its 2023 report, the International Budget Partnership noted that "Cameroon has increased the availability of budget information by increasing the information provided in the Executive's Budget Proposal, increasing the information provided in the Pre-Budget Statement and Year-End Report." However, the IBP report noted that the availability of budget information had declined in some respects and recommended remedial actions to improve transparency.[14] Transparency in management of oil revenue remains indeed work in progress.

The Oil Sector and Socio-Economic Development

The endowment in oil and other natural resources is expected to enable a country to achieve high standards of living for the population. On that yard stick, Cameroon has performed below its potential. If once again we compare Cameroon to Malaysia, the differences could not be sharper (Table 7.8). Malaysia has eliminated poverty in the sense that no citizen lives below the poverty line of $2.15 today. While Cameroon has made strides in reducing poverty, 23% of Cameroonians still live below the poverty line.

According to the World Bank's statistics, the poverty rate in Cameroon (at $3.65 per person per day) declined from 50.5% in 1996 to 23% in 2021. These rates are lower than the average for Sub-Saharan Africa which declined from 57.4% to 36.7% over the same period. The results of the latest household survey indicate that the poverty rate at the national level declined marginally from 40.2% in 2001 to 38.6% in 2021 (Fig. 7.8).

Table 7.8 Indicators of social and economic development in Cameroon compared to Malaysia (2023 or latest reported)

Indicator	*Cameroon*	*Malaysia*
Poverty headcount ratio at $2.15 a day (2017 PPP) (percent of population)	23.0	0.0
Mortality rate, infant (per 1,000 live births)	47	6.7
Share of youth not in education, employment or training, total (percent of youth population)	23.2	9.3
Unemployment with advanced education (percent of total labor force with advanced education)	18.8	4.6

Source World Development Indicators

[14] The IBP recommended the following: (i) Publish the In-Year Reports, Mid-Year Review, and Audit Report online in a timely manner; (ii) Include data on the financial position of the government in the Executive's Budget Proposal and data on the macroeconomic forecast; (iii) In addition, estimates on future liabilities and financial sustainability over at least a 10-year horizon, tax expenditures, and earmarked revenues should be provided.

However, the national averages hide significant disparities between the rural area and urban centers. While over half of the rural population lived in extreme poverty in 2021 (58.3%), only 16.5% of the urban population were recorded as poor. For the cities of Douala and Yaoundé, the rates are as low as 8.3% and 10.8%, respectively. It is also important to stress that while there has been significant progress in reducing poverty, the performance still falls short of the national development target of 30.8%, suggesting that there is still plenty of work to do to eradicate poverty.

Moreover, the results of the latest household survey reveal some worrisome trends. First, while the poverty rates have declined, the number of poor people continues to grow due, "on the one hand, to demographic growth, and on the other hand to the strong internal mobility of populations as a result of insecurity in certain localities, exodus of youths to the cities in search of employment, and climate change especially in the Far-North region" (National Institute of Statistics, 2024, p. 5). The second fact is high vulnerability to poverty. In addition to the 37.7% of the Cameroonian population that are identified as poor, 11.9% of the people are not poor but vulnerable to poverty, and 9.6% are insecure since they are likely to fall into poverty. Overall, only 40.8% of the population is considered non-poor and non-vulnerable to poverty. This implies that the

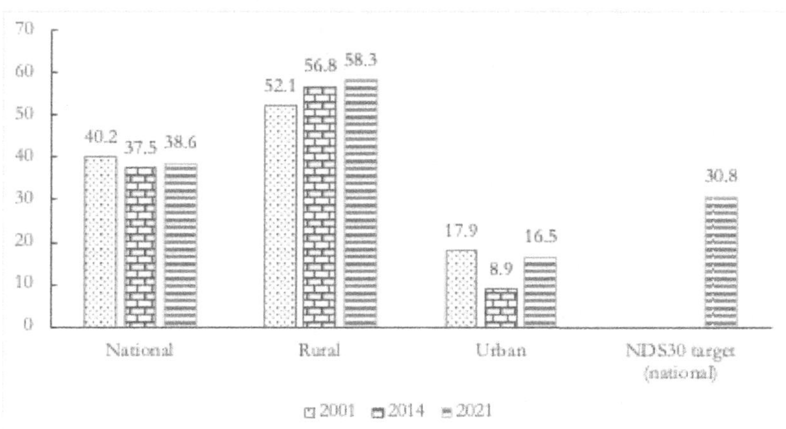

Fig. 7.8 Poverty in Cameroon at the national level and in urban and rural areas, 2001–2021 (*Source* Authors' construction using data from National Institute of Statistics 2024)

standard measures of poverty substantially underestimate the precarity of the living conditions of more than half of the Cameroonian population.

The results of the household survey also show significant disparities of poverty incidence across regions (Fig. 7.9). The rates vary from the highest in the Far-North region (69.2%) to the lowest in the South region (14.9%).

The analysis of the data on poverty raises one important question: has oil endowment contributed to improvement of the living standards of the population? Specifically, are the regions that host oil reserves better off than others in terms of poverty incidence? Oil reserves are in Littoral and South-West regions and at the border of the South region. It turns out that these regions, indeed, have relatively lower poverty rates than regions that are situated further away from the oil reserves (except for the center region which includes Yaoundé). Regions situated further from the oil fields have less possibilities of employment creation directly and indirectly from oil sector activities. They are further disadvantaged as they incur higher prices of oil products due to transport and distribution surcharges. More detailed analysis is needed to explore the mechanisms

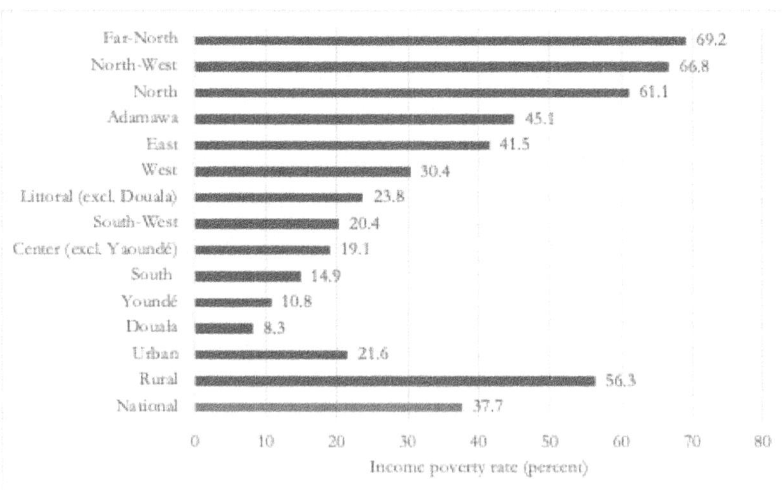

Fig. 7.9 Poverty rates in Cameroon by region in 2021 (percent) (*Source* Survey by the National Institute of Statistics [2014])

through which regions hosting oil reserves may be deriving comparative advantages from oil exploitation in yielding lower poverty levels.

In addition to the poverty reduction goal, Cameroon continues to perform poorly on other dimensions of social development relative to its potential. For example, while infant mortality has declined by half since the 1990s, it is still at 47 per 1000 live births, which is more than six time the rate in Malaysia (6.7% 1000 live births). Moreover, Cameroon faces the pressing issue of youth unemployment. Like other African countries, while Cameroon has succeeded in expanding access to education, it now faces a serious problem of youth unemployment. About one-fifth of college graduates are unemployed, compared to only 4.6% in Malaysia. More than 23% of the youth are not in school, employment, or training and the numbers are increasing steadily, illustrating that the economy is not generating sufficient opportunities for gainful employment in relation to the rate of school completion. This poses both economic problems in terms of underutilization of human capital, but also and very importantly, it creates potential risks of social and political instability. The case of the 2011 "Arab Spring" in North Africa and the Middle East, which was a revolution initiated and led by educated, unemployed, and desperate youth, should be a reminder that youth unemployment is a serious threat to national security and must be dealt with utmost urgency.

Conclusion

The analysis of the oil sector in Cameroon presented in this chapter carries important lessons for Cameroon as well as other resource-rich countries in Africa in terms of the complex challenges they face in harnessing their resource endowment, and in preventing financial hemorrhage through capital flight that tends to plague resource-dependent developing countries. The story of oil in Cameroon is a story of "dual dependence." Cameroon is both a producer-exporter of oil and an importer of crude oil for its refinery (currently on halt since 2019) and processed oil products for domestic consumption. In an odd arrangement, its refinery was initially set up to only process light crude, which the country does not produce. This is a severe constraint to the country's capacity to develop a competitive value chain in the oil sector and reap beneficial terms of trade in the global economy. This has been an important factor for the country's failed economic transformation agenda.

The second face of dependence in the oil sector is the dominance of international companies, a legacy of the pre-colonial era since the beginning of oil exploration. This means that the country only gets a fraction of the value of its oil through the instruments of its fiscal regime. It is, nonetheless, important to note that relative to other oil producers in Africa, Cameroon has set up a regime that enables the government to have a stake in the sector through the SNH which operates both as a regulator and as an associate investor in private oil companies. Thus, the government benefits from production sharing, in addition to the standard fiscal instruments such as oil rents and corporate income tax. However, the analysis in this study and the evidence in the literature have shown that Cameroon still punches below its weight in terms of revenue generation from the oil sector. Despite the important merits of the design of the existing fiscal regime there are serious concerns about the efficiency in the management of government revenue, especially the lack of transparency in the use of the oil revenue (Gauthier & Zeufack, 2011, 2012). The issue then is less a matter of design of the fiscal regime and more a problem of governance of the revenue from oil. Therefore, efforts to improve the performance of the oil sector and to optimize its impact on the national economy and to enhance its role in economic transformation, must be anchored on strategies to improve governance of oil revenue notably through higher transparency and efficiency in its utilization.

The organizational structure of the oil sector that gives an important role for the state-owned SNH provides a mechanism for ensuring that the country optimizes its benefits from oil in terms of foreign exchange earnings flowing into the country. This is a perennial problem in resource-rich countries in Africa in countries where there are no rules about the repatriation of export proceeds, as in Zambia before the establishment of the Bank of Zambia's Export Proceeds Tracking Framework directives in December 2023 (Chapter 5),[15] or where those rules are negotiated on a company-by-company basis such as in the gold sector in Ghana (Chapter 3). Without clear and well-enforced rules on the repatriation of foreign exchange proceeds from exports, it is impossible to ensure that resource export booms generate commensurate benefits in terms of foreign exchange inflows.

[15] As of November 2024, 13 African countries have no specific requirements on repatriation of foreign exchange proceeds. Source: IMF AREAER, November 2024, https://www.elibrary-areaer.imf.org/Pages/Home.aspx.

The analysis in this chapter shows that Cameroon has not sufficiently harnessed its oil endowment to achieve commensurate improvements in the living standards of its population. This is mainly a result of inefficiencies in the utilization of oil revenue and the failure to leverage the oil endowment to fuel economic transformation. The comparison of Cameroon to a country like Malaysia that has similar structural attributes sheds light on the staggering differences in terms of overall macroeconomic performance and social development, illustrating the inability of Cameroon to leverage its oil endowment. It is a manifestation of the "resource curse"; and specifically an "institutional curse" in the sense that the culprit is the poor quality of the institutions, not oil endowment per se. Consequently, efforts to improve the country's development prospects must focus on institutional reforms in general, and on reforms of oil revenue governance in particular.

References

Africa Energy Chamber. (2024). Opinion: Perenco's 'Substantial' Oil and Gas Investments in Cameroon Unlock African Energy Security. *World Oil* (August 8).

Andreoni, A., & Tregenna, F. (2021). The Middle-Income Trap and Premature Deindustrialization in South Africa. In A. Andreoni & F. Tregenna (Eds.), *Structural Transformation in South Africa: The Challenges of Inclusive Industrial Development in a Middle-Income Country* (pp. 237–260). Oxford University Press.

Benjamin, N. C., Devarajan, S., & Weiner, R. J. (1989). The 'Dutch' Disease in a Developing Country: Oil Reserves in Cameroon. *Journal of Development Economics, 30*(1), 71–92.

Cording, M., Nie, W. (2024). *Dealing with Differences: Sinopec's Acquisition of Addax Petroleum (A).* International Institute for Management Development (IMD).

Cossé, S. (2006). *Strengthening Transparency in the Oil Sector in Cameroon: Why Does It Matter?* IMF Policy Discussion Paper PDP/06/2. Washington, DC: International Monetary Fund (March).

DeLancey, M. W. (2019). *Cameroon: Dependence and Independence.* Routledge.

Dietsche, E. (2006). Why the Quality of Institutions Is Not a Cure for the Resource Curse. *Journal of Energy and Development, 32,* 262–282.

Djiofack, C. Z., & Omgba, L. D. (2011). Oil depletion and development in Cameroon: A critical appraisal of the permanent income hypothesis. *Energy Policy, 39*(11), 7202–7216.

DSCN & DIAL. (1993). *L'industrie Camerounaise dans la Crise 1984–1992.* République du Cameroun.

EITI. (2023). *Cameroon EITI 2021 Report*. EITI (online).

——— (2024). Cameroon Achieves Fairly Low Score in EITI Implementation. EIT.

Energy Capital & Power. (2023). Perenco Signs 20 Year for Continued Operations Offshore Cameroon. *Further Africa*. https://furtherafrica.com/2023/06/21/perenco-signs-20-year-for-continued-operations-offshore-cameroon/.

Foka, N. R. M. E. (2024). Hurdles of Technology Transfer in Cameroon's Petroleum Industry. *International Journal of Research and Innovation in Applied Science, 9*(1), 01–13.

Gauthier, B., & Zeufack, A. (2011). *Governance and Oil Revenues in Cameroon* (p. 38). University of Oxford, OxCarre Research Paper.

Gauthier, B., & Zeufack, A. (2012). Cameroon's Oil Wealth: Transparency Matters. In B. Akitoby & S. Coorey (Eds.), *Oil Wealth in Central Africa: Policies for Inclusive Growth* (pp. 155–168). International Monetary Fund.

Grabowski, R. (2015). Deindustrialization in Africa. *International Journal of African Development, 3*(1), 51–67.

Hydrocarbons Prices Stabilization Fund (HPSF) (2021, June 10). Press Release of the 47th Ordinary Session of the Board of Directors. Yaoundé, Cameroon: Caisse de Stabilisation des Prix des Hydrocarbures (CSPH). https://www.csph.cm/new_details.php?p_id=4, Accessed on 24 April 2026.

Imbs, J. (2013). The Premature Deindustrialization of South Africa. In Lin, J. Y., J. Stiglitz, and E Patel (Eds.). *The Industrial Policy Revolution II: Africa in the 21st Century* (pp. 529–40). Palgrave MacMillan.

International Monetary Fund. 2022. *Cameroon: 2021 Article IV Consultation and First Reviews Under the Extended Credit Facility*. IMF staff report.

Keutiben, O., Tatoutchoup, F. D., & Bahel, E. (2022). Oil Revenue Management: Cameroon's Experience. In C. Monga (Ed.), *The Oxford Handbook of The Economy of Cameroon* (pp. 635–647). Oxford University Press.

Mehlum, H., Moene, K., & Torvik, R. (2006). Institutions and the Resource Curse. *The Economic Journal, 116*(508), 1–20.

Mpenya, A. H. T., Metseyem, C., & Ngah, B. (2016). Natural Resources and Capital Flight in Cameroon. *African Development Review, 28*(S1), 88–99.

National Institute of Statistics. (2024). *Fifth Cameroon Household Survey. Situation of Household Living Conditions in 2021–2022. Guidance Policy Note (January)*. Survey Conducted by the National Institute of Statistics with the Government and World Bank Financial Support. Yaoundé: NIS.

Ndikumana, L., & Boyce, J. K. (2022). *On the Trail of Capital Flight from Africa: The Takers and the Enablers*. Oxford University Press.

Ndikumana, L., & Boyce, J. K. (2025). *New Estimates of Capital Flight from African Countries, 1970–2022.* PERI Research Report (January). Amherst: Political Economy Research Institute.

Ndikumana, L. & M. Sarr (2019). Capital Flight, Foreign Direct Investment and Natural Resources in Africa. *Resources Policy 63*, article no. 101427 (October).

North, D. C. (1991). Towards a Theory of Institutional Change. *Quarterly Review of Economics and Business, 31*(4), 3–12.

North, D. C. (1993). The New Institutional Economics and Development. *Economic History, 9309002,* 1–8.

Nting, R. T. (2019). The Political Economy of Mineral Exploitation in Cameroon. *African Research Review, 13*(1), 1–13.

Page, J., Tarp, F., Rand, J., Shimeles, A., Newman, C., & Söderbom, M. (2016). *Manufacturing Transformation: Comparative Studies of Industrial Development in Africa and Emerging Asia.* Oxford University Press.

Parenco. (2023). *Sustainability Report.* https://www.perenco.com/wp-content/uploads/2024/07/2023-ESG-Report.pdf

Perrot, C. (1988). *Energie et Matières Premières. Histoire et Géographie Économique.* Editions Bréal Montreuil.

Pokam Kamdem, M. W. (2022). Devenir pétrolier et le rester. Une histoire de la quête d'hydrocarbures au Cameroun (1904–2000). *Journal Gabonais d'Histoire Économique et Sociale (JGHES),* (9), 61–80.

Presidency of the Republic of Cameroon. (2019). *Law N° 2019/008 of 25 April 2019 to Institute the Petroleum Code.*

Rodrik, D. (2016). Premature Deindustrialization. *Journal of Economic Growth, 21,* 1–33.

SCDP. Société Camerounaise des Dépôts Pétroliers. (2022). *Rapport Annuel 2021–2022. Une Dynamique Post-Covid.* Douala: SCDP.

Tregenna, F. (2016). Deindustrialization and Premature Deindustrialization. In E. S. Reinart, J. Ghosh, & K. Rainer (Eds.), *Handbook of Alternative Theories of Economic Development* (pp. 710–728). Edward Edgard Publishing.

Whiteaker, J. (2020). The State of Play: FDI in Cameroon. *Investment Monitor.* https://www.investmentmonitor.ai/extractive-industries/the-state-of-play-fdi-in-cameroon/

World Bank (2018). The Changing Wealth of Nations 2018: Building a Sustainable Future. Washington, DC: World Bank.

World Bank. (2022). *Cameroon Country Climate and Development Report.* Washington, DC: World Bank. https://openknowledge.worldbank.org/server/api/core/bitstreams/9deeaf4b-a936-5e56-9397-21780f1d764d/content

Zore, M. & Nikiema, R. (2024). Tax revenue instability in Sub-Saharan Africa: Does institutional quality matter? *The American Journal of Economics and Sociology, 84*(1), 153–177.

CHAPTER 8

Conclusion: A New Strategy to Leverage Africa's Natural Resources

Léonce Ndikumana

Introduction

In concluding our 2022 volume on capital flight from Africa, we noted that "In the make-believe world of the perfect neoclassical economy, capital flight from sub-Saharan Africa would be a cruel irony… Natural resources, like oil, hard minerals, and fertile land, would be a sheer blessing, not a curse" (Ndikumana & Boyce, 2022, p. 235). But we pointed out that in the real world, "Natural resources are a hunting ground for rapid wealth extraction and accumulation, and capital flows across borders are driven not by relative scarcity but by the relative secrecy available in offshore havens." We added that "In this all-too-real world, capital flight from Africa … comes as no surprise. It is not ironic, simply cruel." The case studies on Cameroon, Ghana, and Zambia presented in this book provide vivid illustrations of the pernicious connections between capital flight and natural resources in a context of global systems of investment, trade, and finance that enable and perpetuate the plunder of African resources inherited from the pre-colonial and colonial eras and dominated by powerful multinational corporations. It is a bitter reminder that

L. Ndikumana, *Capital Flight from Cameroon, Ghana, and Zambia*, https://doi.org/10.1007/978-3-032-22770-6_8

"there is nothing new under the sun,"[1] in that today's control of African resources by multinational corporations is only a repeat of what has always been. Capital flight is a key mechanism of the perpetuation of the plunder of Africa's natural resources.

The Scale and Costs of Capital Flight

The evidence presented in this book demonstrates that capital flight from Africa is chronic, and in fact worsening, as the volumes of outflows continue to accelerate over time. The three countries covered in this study bear testimony to the financial hemorrhage suffered by African countries. Over the past five decades, from 1970 to 2022, Cameroon, Ghana, and Zambia have lost staggering amounts of $97.7 billion, $85.7 billion and $79.6 billion, respectively, through capital flight. Following established practice in the literature, capital flight is defined as funds that appear to have flown out of the country without being recorded in the government's official statistics as summarized in the country's Balance of Payments. In other words, it is the residual inflows of foreign exchange that cannot be traced in the various forms of use or reserves of foreign exchange.

The losses suffered by African countries from capital flight exceed the annual capital inflows into the continent. Had these funds stayed and been invested in the source countries, they would have expanded the productive capacity of these economies and boosted economic growth. Instead, these funds are stashed offshore and they accumulate value to the benefit of the asset owners. While some of the funds are consumed, the majority is invested in income generating assets such as bank accounts, real estate, and other valuable objects. Using a conservative assumption that the funds have earned interest at the modest US Treasury Bill rate, we find that the stock of wealth accumulated from capital flight from Cameroon, Ghana, and Zambia amounts to $111 billion, $81 billion, and $87 billion respectively. The earnings on this wealth are not taxed as they are held abroad in disguised forms out of sight of the tax authority. The accumulation of such massive private wealth offshore also worsens inequality in these countries given that the owners of such wealth, who are already in

[1] The phrase is attributed to Ecclesiastes 1:9 in the Bible and means that what exists today is only a repetition of what has always been, reflecting a cyclical and unchanging nature of human existence and the world around us.

the top strata of the income distribution, are shielded not only from taxation but also from the impact of depreciation of the national currency. Ultimately, capital flight has adverse distributional effects in addition to the damage done by draining investment capital from the continent.

Even as these countries experience hemorrhage through capital flight, they continue to lag severely behind their development goals, especially the objective of achieving decent living standards for their populations. In Cameroon, over 60% of the population in Far-North, North-West, and North regions live below the poverty line. On average 38% of the Cameroonian population is considered poor. In Ghana, poverty rates are as high as 70% in Upper West region, 61% in Northern region, and 55% in Upper East region. About 60% of Zambian people are considered poor and 48% are extremely poor. The poverty rates exceed 76% in five regions. And in each of these three countries, poverty is either stagnant or rising in some places.

In addition to high and stubborn poverty rates, the three countries studied in this book also portray substantial gaps in access to basic social services that undermine the wellbeing of the population. The funds that leak out of the countries through capital flight, some of which are from the plunder of natural resources, could be used to scale up investments in public infrastructure and vital social services such as education and health. Capital flight from Zambia represents 10% of GDP on an annual basis. This is twice the current total expenditures on health and 4 times government health expenditures.[2] For Cameroon, capital flight (7% of GDP) is more than twice government health expenditures. Similarly, capital flight (3.2% of GDP) is 1.5 times government expenditures on health in Ghana. Clearly these countries could significantly scale up their investments on health and education if they could curb capital flight. Therefore, policy discussions on strategies to improve the provision of social services and accelerate the fight against poverty must incorporate an agenda for fighting capital flight.

[2] The figures on health and education expenditures cited in this paragraph are from the World Bank's World Development Indicators (accessible online).

Natural Resources and Perverse Connections

Being endowed in natural resources is supposed to provide a "comparative advantage" to a country as a basis for long-term development. In *The Changing Wealth of Nations 2021*, The World Bank stated that "Natural capital is a key endowment for lower-income countries, and harnessing nature to invest in other assets is a key component of economic development. But building an economy is not about liquidating natural capital to build other assets. Natural capital per capita increases with income level, but the share declines as other assets are added" (World Bank, 2021, p. 79).[3] Indeed, development requires a smart use of a country's natural capital: "Development is about more efficient use of capital… bringing to bear other assets to increase productivity, together with the strong institutions and policies that make investment attractive" (Lange et al., 2018, p. 9). In the mid-70's, John Hartwick (1977) suggested a simple rule of thumb, that is now known as "the Hartwick rule," stating that countries that depend on nonrenewable natural resources can achieve sustainable development (simply defined as stable consumption per capita) if the rents from nonrenewable resources are continuously invested rather than used for consumption. In other words, the proceeds from natural resource exploitation must be used to build up the production capacity of the economy.[4]

This seemingly simple rule of natural resource management has eluded resource-rich African countries in general, and specifically the three countries that are examined in this book. Their abundant natural capital has not helped to propel them to a path of sustained development. A key reason is that both on the domestic and global sides, the linkages between natural resources and the national economy have been perverse rather than constructive. By perverse connections we refer to the situations where the use and management of natural resources generate unintended outcomes that harm, rather than benefit the national economy, the local communities, and the environment. The three case studies presented in this book have witnessed perverse connections associated with the linkages between African resource-rich countries and the rest of the world. While resource exploitation was expected to fuel beneficial integration of African economies in the global economy, it has primarily benefited

[3] Also see Desai et al. (2011).

[4] See, among others, Asheim (1986).

multinational corporations that own the capital and wield massive political power that enables them to negotiate resource exploitation agreements that are generously biased in their favor. In this perverse connection, resource-rich countries get the short end of the bargaining stick, and their minerals and oil are depleted without proportional gains in terms of government revenue, foreign exchange earnings, and reinvestment into the national economy. During the pre-colonial and colonial periods, Africa's resources were expropriated and made the property of the colonizing state. Thus, the continent's resources were plundered by foreign corporations and served to fuel the economies of the colonial states and feed the coffers of their Treasuries. In the post-colonial era, the unequal exchange has been perpetuated by mining fiscal regimes that provide extensive fiscal incentives to attract foreign capital. Such fiscal regimes have generated limited benefits for African countries in the form of government revenue and foreign exchange earnings, a key reason for the suboptimal performance of African resource-rich countries in terms of economic development.

There are other manifestations of perverse connections related to natural resources. Rather than benefiting local communities, resource exploitation can harm them by destroying land and other sources of livelihood with limited benefits in terms of employment creation and social service provision. This is a major issue observed in the case of large-scale industrial mining as well as artisanal mining, notably in the case of exploitation of gold and gemstones that pollutes water streams and damages agricultural land. Another issue is the unequal distribution of the gains from natural resource exploitation between the central government and the local communities. The revenue from natural resource exploitation can weaken the state-people fiscal compact as it reduces accountability pressures on the government when it can satisfy its needs without levying taxes on the population. Inefficient and non-transparent management and utilization of revenue from minerals and oil have indeed been identified as a major cause of the poor economic performance in Cameroon as discussed in Chapter 7, operating as one of the mechanisms of the resource curse.

Key Lessons from the Case Studies

The three country case studies teach us a lot regarding the linkages between natural resources and capital flight and the causes of the poor performance in leveraging these resources to promote long-term economic development. A few lessons that stand out from each case are described below.

The case of Ghana stands out as an illustration of the critical importance of the fiscal regime for the overall impact of natural resource exploitation on the economy. The fiscal regime determines whether, or not, a country truly owns its resources, and it signals the government's political commitment to protecting the interests of the nation as the legitimate owner of the resources. The analysis presented in this book shows that Ghana has never truly regained ownership of its gold since the Western traders set foot on its territory. Since then, the gold sector has been controlled by foreign investors, and the country's benefits have been limited due to the leniency of the fiscal regime that grants generous fiscal incentives to foreign gold mining companies. In addition, the country's benefits from the gold sector are eroded by systemic export misinvoicing, whereby structural opacity of the gold trade statistics make it impossible to fully track the movement of gold in terms of quantity and value. The gold sector exhibits triple dependence that characterizes other resource-rich countries in Africa, namely dependence of foreign capital, dependence on foreign refineries (in South Africa) to process the gold, and dependence on global markets for the value of its gold. The liberalization of the industrial organization of the gold sector has exacerbated the systemic resource dependence and unequal exchange. At last, the Government of Ghana has recently woken up to the need of overhauling the gold mining fiscal regime by establishing the much welcome Ghana Gold Board (GoldBod) whose mandate is to buy, sell, weigh, grade, assay, value and export gold and other precious minerals in Ghana. But like all institutions, Goldbod will be effective only if it is managed efficiently, equipped with appropriate technological and human capacity, and enjoys genuine operational autonomy.

The cocoa sector in Ghana offers substantial contrasts with the gold sector in terms of ownership, regulation, and direct benefits to the economy and the population. Cocoa is and has always been owned by the Ghanaian people thanks to diligent government control. The organizational structure of the sector enables the government, through its agencies, to ensure oversight of the operations from production to export of cocoa beans. Thus, production and exports are adequately tracked, which has helped minimize the risks of capital flight through export misinvoicing and smuggling. The control of the price setting process by Producer Price Review Committee (PPRC) helps to protect farmers' earnings from speculation by intermediaries and even from the vagaries of international cocoa markets given the government's commitment to ensure that the farmgate price remains at least 70% of the international price of cocoa beans. Moreover, the close regulation of the sector ensures that the receipts from exports of cocoa beans are fully repatriated, unlike the case of gold where companies are allowed to keep substantial fractions of gold export proceeds offshore. The analysis in Chapter 4, however, points out that the overall rewards to the cocoa farmers remain modest. This is because the higher end of the cocoa value chain is controlled by cocoa processing corporations, which are all foreign. There is therefore a need to design incentives and mechanisms to encourage and facilitate investment of Ghanaian capital in the higher end of the cocoa value chain. Only then can Ghana truly claim ownership of its "political crop."

The analysis of Zambian mining sector in Chapters 5 and 6 has documented that Zambia has not benefited from its vast endowment in copper, gold, and gemstones due to four main factors. The first is the dependence on foreign capital and the dominance by foreign corporations that has been inherited from the pre-colonial and colonial eras. Second, the mining fiscal regime provides generous incentives to attract foreign capital, which undermines government revenue mobilization, while facilitating the outward transfer of wealth from Zambia. The third factor is the leakage of wealth from the mining sector through export misinvoicing and smuggling in an opaque trading system whereby Zambian copper, gold, and gemstones cannot be fully traced as illustrated by large and chronic gaps between its export statistics and import records of its trading partners. Export misinvoicing and smuggling are the key mechanisms of the pernicious nexus between capital flight and mineral resources that has plagued the Zambian economy. The three factors imply that the returns from the exploitation of minerals accrue disproportionately to the rest of the world, rather than the economy and people of Zambia. The fourth factor is that the mode of exploitation of minerals has trapped Zambia into a mining-dependent economy whereby resource exploitation has sucked financial and human capital as well as policy attention from non-mining sectors, thereby retarding structural economic transformation. The failure to mobilize sufficient revenue from a foreign-dominated mining industry and to reinvest the proceeds to boost economic diversification has prevented Zambia from leveraging its resources to transition to a path of strong, sustained, and shared growth. Any chance of achieving broad-based and sustained growth in Zambia will require a major overhaul of the organizational structure of the mining sector aimed at increasing Zambian public and private ownership, scaling up the efficiency in revenue generation, leveraging the potential of the long-neglected gold and gemstones, developing domestic value addition structures and systems, and improving transparency in commodity trade to combat capital flight channeled through export misinvoicing and smuggling.

The analysis in Chapter 7 has shown that Cameroon has failed to leverage its vast natural resources especially oil. But to be fair, its poor record is not due to lack of trying. In fact, the government of Cameroon got something very important right, which most African resource-rich countries have failed to do, except Botswana,[5] which is the establishment of a management regime that ensures direct government shareholding in private oil exploitation corporations. This design ensures that the government generates revenue from shares in production and profits, beyond the usual fiscal and non-fiscal levies. Thus, the government is truly invested in the oil sector where its assets managed by the Société Nationale des Hydrocarbures (SNH). Yet, Cameroon has not boasted strong long-term economic growth commensurate with its vast endowment in natural resources in general and oil in particular. The biggest issue is not so much the pernicious nexus between capital flight and oil that plagues oil-rich countries, as capital flight through oil export misinvoicing appears to be comparatively limited. Cameroon's problem is rather the "institutional curse" manifested in the design of the exploitation of the sector and the management of oil revenue. On the design side, the country has suffered an "original sin" whereby the government established an oil refinery designed to process light crude oil which the country does not produce and must import, while exporting its heavy crude oil that its refinery cannot process. In addition to creating structural dependence on imported crude oil, the design also created structural currency mismatch that jeopardizes the financial sustainability the national oil refinery.

[5] See, among others, Bakwena (2023) and Besada and O'Bright (2018).

On the management side, Cameroon's problem is the opacity and inefficiency in the management of government revenue generated from oil. As laid out in Chapter 7 and in the literature, concerns have been raised about the lack of transparency in the management of government revenue, which undermines accountability vis-à-vis the citizens. The country has also failed to leverage oil revenue to boost investment in non-oil sectors to stimulate economic diversification. These are indeed the various manifestations of the "curse" that has plagued resource-rich Cameroon, in that sense making it indeed an "Africa in miniature."

Recommendations

The analysis presented in this book suggests that African resource-rich countries must undertake game-changing policy reforms—not just marginal adjustments to the status quo—if they hope to fully leverage their natural resource endowment to achieve strong, sustained, and inclusive economic development. However, to be effective, the efforts by African governments must be supported by reforms in the global trade and financial systems as well as national regulations in the Global North which is the primary destination of Africa's natural resources and capital flight. Below, we highlight some of the key areas of focus of the reforms.

Abolish or Severely Overhaul the Mining Concession Model

Most African resource-rich countries use the mining concession model whereby they collect revenue from taxing multinational corporations that are granted mining rights over extended periods. It is estimated that 80% of entities making payments to governments in Sub-Saharan Africa in the extractive sector are foreign-owned multinational enterprises (MNEs) (Albertin et al., 2021). Thus, the benefits from increased mineral production, price, and export booms accrue disproportionately outside of the African continent. Clearly, the mining concession model and the associated fiscal compact between extractive multinational corporations and national governments has not served Africa and its people; it must therefore be either abolished outright or severely overhauled.

To benefit from mining, African countries—through their governments—must be invested in resource exploitation as shareholders. Mining development agreements must be designed to provide better rent sharing arrangements with a minimum of 15% government's stake in the capital of mining and oil companies, in addition to the usual tax and non-tax levies. In addition, the government could negotiate joint ventures with private companies in new exploitation and trading of minerals and oil. African governments can pay for their shares forward from their shares in future production and future tax and non-tax levies. This arrangement is thus financially feasible as it does not face any challenge related to the government's liquidity constraints. Botswana offers an example for such a win–win mining regime whereby the government owns 15% stake in De Beers and can engage in 50–50 joint ventures with De Beers in mining and trading of diamonds. Under such arrangements African countries could reasonably claim true ownership of their natural resources.

Taxation of Extractives as a Balancing Act

The fiscal regimes governing extractive industries in Africa are primarily driven by the desire to attract foreign direct investment (FDI) while mobilizing government revenue. The evidence, however, shows that what deters FDI in Africa is not taxation, but rather a bad business environment and high production costs (Coulibaly & Camara, 2021). Rather than engaging in a race to the bottom by cutting tax rates and non-tax levies, African resource-rich countries should invest in improving public infrastructure, simplifying and enhancing the efficiency of the regulatory frameworks, rooting out corruption, building rich and up-to-date geological information databases on natural resource reserves, stabilizing the macroeconomic environment, and developing technical capacity through investment in education with a focus on natural resource management, engineering, science, and technology.

Recently some innovations have begun to emerge across the continent, which could form a basis for broad reforms of the fiscal regimes through peer learning across the continent. One example is the abolition of negotiations of mining agreements with MNEs on a mine by mine basis, which has typically been an avenue for mining companies to game the system and leverage their economic and political power. In Sierra Leone, a newly elected government introduced a reform under the Extractive Industries Revenue Act (EIRA) that abolished negotiations of fiscal terms with corporation on a mine by mine basis, which reduces corporations' ability to take advantage of information asymmetries to extract special deals (Albertin et al., 2021, pp. 37–38). Another example consists of setting limits to interest deductions, notably to combat "thin capitalization" aimed at eroding the tax base, in the cases of South Africa and Nigeria (Albertin et al., 2021). We have already mentioned above the case of Botswana's mining governance regime that involves government shareholding in DeBeers and joint venture in mining and trading of diamonds. Such innovations not only increase government revenue generation from resource exploitation, but they also increase the overall impact on the economy, ultimately enhancing true national ownership of natural resources.

Trade Misinvoicing and the "Missing Minerals"

The analysis presented in the cases of gold in Ghana and copper and gold in Zambia has shown that trade misinvoicing is a major channel of massive losses in foreign exchange and government revenue. Trade statistics for Ghanaian gold and Zambian copper and gold show both evidence of export underinvoicing as well as "missing minerals" whereby some of the minerals recorded as exported by Ghana and Zambia are not traceable in their importing partners' records. While export underinvoicing has generated more attention because it is a major mechanism of capital flight, the issue of "missing minerals" is also critically important for African countries. The phenomenon reflects structural deficiencies in the recording of transactions throughout the mineral value chain that make it impossible to assess the true value of mineral exports captured by African countries and to gauge whether these countries are receiving a fair share of the market value of their minerals.

Addressing these problems requires concerted efforts in source countries, trading partners, and the global trading system. Exporting countries need to invest significantly to increase their technical and technological capacity—especially taking advantage of digitalization—to improve the reporting and tracking of transactions on minerals and oil throughout the entire value chain. This involves building searchable data platforms that enable access to real-time information on the quantities and prices of mineral exports as well as the corresponding flows of foreign exchange. This will not only help reduce export misinvoicing but also crack the veil over the practice of dissimulation of the proceeds of mineral exports in offshore financial centers. At the destination side, there is a need for systematic automatic country-by-country exchange of trade and finance information related to minerals and oil transactions. This involves both governments and special zones such as the so-called "trading hubs."

Only coordinated efforts between African governments and their trading partners can dismantle the global architecture that facilitates trade misinvoicing around the world.

Some of the Ghanaian and Zambian gold exports "fall out of sight" in the process of moving to South Africa where gold is refined at the Rand Factory before final exporting. The South Africa node of the value chain is a "black box" where Ghanaian and Zambian gold is not recorded as either imports on its way in or re-exports on its way out of South Africa. This problem seems to be systematic and has been identified in the case of other gold exporters with linkages with South Africa (see Ndikumana & Boyce, 2022). There seems to be very little chance of ever shining a light inside that "black box." A practical and efficient solution is for Ghana and Zambia to "domesticate the gold" by establishing their own refineries. This would not only reduce the opacity in gold trade statistics, but it would also enable these countries to capture a much larger share of the value of gold by moving up the value chain. Moreover, such a change would increase employment creation as well as these countries' share of the world market value of their gold. This recommendation holds for all other minerals as well as oil. Investing in domestic processing of natural resources is a game changer that will allow African countries to diversity their economies and embark on a resource-fueled takeoff toward strong, sustained, and shared long-term growth.

Leveraging the Potential of Artisanal and Small-Scale Mining

National mining development strategies in Africa have typically focused on modern large-scale mining while largely neglecting the artisanal and small-scale segment of the mining sector, especially for gold and gemstones. Yet, if properly regulated and incentivized, this segment has substantial potential to boost mining production and the overall development benefits of natural resource exploitation. In many countries production from artisanal and small-scale mining is either not reported or poorly reported, so that we do not even know how important the subsector is currently. In the case of Ghana (Chapter 3), official data indicates that small-scale mining contributes over 30% of total gold exports. In the case of Zambia, until recently, artisanal and small-scale mining of gold and gemstones remained outside the policy maker's radar screen and at the margin of mining sector development strategies. Yet, the limited data on the subsector suggests that production is substantially under-reported and exports are subject to significant smuggling. During our fieldwork in Zambia, we were constantly told that small-scale miners "seek but never find"; but, quite oddly, they keep digging. Yet, digging costs money. So, the question we must ask is: By what financial calculus do these miners justify pumping more of their hard-earned savings and costly loans into a supposedly unprofitable enterprise? If miners are rational agents, as we must assume, either they are relying on very poor information and limited technical expertise, or they have very high tolerance for risk and incredible patience, or they seek and find but don't tell. Whatever state of the world they operate in, informal and small-scale miners can play an important role in the mining sector, provided they receive appropriate regulatory oversight and technical guidance, as well as assistance in securing low-cost sources of financing to invest in exploration and exploitation. Thus, the Ghana and Zambia economies would benefit from a transparent and productive small-scale mining subsector.

Transparency and Rules

Under the pre-colonial and colonial regimes, mining was a privileged domain of the ruler and the private investor. There was no formal obligation to inform the public about the nature of the mining deals, or to report on the fruits of the investments in the sector and how such fruits were shared between the country and external parties. The post-colonial African states inherited this tradition of opacity, considering mining as *la chose de l'État* (government's affairs) whereby the government is deemed to have no obligation to report to the public about what is happening in the extractive sector. Regrettably, this tradition has not ended, as there is still substantial opacity in the reporting of mining sector operations in Africa. African countries have joined frameworks that promote transparency in extractive industries in the hope of addressing this problem. Since 2007 seventeen African countries have joined the EITI,[6] with a commitment to systematic reporting of information on payments by mining companies to the government. But a lot more needs to be done to break the tradition of opacity in natural resource management.

[6] EITI members include countries that are not rich in minerals or oil such as Ethiopia and Seychelles. https://eiti.org/countries.

Transparency must be systematic and applied at all the nodes of the entire value chain of mining starting from exploration all the way to reporting on exports and foreign exchange earnings. African governments should publish mining development agreements and encourage and be receptive to comments and inputs from experts, civil society, and members of the public. Reports on development outcomes of mining exploitation should be broadly accessible and disseminated in national and regional economic development fora. In the end, natural resources belong to the country, so the citizens are entitled to know how the resources are managed and how the proceeds from resource exploitation are used. Transparency is critical for the accountability and credibility of the management of natural resources.

One important instrument to foster transparency is setting clear and publicly known rules on the utilization of the proceeds of natural resource exploitation. Clear rules can also improve efficiency in the use of revenue from natural resources to maximize the impact on economic growth and to drive economic transformation. In the spirit of the Hartwick rule, African resource-rich countries should institutionalize a rule requiring that a given fraction of the revenue from natural resource exploitation is to be saved and used to finance public investment. Botswana provides an excellent example of this investment rule that other African resource-rich countries can emulate. Indeed, Botswana has been able to channel resource rents into public infrastructure, health, and education, with the support of good governance and sound macroeconomic policies, making it a real success story of resource-based economic development (Acemoglu et al., 2001; Robinson, 2013).

In the same spirit, windfall gains from positive shocks to commodity prices and demand should be channeled into a long-term investment fund to be tapped for financing public investment. Such funds would finance new public investment as well as maintenance, thus solving a chronic problem in Africa where, quite often, public infrastructure (e.g., roads) is built but not maintained due to lack of appropriate budget allocations to maintenance. Increased availability of quality of public infrastructure will reduce production and trade costs, thus fostering economic transformation.

A second rule is to specifically dedicate a fraction of government revenue from natural resources to investment in human capital with a focus on engineering, science, technology, and other related fields such as law, finance, and economics applied to natural resource management.

This entails both a reform of the management of natural resource rents as well as a reorientation of national education systems, most of which are still stuck in the past where education served to prepare the youth to enter the civil service, in which case it did not really matter what anyone studied in school. Such reforms will enable African resource-rich countries to slowly graduate from dependence on imported technical expertise and leverage their capacity to negotiate resource exploitation agreements on a level playing field to generate win–win mining contracts.

To the extent that Cameroon, Ghana, and Zambia can implement such rules of transparency and make strategic investment of the proceeds of natural resource exploitation, they could be launched on a path of economic transformation, thus better leveraging their natural capital. The combination of an economic transformation-oriented investment strategy and a new resource exploitation regime where the government is a shareholder in resource exploitation ventures will increase the benefits from natural resource exploitation in terms of government revenue, foreign exchange earnings, and strong, sustained, and shared economic growth. Only then will Cameroon, Ghana, and Zambia be able to claim real ownership over their natural resources.

References

Acemoglu, D., Johnson, S., & Robinson, J. (2001). An African Success Story: Botswana. In D. Rodrick (Ed.), *Search of Prosperity: Analytic Narratives on Economic Growth* (pp. 80–119). Princeton University Press.

Albertin, G., Yontcheva, B., & Devlin, D. (2021). *Tax Avoidance in Sub-Saharan Africa's Mining Sector* (Departmental Paper No. 2021/022). International Monetary Fund.

Asheim, G. B. (1986). Hartwick's Rule in Open Economies. *Canadian Journal of Economics, 19*(3), 395–402.

Bakwena, M. (2023). Diamond beneficiation and economic diversification in Botswana. In I. Mogotsi & N. Namwoonde (Eds.), *Economic Diversification in Africa: Lessons from Botswana* (pp. 115–129). African Books Collective.

Besada, H., & O'Bright, B. (2018). Policy Impacts on Africa's Extractive Sector: Botswana, Diamond Dependence, and Diversification in the Post-diamond Period. *Revue Governance, 15*(2), 86–105.

Coulibaly, S., & Camara, A. (2021). *Taxation, Foreign Direct Investment and Spillover Effects in the Mining Sector* (Working Paper No. 354). African Development Bank.

Desai, D., Lange, G.-M., Hamilton, K., Ruta, G., Chakraborti, L., Edens, B., Ferreira, S., Fraumeni, B., Jarvis, M., & Kingsmill, W. (2011). *The Changing Wealth of Nations: Measuring Sustainable Development in the New Millennium*. The World Bank.

Hartwick, J. (1977). *Population Growth, Technical Progress, Intergenerational Equity and the Investment of Resource Rents* (Working Paper No. 280). Queen's University, Department of Economics.

Lange, G. M., Wodon, Q., & Carey, K. (2018). *The Changing Wealth of Nations 2018: Building a Sustainable Future*. The World Bank.

Ndikumana, L., & Boyce, J. K. (2022). *On the Trail of Capital Flight from Africa: The Takers and the Enablers*. Oxford University Press.

Robinson, J. (2013). Botswana as a Role Model for Country Success. In A. K. Fosu (Ed.), *Achieving Development Success: Strategies and Lessons from the Developing World* (pp. 187–203). Oxford University Press.

World Bank. (2021). *The Changing Wealth of Nations 2021: Managing Assets for the Future*. The World Bank.

Index

L. Ndikumana, *Capital Flight from Cameroon, Ghana, and Zambia*, https://doi.org/10.1007/978-3-032-22770-6